ACCLAIM FOR GINGER BURR'S
That's So You!

"*That's So You!* takes a fresh look at your wardrobe woes and brings joy and ease to the experience of getting dressed every day."

—Lynn Robinson, author of *Trust Your Gut and Divine Intuition*

"Ginger's warmth, wit and wisdom come through on every page. Now you can experience Ginger's magic manner as she helps you feel and look radiant."

—Jodi R.R. Smith, author of
The Etiquette Book and Manners for the Modern Woman,
mannersmith.com

Create a Look You Love with Beauty, Style and Grace

That's So You!

Ginger Burr

BALBOA
PRESS

A DIVISION OF HAY HOUSE

Balboa Press books may be ordered through booksellers or by contacting:

Balboa Press
A Division of Hay House
1663 Liberty Drive
Bloomington, IN 47403
www.balboapress.com
1-(877) 407-4847

Printed in the United States of America

ISBN: 978-1-4525-6873-7 (sc)
ISBN: 978-1-4525-6874-4 (e)
ISBN: 978-1-4525-6875-1 (hc)

Library of Congress Control Number: 2013903052

Balboa Press rev. date: 03/07/13

For my mom
with love and appreciation

Table of Contents

Foreword

I WAS RAISED BY a grandmother who loved clothes. She would charmingly misquote 1 Corinthians and say, "Your body is a temple, and you're supposed to decorate it." Her influence, and a string of others, led me to fashion school in London at eighteen. I kept a color-coded calendar then to alert me to the date each major fashion magazine would hit the newsstands: British *Vogue*, French *Vogue*, American *Vogue*, Italian *Vogue*....

Although I was an expatriated Midwestern teenager with a student budget and a weight problem, I took fashion seriously. In my mind, looking good was a right and a responsibility. I felt a blessed connection to good fabrics, well cut and suited to one's individual style. People talked about traditional style, romantic style, preppy style and bohemian style, but I knew mine was something else: Parisian, but more Left Bank than Champs Élysées. It was challenging to find clothing and accessories in sync with that style, but when I settled for less and wore what I'd settled for, there was invariably less joy in my day. If *That's So You* had been around then, I'd have learned early on never to settle.

Ginger Burr knows fashion and how it translates to real life—without trading bodies with a supermodel or cashing in the IRA. First, she'll have you "shopping" (and discarding) from your own closet. Like the statue of David that remained after Michelangelo chipped away at everything else, there's art in your closet already. It's just competing with lots of other things. Or maybe you haven't yet discovered the belt or blouse or scarf that would make that simple black skirt or pair of dark denim jeans a masterpiece. Ginger will make sure you know it when you see it.

Reading *That's So You* is like having an image consultant on call, answering every question you have and plenty you didn't know you had. Its author knows as much about the female psyche as she does about pencil skirts and pantyhose. She gets it that each of us is unique and that our quirks and preferences and predilections make us who we are. There is no one size fits all.

Ginger's take on the what-to-wear question is totally up-to-date yet based on the timeless principles known by women such as Audrey Hepburn, Katherine Hepburn and the Duchess of Windsor. They looked amazing—and their photographs still do—because each had a look that was "so her." With the information and inspiration in *That's So You,* you'll develop the look that is uniquely yours, so you can feel more confident than ever in how the world sees you.

And while you're *looking* good, this book will give you the opportunity to *do* good with its introduction to the concept of cruelty-free fashion and beauty. Ginger Burr's image consulting firm is called *Total* Image Consultants, and the part of her book about the ethical side of elegance gives those of us who read it the chance to be *totally* attractive—inside and out. Once you know their origins, fur, down, leather and cosmetics painfully tested on animals in laboratories aren't pretty anymore. But don't worry that learning some of the gory details about animal abuse will mean you are left with cheap plastic shoes and only four lipstick colors in all the world. Not anymore. Compassionate fashion and beauty have come into their own, and no one knows more about them than Ginger Burr. She also knows—and tells—how you can incorporate them, all at once or over time, into your personal style.

This book is as complete as any I've ever seen, and although you'll refer back to it time and again for another well-dressed tidbit, it reads like a novel. So, get started on a truly delightful read. The way from here to fashion forward: turning the page.

—Victoria Moran, author of
Creating a Charmed Life and *Main Street Vegan*

Preface

So MANY WOMEN LOOK at me and think, "It's easy for you; you know what you're doing." Or "You're slim, and everything looks good on you." While there is certainly truth to both of those statements, most people are surprised to learn that I spent the first half of my life making tons of fashion mistakes and that it looks easy for me because I have learned about my body and how to dress it.

When I was in my teens and twenties, I felt so lost when it came to how to dress. I remember back in 1980, when I was at my sister's bridal shower, I overheard my mom tell a friend that I looked like I was wearing my pajamas. Sadly, she was right. No, I wasn't actually wearing my pajamas, but it was close. I had on a shapeless, flowy earthy–crunchy dress that was unlike anything she had seen me wear before.

Did it look good on me? Not really. Did I feel good wearing it? No, mostly I didn't. So, why was I wearing it? Because I was searching for my own personal style and this was one step along the way. I had found one more style that didn't work!

At the time, I was very active in the folk dancing scene, and I loved how comfortable the other women looked in their cotton dresses and pretty flat sandals. They exuded an ease and comfort that was so natural and free-spirited. I wanted to feel that way, too. So, I imitated what I saw but never felt completely at home in that look.

In retrospect I see all the clues that would have helped me refine my look to align my inner and outer beauty, but at the time, I didn't have the guidance or resources to help me see those clues clearly. I was imitating women who were very low maintenance and reveled in that part of themselves. They washed their hair and let it air dry while I had styled my hair every day since I was ten. Most of them either danced barefoot or with flat sandals while I was thrilled when I found a pair of vintage high-heeled oxford shoes to dance in. And, when everyone else was wearing T-shirts and jeans or long cotton skirts and peasant blouses, I was searching the racks at thrift stores for beaded cardigan sweaters.

If I had known then what I know now, I would have realized that who I was on the inside was not being fully reflected in the style choices I was making. I wanted to fit in, so I tried dressing like everyone else. But my inner essence, that part of me that makes me who I am, was not happy. Mostly, I felt like an imposter. I didn't feel like part of the crowd, yet I also didn't feel like I was expressing myself fully, either. I was stuck somewhere in the middle and didn't know how to get where I wanted to be.

Thankfully, when I was nearly thirty I was lucky enough to meet the very talented and beautiful Nevena Cranney, who taught me how to tap into that part of myself that was longing to come out. She exuded a sense of self-confidence that was captivating and inspiring. I knew I wanted to feel that myself and help others access their inner beauty as well. Since then, I have done just that—cultivated my own sense of style and shared my expertise with other women who are as lost as I was back then.

Every section in this book is a result of my personal experience. I know that all of this is learnable because I had to learn it myself. This journey takes time and effort, but there's a freedom that comes with each step you take toward creating a look you love from the inside out.

As you begin, the most important thing is to be sure your personal style is motivated by your own self-confidence and comes from a place of genuine delight and a love of beauty. Allow a new sense of joy and freedom to unfold as you go through the chapters and put the lessons into practice. Watch as old habits and unnecessary expectations give way to fresh, new ideas and ultimately, yes, a wardrobe you love—a wardrobe that's *so* you! That is my wish for you and the main reason I am sharing all of this with you. I am honored to support you each step along the way as you create a look you love with beauty, style and grace.

Acknowledgements

WRITING THIS BOOK HAS been a joy from start to finish, and there are so many wonderful people to thank for making it a dream come true.

I have to go back a long way to one of my music professors in college, Pamela Susskind (now Pamela Pettler) who, after reading one of my papers told me, to my surprise, that I was a really good writer. Her coaching and encouragement changed my life, and I have been writing ever since.

Although it is one thing to write articles for my blog, it is another thing altogether to write a book. My editor, Marijane Leonard, has been helpful beyond words. Her insight into how to organize the chapters and make the information flow has made this experience even more fun and rewarding than trying to do it all on my own. I also must give special mention and heartfelt thanks to Leora Tec who offered her enormously valuable insights and suggestions in the final two months of the project. Her contribution went well above and beyond my wildest expectations, and I am forever grateful.

Special thanks go to my friends and clients who read my book in various stages of completion and offered their recommendations, expertise and support. Jodi Smith, an author herself, knows the joys of writing a book and graciously shared her wealth of knowledge and experience. Priscilla Feral and Lee Hall, champions of animal rights at Friends of Animals, offered wise suggestions and guidance for the vegan fashion chapter. Stefanie Frank, Wendy Yellen and Jackie Davis each brought her own wisdom to the editing process. I could not have had a better group of women supporting me through this journey, and I am extraordinarily appreciative.

For the past three years, I have had the good fortune to work with my amazing coach, Heather Dominick. For her brilliant, "Energyrich" coaching and unwavering belief in me, I offer my heartfelt gratitude.

Thank you also to all of you who regularly read my articles and take the time to let me know the information I share inspires you. You make it fun and rewarding, and you are the reason I wrote this book.

A special thank-you goes out to three fabulous women: Jackie Davis, Diane McKay and Amanda Sobel. Not one of them hesitated for even one moment when I asked her permission to use her before and after photos on the cover of this book. Each of them is just as beautiful on the inside as you see on the outside. And, to the gifted photographer Meri Bond, who captured each woman's inner essence through the lens of her camera, I express my sincere thanks.

Lastly, I want to thank my life partner, Marion Davis, who has believed in me from the beginning. She inspires me with her life's mission to empower women by building their self-esteem. She makes me laugh every day at the quirkiness of life and shares my love for beauty and compassion. Thank you from the bottom of my heart.

Introduction

GLORIA DROPPED HER BAGS of clothes on the floor and started pulling things out. "What do I do with this?" she said as she pulled out a sleeveless blue-and-purple tie-dyed tank top. "I bought it when I was in Miami Beach and needed a top for a dinner out. I never wore it again. Somehow it just never felt right. And what about this floral cardigan? I used to wear it all the time but then saw a picture of myself in it, and I couldn't believe how dowdy I looked. It's so depressing to think that I wore that all those times and looked like that! My whole wardrobe seems to be made up of a mishmash of items, and there's no cohesiveness. Nothing makes sense together, so getting dressed is so exhausting and discouraging!"

If you nodded your head as you read Gloria's story and thought, that's me, that's me, then you know firsthand how frustrating it can be to get dressed every morning when nothing seems to work right. You wonder if you don't have the right stores, a big enough budget or a sleek enough body. Something always seems not right. Your intentions are good, and you know somewhere deep down inside that you can have a personal style you love. But as you search for those curvy jeans or wonder what to put over that sleeveless dress, you just feel lost.

Your wardrobe is meant to be a source of joy and personal expression, not aggravation. Life is too short to spend every day feeling disempowered each time you get dressed.

Creating a wardrobe you love is all about aligning your inner and outer beauty. When you reflect your inner sparkle—the part that makes *you* special—in the clothes you wear, you create a personal style. This book is designed to take you step by step through that experience.

The truth about style is that it is not an exact science. You cannot make everyone around you happy with the choices you make. Just watch some red carpet commentary, and you'll see that many fashion gurus can't agree on who is the best and worst dressed (not that I ever encourage judging others' wardrobes). Add to that the fact that no two bodies are exactly the same and that personalities, lifestyles and general likes and dislikes vary widely. I can safely say that my friend's sixty-nine-year-old mom who loves long belted vests over leggings with boots would not feel comfortable wearing my forty-year-old neighbor's flowy skirts and ruffled tops. It's no wonder so many women get overwhelmed when they think about putting together a wardrobe they love. There are so many choices and so many ways to coordinate those choices that it all can easily feel overwhelming.

So how do you navigate all the variables that go into creating a personal style that truly, honestly, deep down to your toes reflects who you are? If you have been in a fashion rut for a while, it probably has as much to do with inner obstacles as it does with what styles work for your body. This book will address both. When you create new awareness around things like your body image, the positive or negative influences that have affected your clothing choices up to this point, and your fear of looking inappropriate or silly—all of which have kept you stuck—you can loosen these strongholds on your personal style.

That's why the book begins with a chapter on identifying and addressing your inner obstacles. Once you're aware of what's going on inside, it is easier to look at your wardrobe with new eyes. Then you can begin to tame your closet and purge garments that aren't serving you with a freedom and awareness you've never known before. The book then moves into some of the more real-life aspects of dressing such as creating a signature style, harnessing the power of color, and knowing when to wear (and how to choose) a cardigan or a jacket. You will also learn to navigate stores more efficiently to have productive shopping experiences. After that, you can explore adding pizzazz with accessories, mastering the art of dressing casually with style and creating a professional wardrobe that also has personality. As if that's not enough, this book also looks at beauty from a new perspective by introducing you to the concept of adding compassion into your wardrobe choices. And, finally, the book concludes with the topic of aging and takes you through all the complicated expectations and complex choices that go with that.

The most important thing to keep in mind while reading *That's So You* is that everything you will read here supports you in creating a wardrobe you adore. Will you have to put some thought and energy into your personal style journey? Yes. As one client recently said to me, "Thank you for encouraging me to think more deeply about issues and then act on them." You *can* make positive changes in your wardrobe and personal style one baby step at a time. If you internalize and use the information in each chapter, you will see your new wardrobe (one that feeds your soul as well as meets your lifestyle needs) take shape little by little. The payoff will be great.

Throughout the book you will find stories of women I have worked with whose experiences highlight specific points. In most cases, I have changed their names or merged several experiences into one out of concern for their privacy.

The success stories below are from women who thought they could never have a look they love.

> "I feel more grounded and confident in how to put things together and also know better what questions to ask when I don't know." —Tammy

—

> "I still can't believe I have clothes I love. I thought I'd always be in mediocre clothing limbo. I'm now learning to be more proactive in wardrobe selection and am trying to figure out what the different types of situations I need to dress up for and trying to get the right clothes for each situation. I'm even getting used to putting together outfits. The reality

is, it takes a while, and it's not all going to be fixed in a few weeks, but I've already noticed a vast improvement in my wardrobe, and (even better) how I feel about things in general. It's so nice working with you because not only was the process successful, it was smooth and seemingly effortless, though I well realize your experience made it feel easy. Most importantly, I can't believe I finally have jewelry and clothes I love!" —Carol

— —

"I rushed home from work today because a friend was coming over for dinner. I took off my suit and threw on a pair of jeans and one of my new tops (oh, and a pair of beautiful earrings!). I felt so much more pulled together than I ever have when dressed this casually before, and the best part was that it was no harder than wearing any of the dull, ill-fitting, unflattering T-shirts that I used to own! Thank you!" —Kate

— —

"A few weeks ago I was headed to my Pilates class. I was walking into the building with another woman who teaches yoga there. She looked at me and said, "You look so nice and pulled together!" I was delighted. It was the last thing I ever expected someone to say as I was heading to a workout class. Yay! Since working with you, Ginger, I have picked up so many things in "my colors" including dark brown workout pants for Pilates and tops in various colors that work for me along with coats to finish off the look in cold weather. It's wonderful to know I don't have to be dressed up in order to look nice." —Teresa

Do you dream of having the same experience as these women? The truth is that you can have a closet full of clothes you love. Yes, it is possible to pull together a fabulous outfit in three minutes (if that!). You *can* have just the right number of clothes and wear everything in your closet, and you will receive unsolicited compliments. The best part, however, is that you will know in a genuine, heartfelt way that you look great.

It's your turn now, so let's get started!

Before you dive in, here are some guiding principles to follow during your personal style journey. Jot these down on an index card and keep it handy.

- **Allow yourself the time to read and re-read each section** as often as you need to internalize the message. When you're learning something new, repetition is key. Every time you do this you will pick up something you hadn't seen before.

- **Share this only with those who will be supportive.** Be sure that whomever you share this with is as excited about your journey as you are and wants to help you celebrate your successes (or, maybe even join you) along the way.

- **Practice what you learn.** It's OK if these ideas seem new and a little foreign at first. That's where the practice comes in! The more you practice, the more they feel familiar and fun.

- **Expect, welcome and celebrate the learning curve.** Chances are good it has taken you a while to get stuck (it doesn't usually happen overnight). So, give yourself a break and celebrate each new success no matter how small. Each time you do you set yourself up for more and more success – the universe just works that way.

- **Be kind and patient with yourself.**

If you, like Gloria, have been struggling with your wardrobe—not loving what you have but not knowing how to change it—this book will help. Let me guide you through each step of your style journey so that you can create a wardrobe you love with beauty, style and grace.

Chapter 1

Tapping Into Your Inner Beauty

WHO ARE YOU? I ask because this is an important aspect of creating a look you love. When you dig really deep down inside, who do you see? Don't worry if your answer feels a bit unclear right now. You're here because you want to figure out the answer, and this chapter will help you begin.

Tapping into your inner beauty means addressing inner obstacles that keep you stuck—all those learned behaviors and limiting beliefs that do not serve you but have dictated your wardrobe choices up to now. It means looking at what makes you special and being sure your personal essence is reflected in the wardrobe and style choices you make.

I know that this is often an unfamiliar step, and that's exactly why so many women regularly wear clothes they don't love. Did you know that every time you enter a room you make a statement without saying a word? This statement is first and foremost visual, and so many people are, at most, only vaguely aware of the statement they are making. In fact, often they hope to be as invisible as possible, and they figure that if they just blend in no one will notice them. But the statement you make is about more than how you look. People pick up on your energy— how you feel about how you look. When you feel tentative about the statement you are making with your wardrobe choices or you don't like how you are dressed, others can often sense that discomfort.

This is not about dressing the way you think you *should* look or how you think others expect you to look; it's about purposefully creating the

1

visual image you want to project. When you do this in an authentic, heartfelt way (that's where tapping into your inner beauty comes in), it will give you confidence and a more empowered presence and offer others valuable insight into who you are. Plus, when you look in the mirror, and you will feel good! This, in turn, boosts your self-esteem, bolsters your confidence and draws people to you with a very clear message about who you are.

Are you ready for some realignment? Take a deep breath, open your mind, open your heart, and let the new you emerge. Welcome to the first step in your magnificent journey!

Does How You Look Really Matter?

IT'S NO SECRET THAT our society is obsessed with image. We hold women to an unrealistic standard of beauty with the expectation that every woman should be young, tall and thin. Really? It's no wonder so many women feel excluded! But, as you know, this is nothing new. In fact, over three decades ago, when I was in my early twenties I realized this and rebelled. I outright rejected the idea that someone else would tell me how I was supposed to look in order to fit in. I decided to do something about it, so I stopped shaving my legs, wore androgynous clothes and relinquished my mascara. I know that doesn't sound all that impressive, but since I have blonde eyelashes mascara was the only makeup product I wore, and it significantly changed my appearance. It was a bigger sacrifice than you think.

This rebellion lasted about three months, and then I had an epiphany. It was an awakening that eventually influenced the work I do now. I realized that even in my rebellion I was letting others direct the choices I made rather than letting my personal preferences and inner spirit guide me, and as a result, I felt out of sorts. I started paying more attention to what made me happy and less to what others expected. That mindset has served me well ever since.

So the question remains, does how we look really matter? You bet it does. But maybe not in the way we've been led to think it does. Let's talk about this some more.

In the show *Wife Swap*, two wives switch families for two weeks: In the first week, they live by the new family's rules, and in the second week, they set their own rules by which the new family must live. For the sake of dramatic tension, the producers choose families whose values and philosophies are diametrically opposed.

I don't watch the show much because it often feels mean-spirited and just too stressful, but I remember one show where the wives expressed their views about personal image. One woman believed that how you look is all that matters. The other, who felt strongly that beauty comes exclusively from the inside, was appalled at how much time her temporary family spent on grooming and dressing and was very outspoken about it. She rarely brushed her hair, never cared if her clothing matched, and shopped exclusively in thrifts stores and only when absolutely necessary. (As I said, the show is about extremes.) As you can imagine, much drama ensued!

So, who is right? Does how we look matter above all else? Do clothing, makeup and hair choices have that much influence? Or should our personality and inner essence be our primary focus with no attachment to how we look on the outside?

Over the years the most important thing I have realized is that the key to feeling deep satisfaction with how you look is matching your outer appearance with full appreciation for and expression of who you are on the inside. Here are three steps to get you started:

1. **Dress with intention:** Many women have fallen into a state of unconsciousness about how they look. Is it any surprise when you consider the factors working against us (e.g., body image issues, social pressure, compromised self-esteem, disinterest in fashion)? Women are bombarded by messages about how we "should" look and what we "should" wear. After a while, many give up and resort to dressing in what is safe and easy.

   After this pattern is repeated enough, dressing becomes an unconscious act. If this sounds familiar, take a look in the mirror, and ask yourself this: "If my clothes could talk, what would they say about me?"

   Do you like the answer? If not, it's time to make changes. Ask yourself what you would like your clothes to say about you.

   Then, keep that message front and center as you go through the rest of this book. It is a very clear and important message for you to heed and is part of what will give you great satisfaction when you get dressed each day.

2. **Know the rules:** I once spoke to a large group of young professional women. Most were incredibly appreciative of what I shared, but a couple of them were up in arms and called my talk sexist. They said that the organization that brought me in would never do the same for a group of men. Wouldn't they be surprised to know that, yes, it would?

   Little did they know that I am a feminist from way back (possibly, yikes, before they were born) and that my passion has been and still is to empower women. Knowing the rules—both spoken and unspoken—of how to dress for the workplace can be critical to professional success. And who would want to risk that—especially because they didn't know any better (talk about disempowering!)?

   If you understand the rules about dress, then you are well equipped to make choices that serve you. Knowing the expectations, you can then make a conscious decision to disregard them if you choose to and are better prepared to deal with, or circumvent, the consequences.

3. **Show respect:** Take pride in how you look. Good grooming habits are essential and have nothing to do with where you shop or how big or fancy your wardrobe. Others notice when you take good care of your body and your clothes—and when you don't—and, most importantly, you feel best when you give yourself some TLC.

   Fair or not, people will make assumptions about you based on what they see, so you must feel confident that you are creating visual cues with authenticity--which is not what I was doing when I rebelled many years ago. Let me assure you that it is not possible to meet everyone's expectations, but one thing is for sure: You *can* meet your own expectations. That's what we'll be focusing on for the next nine chapters.

Are You Settling for Good Enough?

When you choose a doctor, do you want the best, or do you say, "What the heck, good enough is good enough"? Of course you don't!

When you help your child with her homework and she tells you that two plus two equals five, do you say, "Oh, sweetie, that's good enough"? I doubt it!

When you go out for dinner and order spaghetti and they bring you lentil soup, do you send it back or say, "That's good enough"? Chances are good you send it back!

So why do you get dressed every day in something that is just good enough?

Recently, I was shopping with Tracy for the first time. We had a number of outfits with us in the dressing room, and the first thing she tried on was a magenta top. As she looked in the mirror and assessed what she saw, I could sense her mind whirling. I asked her how she liked it. She hesitated and then said, "I'm not sure I like the fabric. But it fits well, so I think it's good enough."

Oops. I think not! That was her old way of doing things, but I was there to help her move beyond that and never settle for less than great or fabulous or terrific. There is never a time when good enough is good enough!

Tracy looked relieved, although maybe a tad skeptical as well, when I explained this to her. Up until then, good enough had been her default. She always felt thankful when she at least met that (low!) standard.

When you think of Bette Midler, what do you picture? Perhaps it's a woman with incredible energy, a quick wit and a quirky style. You have to admit that whether you love her style or cringe when you see it, her message is something we can all admire. Bette is Bette—loud and clear!

There is a somewhat famous quote attributed to Bette: "I have my standards. They're low. But I have them."

This is probably more her quick wit speaking than her own fashion sense. However, I don't personally know Bette, so I can only guess. Regardless, I know she speaks for many women when it comes to creating a wardrobe: You have your standards. They're low. But you have them. The question is why are they so low?

It is not unusual for new clients to tell me that I really don't need to see their wardrobe. They can show me a couple of pictures, or I can just look at what they are wearing now; that's their "uniform." They've settled on something that gets them out the door in the morning, doesn't stand out too much and is comfortable.

A "uniform" certainly gets the job done, but what happens to their soul, their heart, their inner beauty? They finally rebel! One day these women take a peek in their closets and think, "I don't want to do this anymore." But then what?

Over the past twenty-six years of working with women on how they look (and, of course, thirty years of my own personal reflection before that), I have found that there are at least four reasons why women settle for less—often wearing the same few personally uninspiring outfits day in and day out. See if you can relate to any of these:

1. **You feel clueless.** You do not know how or where to begin to create a wardrobe you love. Although you long to look in the mirror and feel great about how you look, you mostly feel lost and overwhelmed.

2. **You hate to shop.** You do not like shopping, primping or any of the planning that goes into creating a wardrobe, not to mention whether you even know how. You want to be comfortable, and you want to get through the process quickly. As a result, personal expression takes a backseat to comfort or ease.

3. **You do not like your body.** Your first inclination is to cover it and hide until you feel better about how you look. This, of course, perpetuates the bad feelings about yourself, and the

cycle continues. For you, shopping is a nightmare experience. Finding things that fit properly is challenging, and because you feel uncomfortable with your body, you cannot imagine loving anything that would actually fit anyway. Besides, with a body like yours, you do not think you deserve to buy something you love. This is a common underlying theme I hear often.

4. **You do not have time.** This is usually present in conjunction with at least one of the other three reasons. You buy things on the run, often settling for something adequate rather than extraordinary because it is quicker. You do not have time to organize your wardrobe, and exhaustion causes you to toss things haphazardly into your drawers and your closet at the end of the day. Even if you do own pieces you love, finding them and coordinating them just takes too much time and effort, and, of course, more important obligations take precedence. You keep thinking that someday you will get to it, but someday never comes.

Does any of that ring a bell? Have you settled for less because you are unsure how to take a step forward that feels good and all of your attempts so far have been frustrating?

Here are three steps to help you get out of your Bette Midler rut:

1. **Become aware.** Congratulations! Yes, you have already taken a giant step forward. Not only have you acknowledged that you let your standards slip a bit, but you have also not given up—or you would have stopped reading a long time ago. Yay for you! The important thing now is to do something to move you forward so you don't fall back into "good enough" thinking.

2. **Build on what *is* working.** Chances are good that not everything in your wardrobe is a complete disaster. Almost always when I go into a client's closet after she has told me she doesn't like anything in there, she will come across something she loves. Maybe it's a pair of shoes, a favorite jacket or a scarf.

It doesn't matter. The point is that she owns and can identify something she enjoys wearing.

Now it's your turn. Take a peek in your closet and pull out one thing that delights you (even if you can't complete the outfit—sometimes that's the biggest frustration, but let's not go there yet). Analyze it. What is it about it that you love? The color, the fabric, the pattern, texture, style details, the way it shows off your waist or legs or shoulders? You get the idea.

Do this with three or four items. Write down what you discover and then see where you can find commonality. Maybe you'll find out that you love paisley or a particular collar design or a specific fit. Maybe everything you chose is made out of linen or has a similar texture. This is invaluable information.

3. **Practice, practice, practice.** Make a list of what you learned and write it on an index card. Keep it handy in your handbag. Now, go shopping. It doesn't have to be a long shopping trip. Just venture out to your favorite store and wander through, or really branch out and try a new store altogether!

   Look for the things you discovered you loved about your favorite items in your wardrobe. Try on some things. Even if you walk out with nothing, pat yourself on the back for practicing what you've learned (and for leaving without buying something that wasn't great if that's what happens!). Afterward, take a few minutes to jot down what you learned.

   Practice is the only way you will make any changes, so keep it as positive as possible and try to make it fun instead of work. Each time you do this you will get closer to your goal.

One last word: **Go into this exercise (or go back and do it again) with an open mind.** Imagine that as you take these three steps, you will find a key that will help you move forward. You don't have to know in advance what that key is, just go in and explore. Let it reveal itself.

If you go in thinking, "This won't work. I already know that nothing in my closet is any good and nothing looks good on me. It's all hopeless," then that's what you will find. If this is your natural tendency (and trust me, it is for many of us!), take a deep breath, and go explore your wardrobe with a newly open mind!

This is the kind of exercise you can do over and over and learn something new each time. Creating a wardrobe is as much an inner experience as it is an outer one.

Pam, one of my clients, put it very well:

> "Building a strong sense of ourselves gives clarity, especially for those moments when it's important to stand up for ourselves and make the right choices for us. Your work has certainly helped me with all this, and I am more aware of saying YES or NO, embracing or discarding, rather than just going with the flow."

> Here's the bottom line: Since you spend time every day of your life (at least once a day) getting dressed, you deserve to have this be a joyful—or at least peaceful—experience. If it isn't, you are missing a delicious opportunity for self-expression and creativity.

I cannot emphasize this enough. You can have a wardrobe you love no matter what your body shape, age, size, coloring or budget (yes, budget!). This is not a hopeless situation for anyone.

A couple of weeks from now, check in with yourself. Are you and Bette Midler still best friends, or have you parted ways? All joking aside, let Bette inspire you to raise your standards and find a personal style that increases your joy factor each time you go into your closet.

Are There Hidden "Costs" Lurking in Your Closet?

"I DON'T HAVE TIME to go shopping and put together a wardrobe." I hear this all the time! Perhaps you have said it yourself.

Often, what you are really saying is, "I do not have time to walk around the mall or a store futilely trying things on that look terrible or don't fit only to leave the store empty handed and miserable."

Yikes! Who would want to set aside *any* time for that kind of punishment?

Yes, we all have super-busy schedules with work, family, a few cats or dogs, school, friends and a host of other responsibilities (take your pick) pulling us in a million different directions.

True, most of us have enough on our plates without adding one more thing—especially when that one thing has historically been unpleasant and often unproductive. It's better just to make do, tuck it under the rug and manage as best you can. Sure, this will work for a while but at what cost?

It is human nature to prefer to set aside time to do something you enjoy (or that is urgent) than to do something you dislike. That is why messy basements stay messy, writing a paper for a class you do not like gets put off until the last minute, or cleaning the refrigerator doesn't take precedence over taking your children to soccer practice or having tea with a good friend?

But there is something very important to consider: Living with a wardrobe you don't love has substantial hidden costs. Like stress, these costs add up over time and eventually take their toll.

When you live with a wardrobe you don't love, you are:

Undermining your spirit. Tolerating an uninspiring wardrobe takes a toll on your psyche. You get dressed every morning and sometimes more than once a day if you have more than one engagement. When you start your day off feeling frustrated, annoyed, hopeless or overwhelmed, this feeling weighs on your psyche and can affect the rest of your day. As Louise Hay says in *You Can Create an Exceptional Life*, "How you start your day is how you live your day." How is your experience of getting dressed affecting your life?

Sacrificing your dreams. Every woman wants to feel good about herself every time she gets dressed. Some women have had that and lost it over time due to body changes, lifestyle changes or just general aging (wondering what's age appropriate or dealing with a body that has shifted a little); others never had it to begin with. In either case, it is a dream lost. Perhaps it is just buried deeply, but it feels lost forever.

Wasting your time. When your wardrobe and style are not working for you, then you spend a significant amount of time trying to make things work when what you really long for is to get dressed effortlessly and, dare I say it, with joy!

Uninspired wardrobes happen. It has nothing to do with your age, weight, profession, location or financial situation. A frustrating wardrobe is an equal opportunity annoyance!

So what can you do?

Take a few minutes to jot down what having an uninspired wardrobe is "costing" you. Refer to the list above and add your own. Just let it flow. As you write and reflect, you are certain to uncover hidden costs and frustrations you didn't realize were bugging you so much! Perhaps you aren't attending a special event because you don't have anything to wear--this is a much more common experience than you might expect. Or you attend the special event dressed in something you don't feel great in and you feel self-conscious the entire time. Maybe the time you spend trying to figure out what to wear is time you would rather spend playing with your children or reading quietly before you have to leave for work in the morning.

Keep those notes handy (perhaps on your bedroom bureau) and add to them over the next few days or weeks as things occur to you.

The more you make changes as you go through the book, the more you will become acutely aware of what toll these inner "costs" have taken over time.

Once you have done this, take a deep breath, keep smiling and give yourself enormous credit for looking at this deeply. That was a very big step (so many women just live with the frustration indefinitely) and you are on your way!

Here's the good news: Creating a personal style you love can not only be fun, but can also take much less time than you think. As you learn more about how to create a wardrobe you love, those hidden costs will subside.

Do You Love Your Body?

NOT TOO LONG AGO I was attending a social event and was introduced to two lovely women who arrived together. We struck up a conversation about (what else?) fashion, and at one point one of the women turned to her friend and said, "I wish I had your body." Without missing a beat, the other woman rolled her eyes and replied, "Oh, please!" and then launched into a litany of reasons why no one else would ever want her body.

Does this scenario sound familiar? Have you witnessed it or been an active part of it many times over the years? We are often unaware of the damage these statements or experiences have on our psyche, our self-esteem and our ability to create a wardrobe we love. It seems that we are often trained from a young age to belittle the way we look. Sure, we often use humor, which can offset the sadness and mean spiritedness of what we say, but the essence of our words still lingers. Unfortunately, when it comes to body image, women have cornered the market on self-deprecating remarks.

This is not a good thing. As Louise Hay will tell you, language is a powerful thing. According to her, "Self-approval and self-acceptance in the now are the main keys to positive changes in every area of our lives." Hay is one of my favorite mentors in this area. Check out her books (www.louisehay.com) for guidance in learning how to bring more personal kindness into your life.

I have had to learn how to feel better about, and be kinder to, my body, and her books have helped me immeasurably. Here is my story:

As a teenager, going to the beach was an ordeal for me on many levels. First of all, I'm white as white can be, so while my friends basked in the sun all day and came away with a glowing tan, I'd be burned to a crisp within about thirty minutes. But, that wasn't all.

While I was sitting on the blanket wrapped in several towels, a sweatshirt and a hat, I would watch the other women sunbathers and, you guessed it, I'd compare myself. Trust me, to my way of thinking I *never* measured up.

Mostly, I would study the legs of the women walking by. Did I see bikini-clad bathers confidently walking the beach who were knock-kneed? Nope. Never. So, I always, *always* felt self-conscious walking on the beach. I just imagined that everyone who saw me snickered at the shape of my legs.

Of course, the key word there is *imagined*! Never, ever in my whole life has anyone pointed to my legs and laughed—at least that I've been able to see. I, however, am excruciatingly aware of the fact that my legs are not straight.

I used to cringe at the thought of wearing shorts for gym class in high school and college, and I spent the 1980s, when short skirts were the only kind to wear, standing with my left knee bent so no one could tell it was crooked. It's a habit I catch myself falling into occasionally even now.

What are you saying to yourself about your body that keeps you stuck in a rut? Be careful about shrugging it off as good-natured kidding or insignificant conversation. These comments are much more damaging to your psyche than you might know.

Thankfully, I have come to terms with the fact that my legs are unique and have learned to appreciate that they are long and healthy. Sure, I would be delighted to wake up one morning with straight (and could they be a little less white, too, please?) legs, but it is more a fun fantasy than a sad longing.

It saddens me to think of the amount of time I spent feeling uncomfortable about showing my legs when all the time my friends would say: "We don't see it. You must hide it well. It's barely noticeable, so what are you so worried about?"

What about you? Do you find yourself readily comparing your body to that of women whose bodies you perceive as more beautiful than yours?

If so, take a few minutes to reflect on these questions:

1. What body part do you scrutinize on other women and compare to your own body?

2. How does that make you feel?

3. Do you blow it out of proportion? Be honest!

4. What would happen if you stopped hyper-focusing on it?

5. Do you know what triggered it originally or what triggers your insecurity around it now?

What do you do next?

Admit that it bugs you, and commit to making peace with it. Visualize yourself smiling compassionately at that body part. I know, it sounds a little out there, but it really does make a difference. Acknowledge the uniqueness of who you are and that this is part of what makes you special (think Barbra Streisand's nose, Cindy Crawford's mole or the gap between Lauren Hutton's teeth). Commit to learning how to dress to honor that part of your body. This means not trying to eradicate it or hide it under layers of fabric but acknowledging its preciousness as part of *you* and not dressing as if you think it's an eyesore!

Stop whining. OK, maybe *you* don't whine, but I did for years. Oh, poor me! I have knock-knees. Of course, since there's nothing I can do about them, whining does nothing other than make me feel bad about my body. Have I learned how to dress my body in a way that minimizes the crookedness of my legs? Yes. Do I sometimes wear things like skinny jeans or leggings even though the bend in my legs is noticeable? Yes. Are there some days when I feel more comfortable doing that than others? Yes, and that's OK.

Become a master of drawing focus somewhere else. Acknowledge two or three body parts that you love. Do not skip this part! Learn ways to draw focus there by using color, detail, pattern, accessories, texture, etc. to make a statement. And, by all means, do not sit around looking uncomfortable because you are afraid someone will notice the offending body part, and do not run from having your picture taken. Dress in a way that makes your heart sing, hold your chin up, and smile! I can guarantee that others don't notice any of it as much as you do.

Years ago I was playing the piano at an event for hundreds of people. It was the first time I had performed for such a large audience, and I was incredibly nervous. At one point in the song, I accidentally repeated a page. I was mortified and was sure everyone was snickering or gasping. Instead of letting it go by pretending that I had done it on purpose, I made a face. I wanted everyone to know that I knew I had made a mistake. My mother told me later that no one would have noticed my error if I had not wrinkled my nose, and I know she's right.

It's the same thing with our bodies. If you keep fidgeting with an outfit to try to cover the seemingly offending body part, you will draw more attention to it than if you dress in way that makes you happy and forget about it.

After you gain some inner peace about your least favorite part, take things a step further and work on total body acceptance.

How can you begin to feel better about your body? First answer these questions: When someone compliments you, do you explain that it's a fluke or look at the person like he or she is nutty? Do you regularly commiserate with other women about self-perceived body flaws?

You probably answered yes to both. The good news is that these are habits you can change immediately. Here's your homework:

Learn how to take a compliment. When someone compliments your hair, do you say, "Oh, wow. It's driving me crazy today. It never seems to do what I want it to, and the humidity just makes it…." Or when someone admires your sweater, you say, "Thanks. I wish I didn't have to wear it. I'm hot, but my arms are so flabby that I don't feel comfortable exposing them." What if you just smile and say, "Thank you! You made my day!" Then, take a deep breath and, inwardly, maybe take it one step further. You don't have to say anything else aloud. Instead, think to yourself, "Wow! How fabulous that my hair looks good on such a day. That's great news since my hair appointment is still a week away." Find a way to make it feel good. When you respond to compliments this way, you will also be modeling healthy behavior to others. This is especially important if you are raising young girls. What a gift!

Stop the gripe sessions with your friends. Tell them you are on a new path to self-acceptance, and invite them to come along. Challenge them to say something loving about themselves, and get them started by offering each person a genuine compliment. They will love doing the same for you.

Life is too short to spend bemoaning what you don't have. Celebrate what you do have, and you will always feel and look better! This does not mean you have to go around saying happy things about the parts of your body you aren't in love with to everyone you meet. It just means don't say negative things about them. And do not berate yourself if you forget, or you will feel overwhelmed and give up. Just practice regularly so that little by little you are kinder when you talk about your body.

This book is designed to help you address these concerns so you *can* confidently create a wardrobe and feel great about how you look even when certain body parts do not measure up to your ideal. When your clothes begin to express your inner essence, you like what you see—even if you still have twenty pounds you'd like to lose or a little extra underarm dingle-dangle.

Are You Dressing for You or Someone Else?

ON A REGULAR BASIS a woman will call me saying something like,

> "I didn't really think my style was that bad but my _____
> (teenage daughter, husband, boyfriend, mother, best friend,
> sales woman) keeps telling me that my _____ (hair,
> favorite outfit, what I'm wearing to work, bathing suit)
> doesn't look good. At this point I'm afraid to get dressed!"

Not only does she have to ponder the ever-changing world of fashion as it relates to her body, personal style and lifestyle, but also she has to ward off negative comments (however well intentioned) from others along the way.

For some women, creating a wardrobe has always been a source of frustration while for others their discontent has evolved as their bodies have changed. Add to that being bombarded with messages that how they look is not OK, and you have a giant mess!

Believe it or not, when it comes to how you feel about how you look, more harm is done by those closest to you than strangers or acquaintances. Several years ago I surveyed women about the hurtful comments and unwanted advice they still carry with them. The input was overwhelming and often heart wrenching. Let me share a few examples of how these comments can have long-range implications.

> "When I was a teenager, my mother looked down toward
> my feet and said, 'My ankles are thinner than yours!' I
> didn't even know what my ankles were supposed to look
> like but interpreted her remark to mean mine weren't as
> good as hers." —Phyllis

——

"I'm constantly being told how tired I look. While it may be true, do these supposedly well-intentioned people not realize that if I WERE tired, I would be the first one to know and really not need them to point it out?!" —Meg

The feedback I received included simple, seemingly benign comments such as those above and much more insidious and mean-spirited ones such as what Hillary shared:

"I had spent the previous year since my third baby arrived getting back into my pre-babies body shape. Through diet and a serious exercise plan, I'd lost fifteen pounds, was down to about 107 pounds, back into a comfortable size 4 and feeling really great about myself. I actually went and bought my very first bikini for a vacation and some formfitting (but still conservative) clothes to highlight all the good parts of my body. Everybody had been complimenting me on how great I'd been looking.

"When my family arrived for Easter, I was wearing a cute, flirty little skirt (just the type of thing Mom would pick our for me, too!), and she immediately pats my belly and teases me about looking like I'm pregnant! I had long since thought that I was immune to my mother's criticisms, but that day, I cried. Couldn't she have pointed out how great my hair was? Or how nice the outfit was? She did like the outfit by the way. It's just that for whatever reason, she just can't resist making some kind of negative comment, even in jest."

Have you experienced something similar? Does it still influence your feelings about your body and your wardrobe? Even when you are very insightful and logical about these kinds of comments, they can still have emotional impact as Hillary went on to explain:

"I am rational enough to recognize that my mother has her own inferiority issues that she has obviously struggled with throughout most of her life (the stories I could tell!), and I feel pity for her about that, but the fact that she feels the need to make herself feel better by always (and probably unconsciously) belittling me is awful. I know it's more about her than it is about me, but I still bear the marks of it all. I have struggled with my own inferiority complex all my life—probably inherited from her—and have finally reached a place where I feel like I've made real progress to overcome it. But it still doesn't make those hurtful comments any less painful when they come, even though I can rationally talk myself through them and have a network of wonderful friends and a husband to provide positive reinforcement as well."

It is important to address the hurt so you can move forward and feel good about how you look. To truly delight in who you are, it is a very necessary step to unburden yourself. Whether you do it with a good therapist, energy healing or some other personal growth work, the rewards are great. You will bring your psyche and your personal style back to a heart-centered place and truly enjoy who you are and how you express yourself in the world.

Once your awareness has set this journey in motion and you have a newfound sense of empowerment, there are a few things to remember:

Please yourself first. What you wear and how you present yourself visually is a very personal decision. You—not your daughter, your husband, your best friend or your mother—get to choose! And here's the clincher: When you feel fabulous about how you look, even if others do not totally agree, their unsolicited comments hold much less charge. When you reconnect with your personal power and can honestly experience that special part that makes you *you*, discovering your personal style will feel more organic. Whether you do it on your own or with support, this step is critical to disarming the hurtful comments.

Just say no! Some people have a bad habit of imposing their personal views on others and think that being a family member or close friend gives them free reign. It does not! When you receive a hurtful comment or unwanted advice, let the person know—with grace and love—that what they are doing is not acceptable. If you are having trouble verbalizing this, I highly recommend reading books by Cheryl Richardson or Louise Hay (or the book they wrote together, *You Can Create an Exceptional Life*). They will guide you in setting boundaries so you get what you need *and* feel good about it.

Surround yourself with support. You deserve to have your life filled with people who cherish you for who you are and are not trying to change you to fit their mold of what is right and acceptable. When you have this kind of support, you are more likely to ask them for advice because you know it will be given with kindness and love.

The premise for much of this unwanted advice is "I know better than you about your own body." Here's an example.

I once went on a shopping trip with a mother and daughter. The daughter was in her mid-twenties and was about to start interviewing for a job. The mother wanted the daughter to be prepared and thought that an outside expert could help. What I found out was that the mother was using me to push her agenda. I knew we were in big trouble when, as we were walking through the department store's athletic clothing section, the daughter slowed down and said, "Oh, these are my kind of clothes!" Uh oh. Her mother was simultaneously making a beeline for the suits. At one point, the mother took me aside and said, "Stop asking her if she feels good in something and if she likes it. Just tell her what looks good on her and what she should wear." I explained that that wouldn't work and that unless her daughter liked the outfit it would just sit in the back of her closet. I did my best to steer the daughter toward things that would make her happy and keep her relationship with her mom from suffering. But at some point the daughter is going to have to speak up and probably shop without her mother as much as possible!

People like this mother feel it is their right and duty to impose their views. You might even feel bullied into making the changes they suggest, but will you ever feel really wonderful wearing those clothes? Probably not. The bottom line: No one knows better than *you*! And, if you don't know how to choose clothes that make you really happy, this book will help you.

If you have people in your life who think they know best criticize you, make peace with them—with the help of a qualified therapist, if necessary. Then, allow yourself to explore your style from a heart-centered place. When you please yourself first, you will transform your state of being and silence your critics both inner and outer.

What's on Your Never-Wear-Again List?

I'M A BIG BELIEVER in never saying *never*. Times change, lifestyles change and personal preferences change so *never* can feel a bit confining.

That said, I also know that every day we make choices and are given an option about pretty much everything we do. At breakfast do you eat pizza or oatmeal? It's definitely a personal preference. Do you drive the latest SUV or a sedan? You get to choose, and you probably know what you like without too much forethought or mental anguish.

When it comes to personal style, it gets a bit more challenging. Take makeup, for example. For some women, their makeup routine is a very important part of their morning ritual. For others it is hit or miss (depending on their schedule or mood), and for some it's not even on their radar. Again, it really comes down to personal preference.

I happen to think that makeup is fun, and having been born with blonde eyelashes and eyebrows, I love what it can do to make my eyes stand out a bit more. But I would never impose my preferences on someone else.

I cannot tell you how many women I know who have ten different brushes, a slew of hair products, a blow dryer and a flat iron, and they know they aren't going to use them or will use them haphazardly with unsatisfactory results. They simply think they are *supposed* to use them or have been told they *must*. What they really want is a wash-and-wear hairstyle. But they end up with something that needs to be "styled" to work because they can't say no.

If this sounds familiar, it is time to take back your power and your right to say never again!

To give you some examples, I have two personal "never" choices to share:

1. **I will never wear shorts**. Oh, how freeing it was to finally allow myself to say that a number of years ago. OK, so last year

I bought a skort (it is kind of like shorts) in case it gets to be a million degrees when I go for a walk in the summer. Did I wear it last year? No. It never got excruciatingly hot enough; I live near the ocean, so that's not a surprise, but I have it just in case.

2. **I will never wear a self-tanner.** Yes, I'm incredibly pale and cannot tan even if I wanted to, but the last thing I need is one more "beauty" ritual and one that only lasts a few days at that! I have been pale all my life and have finally embraced my paleness—or "pale power," as I like to call it.

It is important to know what you will and won't do when it comes to your own personal style preferences. Otherwise it is easy to end up with a wardrobe full of things you will never wear, and that's exactly what you don't want to have happen. For instance, Nancy had a closet full of button-down blouses. Not because she loved them, but because she thought she was supposed to have them. She had read that they were a staple in every professional woman's wardrobe, only she never felt comfortable in them and was constantly fussing with them when she wore them to work. What a freeing experience it was for her to learn she could let them all go and never wear them again.

This is an example of Nancy dressing by someone else's rules and not by what really made her happy. Until she was able to learn that she could just as easily wear a collarless top with a suit and look pulled together was she able to confidently add button-down blouses to her never-wear list.

Where do *you* draw the line? Perhaps you will never wear high heels. Or maybe you will never spend twenty minutes blow-drying your hair. It could be that you've sworn off skirts forever in favor of pants. When you look in your closet do you see items that you do not wear but thought "should" be key elements in your wardrobe? Perhaps you even like them on the hanger or on others but just cannot relate to them on you? Acknowledging that you don't enjoy wearing them, despite their being perfectly lovely garments in general or looking great on your sister, can help you let them go and move them to your never-wear-again list.

You get to decide for yourself. If it is really that important to you, then own it. If you don't, you will end up frustrated by your choices and other people's persuasive powers. And, guess what? You always have the right to change your mind down the road—even if you said you "never" would!

Do You Have a Fear of Standing Out?

As RACHEL STOOD IN front of the mirror looking casually elegant in a beautiful blue sweater and jeans with high-heeled boots that showed off her long legs, I could sense her discomfort. She acknowledged that she looked good, but she said it without conviction. When I probed a little more, we got to the heart of the matter. She felt conspicuous, like the entire world would be staring at her in this outfit. This was a foreign experience for her, and she wasn't sure if she liked it.

Can you relate to Rachel's experience? How do you feel about standing out from the crowd? Does the idea excite you and make you smile, or does the very thought strike terror in your heart and make you cringe? If the latter is truer for you, then what has been your alternative to standing out? Many women describe their style as "beige," "predictable," "decent" or "downright boring." Rarely does a woman purposely choose that look. It is usually a response to her deeply rooted fear of standing out for the wrong reasons, i.e., she would rather fade into the woodwork than risk looking silly or inappropriate. The result? Each time she gets dressed, her self-esteem and confidence take a direct hit.

Some women equate standing out with looking flamboyant, outrageous or ostentatious. But that doesn't have to be true (although those looks certainly do produce a few stares!). Standing out means owning who you are and celebrating that. And if flamboyant, outrageous or ostentatious is who you are, then celebrate it! You can stand out whether your look is subtle and elegant or dramatic and bold or something else entirely. As long as you display *your* personality and inner essence, then no matter how you express it, it just looks and feels right.

Recently, I met with Fiona, who was about to re-enter the dating scene and felt apprehensive. Her most pressing question was, "When should I show cleavage?" Together we did some work and determined that her personality was primarily gentle, heartfelt and radiant. I could tell just by looking at her that the idea of showing a lot of cleavage felt foreign and uncomfortable. Fiona had a predetermined belief, however, that she was *supposed* to expose cleavage at some point in her dating experience, so it came as a great relief to her to learn that she never had to if she didn't want to, especially if it wasn't true to her essence.

What she really wanted to explore was how to look and feel sexy in a way that was authentic for her. Now, that's a different story!

What about you? What is your look saying about you? What motivation is driving you to choose the outfits you do? Are you trying to blend in and hide (this never really works) or stand out in a way that gives you confidence and feels good?

As with Rachel, women are hesitant about standing out, but this is usually because they don't know how to do so in a positive way. If you could use a little support in this area, here's an exercise to help.

The next time you get dressed, rate the outfit you choose to wear on a scale of one to ten. A ten would mean that you are totally celebrating yourself and dressing authentically with no apologies, and a one would mean that you are hiding as much as is humanly possible. Obviously, the goal is to get to ten!

Next, analyze your look. What aspect of your style feels like you are trying really hard not to be noticed? Is it the:

- color (too beige, black or neutral)?
- cut of the outfit (too big, boxy or shapeless)?
- fabric (sweatshirt, or head-to-toe polar fleece)?
- overall style (it looks like your mother, sister or best friend so you can fit in)?
- accessories (or lack thereof)?
- lack of textures or patterns (all smooth solid colors)?

Once you have analyzed your current look, make a concerted effort to tweak just one component at a time. Add texture, a touch of color or some accessories. Keep trying until it feels good and fun.

Remember, you aren't trying to stand out just to stand out. This is about feeling empowered to express your inner beauty and authenticity. As with Fiona above who worried about showing cleavage on her dates, you have to determine what feels right for you in your life right now.

To give you an example, Alexandra describes herself as refreshingly graceful. She wears delicate colors and soft styles. When she wears a jacket, it is not made of bulky, heavy fabric and does not have a lot of hardware. The accessories she chooses are always expressive in a lovely, gentle way. Meanwhile, Jane is quirky and colorful. She can wear deep, bold colors and often wears two chunky necklaces at once without it seeming like too much.

The delicious part of all of this is that both Alexandra and Jane stand out in their own individual way. If Jane toned everything down and tried to be refreshingly graceful and Alexandra wore brightly colored, quirky clothes, they would each feel uncomfortable and self-conscious. They would stand out in a way that felt disingenuous. Remember Rachel? That's exactly what she was worried about. As soon as we swapped the high-heeled boots for flat ones, she relaxed and smiled. Her legs still looked long, and the blue sweater still showed off her eyes. But she felt more grounded and at ease. Her internal peace shined through, and this is something others cannot help but notice. She now stood out in a way that reflected her inner beauty.

The same can be true for you. As you build your personal style step by step and begin to make positive changes, you will find the styles and garments that genuinely reflect who you are. That's the sweet point where standing out as *you* has a whole new, delightful meaning!

What Makes You Sparkle?

Now THAT YOU ARE ready to stand out a little more, let's look at how to do that beyond the basics.

I have to admit that I am addicted to movies on the Hallmark Channel. Don't give me violence, angst and heartbreaking suffering, and especially don't make me watch the news. I won't have any of it. Instead, give me a bowl of popcorn and corny movies with happy endings.

During the holidays Hallmark runs sappy movies almost nonstop, and I love it. My partner and I sit in front of the fire with the kitties piled on the couch with us, drink tea and watch movies that make most of our friends roll their eyes. I don't care. They make me happy.

One of my favorites is a series called *The Good Witch*. It is uplifting and heartfelt and has a fabulous message.

At one point in the series, Cassie, the good witch, gives a beautiful, sparkly necklace to Betty, a woman who runs the local bakery and catering store. Betty is reluctant to accept the gift because she feels like she doesn't have any place to wear it—she isn't used to standing out. But, after a little encouragement from Cassie, who tells her she can give it back later if she wants to, Betty puts it on and wears it home.

To make a long story short, Betty comes back a few days later wearing the necklace and a whole new outfit. Looking lovely but a little sheepish, she mentions that she adored the necklace but worried that it wasn't her and that she was being too flashy; she was so used to being behind the scenes baking and blending in that anything other than an apron felt foreign and over the top. When Cassie exclaimed, "On the contrary, the outer sparkle just helped your inner sparkle shine through," Betty visibly lit up. She wanted to embrace her sparkle, and Cassie's encouragement was all she needed.

That's it! That's what creating a wardrobe and personal style is all about: letting your outer "sparkle" reflect your inner sparkle. Feel free to replace the word *sparkle* with something similar that feels right to you. Perhaps it's *vitality, effervescence, shine, joy* or *pizzazz*. How you express it is also personal. Your sparkle doesn't have to be in the form of jewelry or anything that glitters. Depending on who you are, it can be soft and gentle or wild and crazy. Perhaps you find joy in an interesting combination of colors or texture or in a pattern that makes people smile or evokes curiosity.

The key is to unlock YOUR inner "sparkle" and let it radiate out through the clothing and style choices you make. When you do this, people who will love who you are at your deepest core see and feel *that* part of you before you've ever said a word to them. Let me say it another way: A wardrobe that reflects your inner essence will allow people who are naturally drawn to your personal sparkle feel that part of you before you ever open your mouth.

The power in this experience is extraordinary and underutilized. So, there is no better time than now to let *your* sparkle out of hiding! Not sure how to go about it? Here's a little exercise:

How does "sparkle" interpret for you and your personal style? Is it sequins and crystals, deliciously shiny fabric or a color that others can't help but notice? Maybe it is an outfit that is so perfectly fit to your body that you look like a movie star? If you aren't sure, take your favorite outfit out of the closet and analyze it for the "sparkle." It has to be there, or it would not be your favorite--or you are settling for "not terrible" as your favorite.

Do you wear a little of your interpretation of "sparkle" every day? If not, why not?

How do you plan to add more "sparkle" to your wardrobe? Be specific.

Never underestimate the power of sparkle. Once you have hit upon yours, you will not be able to get dressed without it—you will miss it immediately.

Here is your homework:

Whatever your plans are for the next week, be sure to add YOUR "sparkle" simply by allowing your wardrobe to reflect you. Remember, it does not have to be in-your-face "sparkle" if that is not your style; it just has to be YOU! Every person's sparkle is different and reflects her personality. It could be a subtle silver thread running through your favorite black sweater. Or, perhaps it's crystal earrings that reflect light every time you move. It might even be a delicious velvet jacket that has a warm, luxurious sheen that only velvet has or slightly daring rhinestone heels on your favorite shoes. Your task is to explore what sparkle means for you, and then let it shine every day.

How Do You Add Beauty to Your Wardrobe?

THE TRUTH IS THAT creating a wardrobe you love is a continuous process. It is not something you do once and then it's done forever. I know this sounds daunting. But as discussed at the beginning of this chapter, living with an uninspired or "good enough" wardrobe undermines your spirit, sacrifices your dreams and wastes your time and money. Every woman wants a wardrobe that makes her feel beautiful, but so many settle for much less.

Take Jennifer, for example. Jennifer had gained about twenty-five pounds since she started menopause. Until then, her weight had been pretty consistent most of her adult life. But now, she looked in the mirror and did not recognize the woman she saw staring back. She used to have a tiny waist and always enjoyed wearing dresses that showed off her curves, but when she tried wearing the same styles now, just in a different size, she didn't like what she saw. Most of her added weight had settled around her middle, and the small waist she had once showed off no longer existed. She stopped wearing dresses altogether and lived in black pants and an oversized top in the hopes of camouflaging her tummy.

For Jennifer, having a wardrobe and personal style she loved seemed elusive at best and time consuming and frustrating at worst. If this is true for you, let the next few chapters help you find focus and motivation. The following framework touches on what is to come in the book. Return to it for a guide to making progress any time you are ready to refresh your look.

Identify one element missing from your wardrobe. Please resist the temptation to make a list the size of the phone book. That will only overwhelm you and keep you from moving forward. Choose just *one* for now. Perhaps, like Jennifer, it is pretty dresses. Or, maybe it's flattering shoes, well-fitting pants or a winter coat that doesn't make you look like the abominable snowman. Whatever it is for you, follow these steps:

Focus on what you *do* want. I'm sure there is a good reason you don't, for example, have the shoes you need (wide feet, can't wear heels, orthotics, bunions, long, narrow feet, etc.), but don't go there right now. Focus on a specific desire, e.g., pretty low-heeled shoes to go with pants, a charming pair of pumps to go with a skirt or whatever will make you happy.

People-watch. In Jennifer's case she might want to shift her focus to women with a similar body shape to hers whose look she admires. She hadn't really thought about it before because her focus had always been on women with small waists who wear a size 8. The more she looks, the more she will see plenty of women out there in all shapes and sizes who look beautiful.

If shoes are what you are looking for, see what shoes other women are wearing. Look for ones you like that you think might fit your requirements. When you see someone wearing a pair of shoes you like, stop her. Tell her you love her shoes and want to know where she got them. I bet she will be delighted you noticed and will be happy to share.

Shop somewhere new. I will say this again and again and for good reason. So many women get stuck shopping at the same place over and over. If you don't like the results, it's time to find some new places to shop. Even if you think you have tried everywhere, keep looking. There are always new places popping up and stores that seem to be the world's best-kept secrets. If you are open to finding them, they will appear. And, here's another opportunity to ask around to see where others whose styles you admire shop successfully.

Keep it positive. If Jennifer feels like she is resigned to wearing baggy clothes to hide her tummy, then she will miss all the beautiful possibilities available to her. The same is true for you. If you go shopping with the attitude that there are no shoes out there for you (your feet are impossible, everything hurts, and all the good shoes are too expensive), guess what you will find? That's right. You guessed it; you will get exactly what you expect. Start to change all that now, and do not beat yourself up if you fall back into old habits or do not at first succeed. Just keep going. If your experience has been one way for a long time, just congratulate yourself on every little success (no matter how small) along the way. It will pay off in the end.

Need some help? Start by taking a deep breath in and then letting it out. Close your eyes, and picture yourself wearing the most beautiful pair of shoes or perfectly fitting black pants or whatever you are looking for. Do not get hung up on the specifics. It is not important that you know whether they are black or silver or if the pants are dressy or casual. It is the feeling you are after. Take a moment and really *feel* how delicious it is. Invite in that sense of joy, excitement, delight or deep satisfaction—whatever is right for you. Enjoy that feeling for as long as you'd like before opening your eyes. Keep this picture and feeling front and center as you shop. (Chapter 4 will give you more tips on how to have a more satisfying shopping experience.)

Bonus: Do not settle! Only buy and wear something if you love it and think it is beautiful. There are no exceptions. This is your opportunity to add beauty (if it has been missing) to your wardrobe and style.

This process works if your critical need is a new haircut, a dress for a wedding, a bathing suit or even basic black pants. Be diligent in following these steps, and you will see results. Over time, these little successes add up to big success. The only way you lose is if you give up. We all need little reminders that we can have what we want, and changing your perspective and experience is as much about inviting in positive energy as it is about knowing exactly where to shop. Overcoming the inner struggle is a crucial component. Keep this concept in mind when you are feeling frustrated.

The first thing Jennifer and I did when we got into the dressing room was to activate positive energy. Remember, she had been stuck in a discouraging place for a while, and shopping with that hanging over her head would not help her find things she loved. I walked her through the visualization of experiencing herself trying on beautiful things that made her look and feel terrific. I then encouraged her to stop and pull up that feeling anytime she started to feel discouraged or overwhelmed as we walked around the store. She did this several times, and that day she went home with two wonderful dresses that made her feel beautiful and gave her hope for dressing her new body.

How do you add beauty to your wardrobe? Know what you are looking for and stay focused and positive. Use the guidelines above over and over, and invite into your wardrobe only things that you love and think are beautiful. It can happen, and you deserve it. With a little practice, you *can* feel great about the way you look and actually love getting dressed every day.

— —

Don't be surprised if working through this chapter revealed unexpected insights about yourself. That's not unusual. Most women I know, myself included, have found little gremlins hanging out where their inner beauty used to live. As you have most likely noticed, these gremlins have a tendency to dampen your natural sparkle and encourage you to sacrifice your dreams of feeling good about how you look. But, don't let them! You now have new information and a growing awareness that will support you in keeping the gremlins at bay more often. And, the next eight chapters will reinforce what you have learned so far and build on it. Most importantly, you will find that when you face these gremlins head on and allow yourself to recognize and acknowledge your inner beauty, they retreat. As each gremlin disappears, you open yourself up to new possibilities for creating a look you love.

Take a moment right now to acknowledge your biggest inner beauty aha moment. Savor it, and celebrate it! This is just the beginning, so keep reading.

Chapter 2

Taming Your Closet

ARE YOU STARTING TO believe that wonderful things are on the horizon? It's true, but first you have some more work to do inside—inside your closet, that is. This chapter will help you take a critical look at your existing wardrobe, which includes clothes, accessories and makeup.

Before you get to your closet, there are a few things you need to put in place to help you assess what you have right now. They are important tools at any step in your style journey, so get these beauty basics as soon as possible.

A Mirror

Believe it or not, most women do not have an adequate full-length mirror. If you are relying on the mirror on your dresser that cuts you off at the knees or a full-length mirror on a door you cannot open all the way in a dark corner at the end of a hallway (you think I'm kidding, right?), you need to make a change.

Let me give you an example. I was doing a wardrobe consultation with Stephanie one day. At one point I asked her to put something on so we could look at the fit of the outfit and play with the mixing and matching possibilities. She very readily agreed, and after she changed I asked her to show me her full-length mirror. I followed her down two hallways, across three rooms, and into a closet to get to a mirror in a guest bedroom on the other side of the house!

"Do you use this?" I asked. "Occasionally," she replied sheepishly. Stephanie admitted that this mirror was so inconvenient that she mostly used the mirror on her medicine cabinet in her bathroom where she could see to her waist, at most, if she stood on her tiptoes.

How did she ever tell if something looked OK? She didn't. Mostly, she just crossed her fingers a lot and hoped for the best!

I suspect that you are now mentally taking inventory of your personal mirror collection. The important questions are: Where are they, and are they truly functional? Much like lighting situations (see below), many women settle for substandard mirror options in their homes. Is this true for you?

Having a mirror where you can see from head to toe is not a luxury. It is a necessity, and, thankfully, it does not have to cost a fortune or take up massive amounts of space.

Let's not just wonder if an outfit works. Let's know for sure!

Please take a few minutes to go to your favorite superstore or look online, and invest in a full-length mirror.

There are lots of choices out there from the $10 mirrors found at any basic superstore to an over-the-door mirror you can conveniently hang on the back of your bedroom or bathroom door. I even found an ironing board that has a full-length mirror on the other side!

Keep these five things in mind when choosing a mirror. It must be:

1. **Conveniently located** in your bedroom close to your closet.

2. **Well lit.** It is useless to look at yourself in the dark!

3. **Smooth and straight.** Warped, "fun house" mirrors distort your body and your perspective, and they do not do a thing for your self-image or self-esteem, either.

4. **The right height.** Can you see all of yourself without standing on a chair or squatting? Yes, your head and feet are important parts of how you look.

5. **The right distance according to where you want to stand.** You want to make sure you have enough room to stand back a little bit so you can get a full perspective. It is not useful if you only have two feet between you and the mirror.

Once you have a great mirror, you will wonder how you ever did without it, and it is important to look in it every once in a while and make sure all is well. If nothing else, take a peek at your rear view and make sure everything looks OK from all angles. Others see this view of you all the time, and you want to be sure you know what's going on back there!

Recently, I attended a concert and stopped in the ladies room before heading to the concert hall. While I was there a woman came out of a stall to wash her hands. I noticed that the back of her skirt was tucked up in her underwear! When I pointed it out to her, she was so thankful. Of course, if you are home alone getting ready for work, a quick peek in the mirror before you leave the house will alleviate any worries about something similar going unchecked.

A Camera (preferably digital)

A picture allows you to see yourself and your outfit from a fresh perspective. It is different than looking in the mirror. You can study a picture, and you can get a sense of what others see.

Here are several comments I have heard from clients after they saw a picture of themselves in an outfit they had questions about:

- "Wow, that used to be my favorite outfit! I had no idea it made me look so dowdy."
- "Hey, I do have nice legs!"
- "I thought those two pieces went nicely together but now I can see that the fabrics don't work and the skirt clings in a way that isn't flattering."
- "I need to stand up straighter."

- "I wear a lot of that light-blue color and can see that it makes me look washed out." (And, also the opposite: "Wow, I had no idea I look so good in coral.")

In each case, the picture allowed the woman to evaluate an outfit in a way she could not do in front of her own mirror or in a dressing room. Try it and see for yourself.

Good Lighting

When I travel one of my pet peeves is hotel bathroom mirrors! There is absolutely no doubt in my mind that these were designed by men who never have to apply makeup and never look in the mirror.

Invariably, I try getting super close or standing several feet back to see if I can get the overhead lighting to be a bit more forgiving. I inevitably give up and go to the mirror over the desk in the bedroom or grab a hand mirror (if it's daytime) and go to the window.

What is up with that? It should not be nearly so complicated to apply a little makeup! I hate leaving the room wondering if I look scary.

And, it's not just makeup that can be affected. If you have ever tried matching colors in a dark room or if you have ever left the house wearing one navy and one black sock or shoe, then you know what I mean. With inadequate lighting, colors are not always what they seem, and you might not notice until it's too late to change!

Unfortunately, so many women settle for the equivalent of hotel bathroom mirrors every day when they get dressed and put on their makeup. If you've been putting on your makeup in the dark, you will be surprised by the difference when you have better light and can actually see what you are doing. You will apply your makeup faster and seemingly effortlessly compared to squinting and doing various facial acrobatics!

Here are a few tips to keep you from looking like you got dressed in the dark:

Use natural light whenever possible. The absolute best lighting for getting dressed or putting on your makeup is natural light. It allows you to see everything clearly. No more wondering if your blush is blended well or if the powder under your eyes is accentuating any lines. You will know for sure. Natural light can seem a bit unforgiving at first, but when you like the way you look in natural light, you will love it everywhere else.

Unfortunately, it is not always feasible or convenient to use natural light since not all bathrooms have access to a window, and many closets (and even bedrooms) are very dark. Not to mention that on a cloudy day natural light is so diffused that it is not helpful. Whenever you do have access to natural light, use it—even if it means taking a hand mirror over to the window to check your makeup and outfit before leaving the house. Hint: When you use a hand mirror, always face the window. You will get a splash of natural light on your face and will be able to see everything well.

Banish overhead lighting. Because it is over your head, this kind of lighting casts shadows, which give you dark circles and basically make it nearly impossible to see what you are doing—at least with any degree of confidence. It lights the room, but it does not allow you to see your face clearly. Without that ability, you feel frustrated or just tired after seeing all those light-enhanced dark circles. It is easy, then, to overcompensate by applying more under eye concealer than you actually need.

You do not have to tear out all the existing lighting in your bedroom or bathroom (although that would certainly be ideal) and start over. Just do not apply your makeup or check your colors under its glare. Instead, invest in a lighted makeup mirror and set it on your bedroom dresser or the vanity in your bathroom—wherever it's convenient. These types of mirrors generally have a "daylight" setting that will give clean, clear, and even light for applying your makeup. Just be sure you don't position the mirror directly under an overhead light or next to a table lamp; these can adversely affect the light from the makeup mirror.

Change your light bulbs. Even if your bathroom vanity mirror is lit from the side, you will want to check the type of light bulbs you are using. Most incandescent bulbs cast a yellow glow, which is also not helpful in evaluating color, and let's not even talk about most fluorescent bulbs, which make us all look slightly green.

So what's the lighting solution? Full-spectrum or halogen lighting, which directly mimics natural light. This goes for your bathroom, your closet or anywhere else you apply makeup or get dressed.

I know you're wondering if the type of lighting can really affect what you see that much. Let me share an experience I had that drove the point home for me.

One day many years ago I stopped at the cosmetic counter to buy some nail polish. I wanted a coral color and found just what I wanted pretty quickly. I couldn't wait to get home and paint my nails. As I stepped out of the store into daylight, I took the polish out of the bag to look at it again. Imagine my shock and disappointment when the color turned out to be bright cotton candy pink! I immediately returned the nail polish, but the experience stuck with me. Indoor lights can fool your eye! Most store lighting adds a touch of yellow or green to everything.

It always amazes me that most stores do not pay more attention to how a dressing room is lit. Do we really want to see every inch of cellulite or look overly tired because of the shadows the overhead lights cast? It can be disturbing and discouraging, and I know it results in lost sales from time to time. Or, have you ever danced around the store trying to find a corner where the overhead spotlights do not cast funny shadows or where it is light enough that you can actually see the detail in a fabric? I do it all the time and always wonder why the stores are not more aware of this problem.

The solution is to take your garment over to natural light whenever possible to evaluate the color, inspect the fabric, determine how well it matches what you want to pair with it, etc. If the store does not have any natural light or it's a cloudy day, do the best you can to decide if you like it and consider taking it home to try it on in better light. Of course, you will only want to do this if the store has an adequate return policy.

With these tools in place, your closet awaits!

How Did You Get So Many Clothes?

WOMEN NEVER COME TO me and say, "I want lots of clothes." Really. It never happens. In fact, most tell me that they want to simplify their wardrobes and want fewer clothes that they wear more often.

DOES THIS RING TRUE for you, too? Does your sense of yearning come from feeling overwhelmed by a wardrobe that does not serve your needs or speak to your heart? Have you settled into a look that is "good enough" and then one day notice that you wear the same things over and over because they are easy, and many things hang unworn in your closet?

Multiply this scenario by a million (I suspect it's at least that many), and that is a lot of clothes not being worn, and, more importantly, a lot of women feeling out of sorts.

It is important to know exactly what is in your closet, but first I want you to think about how it got to be so full. Here are ten reasons why women have so many clothes.

1. **You Love to Shop** – You love to shop and enjoy creating beautiful outfits, and the biggest problem you encounter is that you do not have enough days in the week to wear them all as often as you would like. There are some women out there like that for sure, but unless they run out of closet space they are usually pretty happy with what they have.

2. **Someday Syndrome** – This is a biggie. You have rarely, or never, worn it. You are not even sure you like it or that it fits, but, hey, what if you need it someday to complete an outfit? No! No! No! This is a central theme in this book. There is no room in your closet for things you do not love.

3. **Giveaways and Hand-Me-Downs** – People feel good about passing things along, and it feels good to get things for free. But

do not accept these things unless they work for you—I mean *really work* for you!

4. **You Spent Good Money on It** – Many women hold on to pieces that do not work for them because of the price. If you are not wearing something, you are not getting your money's worth, whether it cost $50 or $500. And, the more you learn about what truly works for you, the less likely you will be to have this issue in the future.

5. **Your Weight Fluctuates** – Join the crowd! I can assure you that so many women—especially those of us over forty—deal with this. It's OK. Relax, and take a breath. What is not OK, however, is keeping all the sizes in the same closet. No! Only the clothes that fit you now belong in the closet you use on a daily basis.

6. **You Are Clinging to the Past** – Do you have clothes in your closet from 1992, 1987 or even before? Your closet should only contain what works for you right now. Hanging on to things you used to wear (for a past job or a different lifestyle) will keep you stuck in a rut and will not help you feel authentically you. A special word about the energy of clothes: If some of your outfits are from a painful or unpleasant time in your past, you do not want that energy in your closet. It will only deplete you.

7. **It's Classic** – Yes, some styles have a timeless quality about them, but there are many fewer than you would think. Chanel jackets are one thing, but even something as basic as jeans go through style changes as the years pass. You do want to take good care of your clothes so you can wear them as long as possible. But you do not want to keep them past their expiration date.

8. **Peer Pressure** – There is a fine line between getting helpful advice from your BFF, mother, sister or friendly sales woman and being railroaded into buying something. Your wardrobe should consist only of pieces *you* love that make *you* feel wonderful.

9. **You Are Searching for the Perfect Pieces** – I once did a wardrobe consultation with Jessica who had at least forty white blouses in her closet. Of those, she generally wore one or two. That's it! So why did she have so many? Because someone had mistakenly told her that every woman should have a white blouse in her wardrobe. While white blouses are great for some women, on others the stark white washes them out, or they find most button-down blouses ill fitting or fussy, especially under a jacket. It could just be that they find them boring. Although Jessica had discovered that finding the perfect white blouse was trickier than she thought, she kept buying them hoping she would find one that she loved. She never did.

10. **You Can't Get Rid of Anything** – You might be keeping things for a combination of the reasons above, or your desire to hold onto things might stem from a more deep- seated reason. Holding on to clothes that no longer serve you because of past experiences or because they give you peace will eventually backfire. At some point, your closet will be so overflowing with clothes that any peace you felt from hanging onto the things you cannot get rid of will be lost in the chaos of your closet.

Can you relate to one of more of the above justifications? A closet full of clothes you do not love can be overwhelming and frustrating, and these feeling are some of the big reasons women never do anything about an out-of-control wardrobe. Living with these feelings day in and day out does not make for a happy experience. And getting dressed is meant to be joyful or at the very least easy and satisfying!

To move you out of overwhelmed and closer to joyful, please make a commitment to take one step toward tackling your closet in the next twenty-four hours. Even add it to your calendar. This will support you in getting ready to do some clearing and take your personal style to the next level.

Is There a Stranger in Your Closet?

WHO DO YOU SEE when you look in your closet? Is your mother's face smiling back at you from that ruffle shirt you've never worn? Or is your best friend's favorite dress hanging out in there taunting you?

In response to the question, "Who do you see when you look in your closet," I most often hear:

- My mother
- My sister
- My best friend
- Myself, pre-children
- Myself, pre-thirty extra pounds
- Myself, pre-menopause
- My favorite celebrity
- Whoever was working at the store the day I went shopping
- The store window mannequin
- All of the above!

Guess what? When you look in your closet you want to see YOU—just *you.* You want to see items that make you smile and that you associate with fun times and delicious moments. Maybe the memories are of pushing your daughter on a swing, lunch with girlfriends, a successful business presentation, or a precious date with your sweetie. These are the simple pleasures that make up life. And you want these feelings to be reflected in every aspect of your wardrobe—down to your nightgown and slippers!

So evict the strangers and weed out those garments that make you roll your eyes or cringe. They have absolutely no place in your wardrobe. This exercise will help you make your closet all about you!

1. **Remove one item from your closet that feels more like someone else than you.** If you are near your closet, go there right now and do this (if not, write down the first thing that comes into your mind so you will remember to remove it later). Do it even if you don't know why it isn't you or what to put in to replace it. The very first step is to get it out of there.

   As long as something that is not you is taking up space in your sacred closet (yes, it is sacred because this is where your essence is expressed every day), you will feel overburdened, frustrated, annoyed or discouraged—or resigned to all of those feelings— every time you get dressed, and none of those is good. It is also very likely that you are not wearing this garment anyway. It is more like a security blanket, but the security is a sham.

2. **Identify one garment or outfit that makes you smile the second you put it on your body.** It can be a dress, pair of pants, a pair of shoes or a scarf. No item is too small or insignificant.

3. **Lay the stranger and the item you love side by side,** and get a piece of paper or a notebook.

4. **For the item that is not you, write down everything you do not like about it.** Be as picky as you can. Maybe it's the way the fabric feels. Perhaps the buttons seem overwhelming, or there are just too many of them. It could be that you dislike the pattern or the way it clings. Or perhaps it has a belt, and you do not like belts. Write down everything! If there are a few things you like about it, write those in a separate column. Maybe the color is pretty, but it can't make up for the fact that the style is so shapeless.

5. **Write down everything you like about the item you love:** color, texture, fit, shape, ornamental details, the way it feels or anything else about it that comes to mind. Maybe it makes you feel sophisticated, down-to-earth, spunky or pretty. Whatever it is, write it down.

6. **Use these lists when you go shopping** to help you stay focused. They are your lifelines! The next time you try on an item, run down both lists and see how the garment compares. It is so easy to get distracted by all the choices, the lighting or the helpful "advice" from sales women or your shopping buddies. Remember from Chapter 1: Only buy or wear something if you love it.

What's in Your Closet?

CONGRATULATIONS! YOU'VE TAKEN ONE step toward taming your closet. Are you ready to do more? It's time to get serious about exactly what's in your closet.

Closets are a lot like basements. Allow me to explain.

Several years ago, I moved. All in all, it went very smoothly, and I attribute much of that to one particular step I took early on: I did what everyone who moves dreads doing: I cleaned out my basement. I spent years running downstairs to fill the furnace or grab my bike and all the time ignoring the boxes filled with things like twenty-year-old business receipts, scads of sheet music that had gotten wet when my water heater broke and a bag full of old towels. Who knew when I might need those! I ignored them until that dreaded day when I realized I was going to move and knew I absolutely, positively did not want to take all that stuff with me.

So, I called my assistant and asked sheepishly, "Would you be willing to help me clean my basement?" She enthusiastically agreed (isn't she wonderful?), and we set a date. When the day came, we made our way to the basement, and forty bags later we stopped only because I ran out of trash bags and didn't feel like running to the store. I am telling you this because in the middle of our project, my assistant turned to me and said, "Ginger, I'm not doing anything. I'm just standing here holding bags." I smiled and said, "Yes, isn't that wonderful? If we had not set this date, I wouldn't be doing this, so thank you!"

It's the same with our clothes closets. We go in them every day and ignore the chaos. This takes effort (even if you are unaware of it), and it keeps you from creating a personal style you love. The first step in creating a wardrobe of your dreams is to know what you already have or don't have and be able to locate it easily. If your closet looks like your children regularly have play dates in there or you've been using it as a repository for every article of clothing you've ever owned, then creating order is key.

Since I know that some of you are now hyperventilating at the thought of cleaning out your closet, I promise I'll break it down into manageable pieces! No matter what, please do not just close the door one more time and relegate your closet woes to out of sight, out of mind. I suspect that has not been working for you so far! Let's get to the heart of it now so you can breathe a sigh of relief—and, hey, maybe even feel excited—every time you get dressed.

You have two options. And, no, moving and leaving everything behind is not an option!

Get someone to help you. Even if all she does is sit on your bed, drink tea or sip a glass of wine and say encouraging things (maybe even fold something here or there, too), the support will keep you focused on the task at hand.

Do it yourself over time. You can transform your closet and your wardrobe within a month with minimal effort, and you will get to enjoy immediate results daily. Follow these three steps:

1. **Change your hangers**. Are your clothes hanging haphazardly on a variety of plastic, wooden, quilted, novelty and (gasp!) wire hangers? If so, please recycle all your wire hangers at the dry cleaners and immediately replace all hangers with either notched plastic hangers (like the ones most department stores use) or the huggable hangers that are so popular. The important thing is that you have only one type of hanger in your closet, so choose your favorite style. Why? When your clothes hang uniformly, you can actually see your choices! Not only will this look more organized instantly, but it will also make step number two easier to do.

2. **Every time you open your closet door, remove one item you never wear** (or at least have not worn in the past year). It is that simple. Are you really ever going to wear that sweater that droops to your knees that your mother gave you or the patterned

leggings your thirteen-year-old daughter told you that you had to have? We often hang onto these items thinking, "Well, what if?" Ask yourself this: Has the what-if ever happened? That's what I thought.

If you are not ready to get rid of the garment right away—sometimes it takes understanding why it won't ever work to feel comfortable donating it (see "Unworn Clothing: Love It or Let It Go?" below)— simply pack it away for future reference. I doubt you will ever miss it. If you remove something once or twice each day, you will quickly and easily reduce your closet chaos, and it will feel great!

3. **Ask yourself one very revealing question about everything you put on: "Do I love this and think it is beautiful?"** If you cannot answer a resounding yes, the item gets packed away or goes in the donate pile. While this sounds simple enough, it is not always easy. But this step is critical if your ultimate goal is to have a closet full of clothing you adore. Be ruthless!

These three steps take very little time, so they are extremely doable. Many women tell me that their spirits lighten, their shoulders straighten, and their energy level rises each day when they perform these simple steps.

Unworn Clothing: Love It or Let It Go?

YOU HAVE COMMITTED TO taming your closet. Now we'll confront the big question of this process: How do you know when to keep something or let it go? Every time I am in front of a group of women and ask how many of them have unworn clothing in their closet, every hand in the room goes up. This tells you something. It's a persistent problem, and it is part of what is keeping women stuck in a wardrobe they do not love and do not wear. It's hard to think about bringing in anything new when there's already so much there or you feel like you'll just repeat past mistakes and add to that growing rack of unworn garments.

Trisha had a ready smile, a quick wit and a playful side to her that quickly put others at ease. Six months earlier, she had left her job in a large CPA firm and started her own business helping women with their finances. She was excited about the move but unsure about whether her old wardrobe worked any more.

One jacket she showed me had been a staple in her wardrobe for several years, but she had not worn it since she left her job. She would regularly put it on and take it off but never wore it out of the house. It used to be part of a pantsuit, but she got ink on the pants and had to let them go. She felt like the jacket should still work but was tired of having it take up space in her closet if it didn't. She said she would feel comfortable getting rid of it if she just understood why it didn't work.

I asked Trisha to put it on. While the fit was fine, it was clear right away that the deep honey color of the jacket was not right for her now that she had let her hair, which was once brown with red highlights, go gray. The jacket also had a jewel neckline so the it looked better closed, and this made the patch pockets sit right on her hips, drawing attention to that part of her body.

While wearing the jacket, Trisha stood stiffly without smiling and did not look comfortable. When I asked her how she felt in it, she let out a breath and laughed. She couldn't wait to take it off. She felt too serious and unapproachable and felt such relief when she wasn't wearing it anymore.

When Trisha and I reviewed the pros and cons, it turned out that although the jacket still fit her body, her lifestyle had changed, the color was no longer flattering, and she did not feel good in it anymore. She wanted her wardrobe to reflect more ease, a grace-filled beauty and joy. Phew. It was clearly time for that jacket to find a new home. When she realized that since it was still in very good conditions she could donate to Dress for Success (www.dressforsuccess.org) and help a disadvantaged woman look and feel professional for a job interview, she was delighted. The decision was easy once she no longer wondered if it served a useful purpose in her wardrobe.

One thing was clear: When Trisha could not clearly evaluate and honestly understand why the jacket did not work for her, she kept it in the hope that someday she would find a way to wear it. But once she felt absolutely clear about why it wouldn't work on her anymore, she could easily let it go. This also gave her valuable information for her next shopping trip.

Do you find yourself saying: "But it's in good condition" or "I barely wore it." Another popular one is: "I paid a lot of money for it, so I have to find a way to wear it." Are you convinced that those are reasons enough to keep these garments? Let me assure you they are not.

Everyone has a different idea of what is too much or too little, pricewise, and how much you paid for something does not influence whether it looks good on you. Of course, the more you understand about what works in your wardrobe, the less likely you will be to waste money of any amount on things you do not wear. The ultimate goal with every garment is to wear it so much that the price per wear becomes negligible—no matter what the original cost.

If you spent a lot of money on something that doesn't suit you, now is the time to cut your losses, learn from the experience and allow something fabulous to come into your closet that you do wear a lot and, let's not forget, that you enjoy wearing. Once you understand why it does not work, the chance of your repeating that kind of expensive mistake again drops dramatically.

Here are the steps that will empower you to move an item out with grace and ease when it's clear it is no longer serving you. Ready, set, go!

Take one item that you are not wearing out of your closet. Put the item on (yes, put it on!), and ask yourself these questions:

- Does the color look great on you? (Remember, you're not going for OK, decent or just good enough.)

- Does it fit you right now? If you love the item but it is just not the same size as you right now, see round three.

- Is it in good condition, or, if not, are you willing to do the necessary repairs? (This includes dewrinkling, aka ironing!)

- Does it conjure fond memories or at least have no disturbing memories attached to it? (Please note that fond memories alone are not enough reason to keep it—at least not in your everyday closet.) If it brings fond memories, is a great color and fits you and you love wearing it, then keep going. Otherwise, move it to another closet, and enjoy the memories when you admire it there.

- Does it work with your current lifestyle needs? So many times I have seen women keep clothes from their corporate days many years after they have needed them. Note: If it has been more than two years since you have worn it, move it out.

- Is it comfortable? If not, and the cause of discomfort cannot be remedied, it goes away.

- Do you love it? This actually should be the first question. But there is a lot to consider here, so keep reading.

That was round one. If you can say a resounding yes (not a pitiful whimper) to *all* of these questions, the item moves to round two. If you said no to any of them, it goes in the go away pile to be donated, consigned, discarded or at least packed away in storage.

If the garment passes round one, ask yourself this: Can you make a complete outfit with it? If so, it's a keeper. If not, you have some additional questions to answer.

- How long have you had it? If it has been more than two years since you've worn it, send it to the go away pile.

- Was there another piece that went with it? This happens often. For example, you buy a pretty print skirt and a top to go with it, and then the top gets a hole or a stain so you have to discard it. This leaves you with half of an outfit. Chances are ten to one you will never complete it again.

- If you are still reluctant to let it go, you absolutely must put it on. I know there are some of you who are doing this exercise without assessing the garment on your body and you are missing a lot of valuable information that way!

Believe me, your mind can play funny tricks on you. If you have fond memories associated with the garment, you will feel compelled to keep it—until you see it on your body. Most of the time, it turns out the garment is not as fabulous as you remember. This is not to say it was not fabulous at some point. It had its day, but today isn't it. Perhaps it fits your body differently or maybe not at all. It might feel old-fashioned, as if it came from a different era. You might even discover it has a stain, a tear or some other defect that makes it less likely that you can still wear it. This is all invaluable information that you often will not get without having the garment on your body.

Round three is evaluating the go away pile. I've used the term *go away* for a reason. You do not have to get rid of all the items; you just need to get them out of your everyday closet. If you put something in the go away pile and you are experiencing heart palpitations worrying that you will miss it, relax. Simply pack these "maybe" items away in an empty closet or in plastic bins in the attic. You can do the same with pieces that work for you when your weight has changed. If you decide you want one (although I predict you won't miss the maybes for a second), you will know exactly where it is should you have a change of heart.

If you are still unsure about some pieces after asking yourself all these questions, it is time to get some objective, preferably expert, assistance. Sometimes you are too close to the situation to be objective yourself or you need some expert validation that you are making the right decision for the right reasons. With a little support and guidance, it all becomes crystal clear.

Where can you find help? Ideally, it would be from an image consultant/fashion stylist whose taste you admire. Even if she is not wearing an outfit you would wear, you want to admire how she puts things together. If that is not feasible, you can invite a trusted friend to help. Sometimes just having someone validate what you were thinking or give you a new perspective can be enough to help you let go of something or find a new way of wearing it. The most important thing is that you must feel self-confident enough to say no when you don't agree or you will not feel comfortable with the choices you make. The last thing you want is someone who decides she knows better than you and will not stop until you give in. In the end, you are the only one who gets to say what you love wearing.

Why go through all of this? Because it's a thousand times easier to give something to charity, take it to a consignment shop or discard it if you know it will never work for you. There is a freedom that comes with that awareness, and once your closet is cleared of all the unworn and unwearable clothes, your mind and heart will feel lighter.

So, keep going. The more you pare down your wardrobe to things that make you feel good and express the core of who you are, the better you will be at doing it. You will gain momentum and be adept at understanding what is working and what is not and why. In fact, make this a regular exercise so you don't end up every year or two with a closet full of unworn clothes. Assess your situation on a regular basis, and you will get dressed with joy and ease every day.

What Are You Waiting For?

WHEN I SAW MY mom one Christmas she came bearing a large box. I shook my head. We had agreed no gifts were expected! So, my first words to her were, "You weren't supposed to bring anything!" Just having her visit my partner, Marion, and me was such a special treat that we were not expecting another gift. Of course, no one has ever been able to tell my mom what to do, and I saw immediately that this was no exception!

We had no idea what could be in this box (it weighed quite a bit) and so were surprised and delighted to find it contained her prized china teacup collection. For many years we have admired it on display in her dining room when we visited, and I know how much she enjoyed them.

The cups are beautiful and delicate. So, after a million heartfelt thank you's, I turned to my mom and said, "You know we'll use these, right? We won't just put them on display." We make it a habit to drink out of pretty teacups nearly every day and have for over twenty years, so there is no way the cups would languish on a shelf somewhere.

Why am I telling you this? Because many women use their clothes and accessories the way my mom used her teacups: They don't. Their prized possessions sit in a box or are sequestered in the back of the closet for years and sometimes decades, never seeing the light of day.

Do you have items that you are "saving" because they have sentimental value, are "too pretty to wear," are timeless, or cost a lot of money? I know this is a sticky subject because it is so personal and these items hold such a prized place in our hearts or memories.

Here are three reasons you are saving those items and why you should use them now:

1. **The big what-if?:** The biggest fear people have around using something they cherish (or simply delight in) is that they might ruin it. So, here's the truth: Yes, you might ruin it. We know

that there is a definite possibility that we could break one of the teacups when we use them. Nine times out of ten (maybe 9.99 times out of ten!), this won't happen. As I mentioned, we've been using these delicate teacups for twenty years and haven't broken a single one yet—and, horrors of all horrors, we even put them in the dishwasher!

We get to delight in using them every day, and nothing can take away our memories of how they feel, how beautiful they look on the table and how much we enjoy drinking from them. Somehow having them sit in a box somewhere or get dusty on a shelf just doesn't hold the same magic.

When I suggest using something, I am not talking about delicate slips from 1900 or a hand-beaded heirloom evening bag that needs to be preserved properly—although I still believe they should have a place of prominence and distinction. Rather I'm talking about those special items you keep looking at but are afraid to use.

2. **The myth of timelessness:** Very few (really, very few!) garments are truly timeless. There I said it. Even if you disagree, there is a much bigger concern here. In general, you do not need your clothes to last more than ten years. Clothes are made to be worn, and if you like your clothes enough, that is exactly what you will do—hopefully with enough regularity that they will eventually wear out after having served you well. If, however, you save them for only those special moments, not only do you fail to enjoy them the way you should, but you also run the risk of finding out they are not as timeless or durable as you thought when you finally get around to wearing them. Too many times I have watched a client put on something she thought was timeless only to find that it had yellowed, the elastic had disintegrated or it just didn't fit anymore.

3. **Nowhere to wear it:** This one is often the final excuse. You are no longer afraid of ruining it, and you want to wear it now, but where? This excuse is actually the easiest to overcome. Here's a little exercise:

- Identify a garment or accessory that you have been saving for one of the reasons listed above.

- When you think about using it, do you get excited? If so, continue on to the next step.

If not, see if you can figure out why. That will help you determine if you should pack it away or give it away. Maybe it just needs some repair or the right accessory. Whatever information you can glean will help you determine your next step.

- Find a time to wear it—within the next week! Maybe it means making a plan to go out to dinner with your husband when you can wear that pretty dress you've been saving, even if it is just to the local eatery. Don't be surprised, however, if things change. Recently, Sarah told me that she and her husband had plans to go out to dinner to a simple, casual restaurant nearby. She decided she just had to wear a gorgeous dress and amazing necklace we had gotten during our shopping trip. When Sarah came downstairs all dressed, her husband took one look at her and said, "Wow! We're going to the Four Seasons for dinner instead."

  Or, perhaps call your girlfriends and suggest a girls' night out at your place where everyone wears something she has been saving. Or, maybe it just means taking a few minutes to switch handbags to the one you bought six months ago but have not gotten around to using yet.

As you are reading this, your mind is probably spinning thinking of all the long-forgotten garments or accessories you have tucked away that never see the light of day. There is no time like the present. Stop saving those items of beauty for a special occasion. In most of our lives, those times just do not come around often enough, so we have to make those special occasions ourselves. It can be easier than you think to integrate them into your current wardrobe so you and others vicariously, can enjoy them.

Is Your Jewelry Out of Sight?

YOU MIGHT NOT ACTUALLY store your jewelry in your closet with your clothes, but no matter where it is, keeping it organized and easily accessible will simplify your experience of getting dressed every day. Before we talk about how to use accessories, let's address where you keep them.

Julia had on one of her favorite outfits. While she loved it, she felt like it still needed something to pull it altogether. Naturally, the discussion turned to jewelry. Did she have some? Did she like it? What kind was it—fine, bridge/semi-precious stones or costume? You get the idea.

Finally, I asked to see it. As often happens, it turned out to be a huge ordeal! Some of Julia's jewelry was in a dresser drawer in boxes, some was scattered haphazardly in a jewelry box, and the rest was in another room in a mishmash of boxes, drawers and bags. When I asked if she wore it, she responded, "Not really."

I can tell you right now that if, like Julia, your jewelry is strewn somewhere or neatly (or not so neatly) tucked away in boxes, three things are generally true:

1. It's too much trouble to get to it to wear your jewelry.

2. You probably have things you have forgotten about.

3. You might not love it enough to wear it.

All of these can be remedied if you can create a way to store your jewelry so you can see it. When you do, several things will happen. You will feel renewed excitement at the idea of wearing it. You will be able to find it easily, and this is likely to translate into your wearing it more. And, you will become acutely aware of what you no longer like, what doesn't go with anything and what is out of style. This makes it much easier to purge.

As you know, I spend time in a lot of closets and have come across a number of women who have devised ways of organizing and storing their jewelry so it is readily visible but not in the way. Here are a few ideas I have learned from some very clever clients:

Think outside the box. Find unusual containers and turn them into jewelry holders. Annie, for instance, used a silverware tray to hold her bracelets and necklaces.

Amy took one shelf in her closet to display her necklaces. She attached hooks underneath the shelf above so her pieces could hang freely and in an organized way. This made it easy to see what she had to coordinate with her clothes.

Claudyne lives in a fabulous old house that has a big pole running vertically through her walk-in closet. She attached plastic hooks and hangs all of her necklaces there. She can easily see what she has, so getting dressed and accessorized is simple. And the pole becomes an integral part of her closet rather than being in the way.

Jodi keeps it simple and stores the jewelry that goes with a particular outfit in a mesh bag and hangs the clothes and jewelry together on the hanger. Since this is the primary way she accessorizes that outfit, she eliminates the step of going to find her jewelry when she needs it and makes getting dressed even easier.

Do you enjoy do-it-yourself projects? Here is an easy one for hanging earrings. Find a beautiful frame, attach a piece of wire mesh to the back, and hang your earrings through it. You can hang the frame on your wall above your dresser or in your closet and see all your earrings in one glance. Or, pick up one of those eighty-pocket hanging jewelry organizers. The pockets are clear so you can see your earrings easily, and you can hang it over your closet door or in your closet.

My personal favorite—I have one of these—is a beautiful cabinet that doubles as a full-length mirror. I keep it in my bedroom filled with all my jewels!

Sterling silver does require one extra step. I have not met anyone yet who loves to polish her tarnished silver jewelry. My dear friend Karen

Halaby of Jewelry by Karel shared this valuable tip for taking care of your sterling silver jewelry: It will stay shiny longer if you place each individual piece in a plastic zip-close bag. Squeeze the air out, and zip it. Because it is exposed to less air, it tarnishes more slowly.

In general, it doesn't matter how you store your jewelry as long as you can see it and get to it easily. Like most other things, when it's out of sight, it's out of mind.

Now that you know how to store your jewelry you will want to determine how much of what you have you'll keep. As you are going through it, you are sure to find pieces you had forgotten about, and now you can wear them again. It's almost certain that you will also find pieces that make you wonder why you ever purchased them in the first place.

As you did when you assessed your clothing, you *must* put on any piece you are considering keeping. It's easy to be fooled by something that looks pretty in the box. When you put it on, you might realize it gets totally lost on you, the color is terrible, or it hangs funny and you have to keep fussing with it, which is probably the reason you stuck it in the drawer to begin with.

Use the same checklist from "Unworn Clothing: Love It or Let It Go" (earlier in this chapter) to determine what you will keep and what you'll pass along. It is easy to save more than you should because jewelry doesn't take up much space. But if you do this often enough, you will end up with the exact problem you started this exercise to solve: a mass of jewelry with the items that you really do love and want to wear buried and inaccessible. Stay strong! If you don't love it, pass it along.

Does Your Makeup Need a Makeover?

YOU DIDN'T THINK YOUR makeup was safe from this process, did you? It needs organizing just as much as the other parts of your wardrobe. Here are three steps to take right now that will give you satisfaction, keep your skin healthier and get the makeup part of your style journey off to a clean start!

Wash your makeup sponges and brushes. You use them day in and day out, yet most people rarely think about all the bacteria harbored in those bristles.

You know that powder compact you use every day? The same sponge has been in there since you bought it, right? Give it a wash. Use a little shampoo, facial cleanser, or liquid hand soap. It probably will not ever be white again, but at least it will be free of all the built up gunk. One word of caution: if you have used it for a really long time already, it might fall apart. It is best to wash your sponge every two or three weeks (at least). Once it gets to be too dirty, it won't hold up to the washing. If you fear your sponge is too old, go to the drugstore and find a replacement before you attempt to wash the old one, just in case.

The same goes for your makeup brushes. Chances are you invested a little bit in them, and if they are good quality, they will last. But, not if you don't wash them! Built up makeup, oils from your skin, and dirt will eventually break down the bristles, and you will have to replace the brush sooner than you would if you simply washed it periodically. Rinse the brush under warm water. Put a bit of shampoo or facial cleanser in the palm of your hand and swirl the brush in it. Rinse it well until all the residue is gone. Squeeze the bristles gently in a paper towel, and allow the brush to air dry. You will breathe new life into your brushes, and they'll be so much healthier for your skin.

Replace your mascara. Most women I have talked to do not have a clue as to when they bought their current mascara. This is the one makeup product you don't want to fool around with. The dark, damp packaging is the perfect breeding ground for bacteria. Replacing your mascara every three to six months is important. Tip: If you buy a new tube at the beginning of the year or perhaps when you change your clothes to and from daylight savings, you will easily remember the date and know when it's time to get your next one!

Throw stuff out! Take a look in your cosmetic bag. In fact, empty it out. What's in there? Do you use it all? Is anything more than three years old? Does anything smell funny or have a weird consistency? Do yourself a favor and throw out at least three things--they are in there; I'm sure! Get rid of those weird lipstick colors you got as samples or the light-violet blush you got because it was "in" last spring. How about that eye shadow compact that contains several colors? Are you keeping it even though you used up the one color you really like? Admit it. You will never use the other colors. Dump that moisturizer you bought on a whim when someone told you it would take twenty years off your face, but don't use because it felt too goopy. You will never miss these things, and your load will be lighter.

The steps above are easily implemented. Cleaning your sponge and your brushes can be done while you are brushing your teeth. Buy new mascara the next time you are in the drugstore or your favorite department store, or get it online--that's even quicker! And throw out three things from your cosmetic bag the next time you put on your makeup. What could be easier and more freeing? Oh, and while you're at it, take a closer look at your cosmetic bag itself. Has it seen better days? It's so easy to overlook how grungy it can get from makeup spills and normal wear and tear because you are looking at it often. Now that you have cleared out your old makeup, why not pick up a new pretty bag to store what's left?

— —

As you can see, when I talk about taming your closet I do not mean you have to be neat as a pin. Not at all. Rather, it is about subduing disorder so you can honestly see what you have.

This experience supports you in moving forward and makes it less likely that you will repeat mistakes or continue to be overwhelmed by the sheer magnitude of what you own. When you truly know what garments have taken up residence in your closet, you can more easily evaluate whether something should stay or go. In addition, when you remove items that no longer feel like you, you free up space for bringing in those that do.

And all that order means you can easily access each item instead of having to rifle through piles of clothes, jewelry or makeup to find what you want to wear. Getting dressed just got a little bit easier, and it is only going to get better!

Chapter 3
Real-life Fashion Advice

IN THE LAST CHAPTER, you gathered some style tools and worked on your closet to make sure it contains only things you love that work for you. This chapter is all about helping you decide what new things you will add. It will give you food for thought to broaden your concept of what is possible—and occasionally what isn't!—to help you make sense of all the possibilities out there. The advice is designed to take some of the mystery out of making choices that flatter you.

Creating a personal style is not a one-size-fits-all experience. If it were, fashion magazines would have gone out of business a long time ago, and everyone would be walking around wearing pretty much the same thing. How boring would that be? You know from the first chapter that creating a wardrobe you love is about letting your clothing express your inner beauty and not settling for a preconceived idea of how you should look, which will never feel truly satisfying.

As Martha said to me before she started applying these principles, "I wear the same things over and over because I don't know how to make other choices. At this point, I'm starting at zero and want to do it right. I'm tired of feeling invisible and frumpy."

What this chapter will not do is address every specific body type or tell you to wear skinny jeans if your legs are one shape but not another or when to wear a wrap dress instead of a sheath dress. First of all, there are plenty of books and magazines out there that focus on these tips, but they are just one tiny component of creating a look you love. I have seen many exceptions to every rule, and frankly, if that were all you needed to create a look you love, you would already be doing it and would be perfectly happy. The fact that you are here says you're still looking.

After twenty-six years of working with countless women of varying body shapes, heights, weights, ages and personalities, I can say with great certainty that every woman is unique, and there is no one way of dressing that will appeal to every woman's body, heart and soul. You will have much greater success and ultimately feel more satisfaction when you dress with intention from the inside out and apply that to real-life wardrobe situations, such as creating a signature style you love, discovering the joys of wearing a jacket or avoiding the pitfalls of certain cardigan sweater styles. You have the foundation of the previous two chapters to build on, and that is exactly what you will be doing here and in all the chapters to follow.

Remember, *you* are the most important person to make happy. When you are happy with how you look, others pick up on the energy of your newly found self-confidence and delight and they reflect it back to you. You are now ready to start developing your signature style. Let's go!

What's Your Signature Style?

The desire to look good does not fluctuate with the economy. Through good times and bad, it is human nature to want to feel good about how you look. Resources might change, but desire does not. In fact, this might even get stronger when times are tough!

Before you add another item to your wardrobe, let's talk about creating a signature style. This is a look that people associate with you because it is consistent and memorable. A signature style expresses your personality, makes you smile every time you get dressed, and gives the world a clue from the outside as to who you are on the inside. And you want to be sure you are giving them the right message! Understanding your style will make you a savvier shopper and a smarter dresser.

Remember that creating your style is an ongoing journey, not a final destination. Your body will change, and fashion will change, but if you take one step at a time and celebrate each change that makes you feel good, you will get there.

These ten steps will allow you to move in the right direction. Take notes as you do these. These insights will be invaluable when you shop.

1. **Hold it right there!** The first step is awareness. Fully allow the realization to surface that you aren't happy with your wardrobe right now. Do not wallow in it, but fess up and take responsibility. Agree that you will no longer support this habit that is not serving you. Every woman, no matter her age, weight, height or coloring, can look fabulous. You are no exception. Sure, you might have to come to terms with the fact that you are not going to grow five inches taller or that your weight has stabilized higher than you want it to or that you will always have slightly bowed legs no matter how toned they are. But, you can always dress in a way that minimizes the parts you don't love

and maximizes what you do love. Always--even if you don't believe that right now.

2. **Go beyond comfort.** I am not saying sacrifice comfort. I'm saying allow for other aspects of your ideal wardrobe to be present *along with* comfort. Yes, you can wear a dress that is comfortable, *and* it can be beautiful and reflect who you are. Comfort and personal beauty are not mutually exclusive. (For more on this, see Chapter 6 Casual Matters.)

3. **Be yourself.** Many women have a wardrobe that looks more like everyone but them. (Remember the strangers in your closet from Chapter 2?) As a result, what they have does not delight them. They are bored or uncomfortable!

When I say be yourself, I'm talking about who you are at a gut level, not whether you are an entrepreneur, mother, wife or speed skater. Are you radiant, down-to-earth, quirky, fun, bold, gentle, spunky, elegant, unconventional or something else entirely? If you are over forty, how have you changed, grown and evolved from when you were in your twenties? What positive words would you use to describe yourself now? These traits *must* be reflected in your wardrobe, or you will never feel fully satisfied.

If your wardrobe doesn't reflect your personality, do not berate yourself. Exploring different styles helps you determine what you like and what you don't. What often happens, however, is that if you are at all uncertain, you assume others know better. It is now time to take back control of your own style!

Before you go any further, take a few minutes to think of three or four positive words to describe yourself. Think big! Use a dictionary or thesaurus for inspiration. For example, are you dynamic, impish, enthusiastic, fiery, poised or saucy? Ask a friend to help—just be sure the words resonate with you, not just your friend, because you want them to be reflected in your wardrobe. Note: When you are choosing your words, do so without imagining how they will translate into clothing. That part will take care of itself later. It is easier to see how a wardrobe can be colorful, sweet or down to earth than it is to imagine clothing that is humorous, determined or sensitive. Do not get sidetracked right now; focus on words that best describe you.

These words can tell you a lot. If, for example, one of your defining words is *luminous*, and you dress in all neutral colors, perhaps it's time to add some pizzazz! Or, if you are wise but your wardrobe consists of pastel T-shirts with silly sayings on them, it might be time to bring in more rich colors, textures and styles.

4. **Know what you have.** Pull three or four of your favorite outfits out of your closet. What do they have in common? Look for these themes:

   - **Color**—Do you love to wear color, or are you a black and white or neutral person? If you wear color, are there particular ones you favor?

   - **Fabric**—Do you like fabrics with body and structure, or do you prefer soft and airy or flowing and drapey?

   - **Fit**—Do you like fitted, loose, flowing or softly tailored?

   - **Solids vs. Prints**—Do you wear one more than the other?

5. **Know what you want.** What characteristics do you feel are missing in your current wardrobe that you wish it had? Pizzazz? Elegance? Beauty? Drama? Femininity? Spunkiness? Or something else?

6. **Know your accessory style.** Consider how frequently you accessorize and the types of accessories that interest you.

   - Do you always or never wear jewelry?

   - Do you like scarves? Do you know how to tie them?

   - Are shoes your passion or just a necessity?

- How do you feel about handbags, eyeglasses and even your hair?
- What makes your accessories distinctively you?

7. **Know your dislikes.** Perhaps you cannot imagine wearing ruffles, anything embroidered, turtlenecks, or polo shirts. It's up to *you*! What you do not like can tell you as much about your style as what you do enjoy wearing. (For additional inspiration, reread "What's on Your Never-Wear-Again List?" in Chapter 1.)

8. **Let the universe inspire you.** Spend five minutes a day visualizing yourself wearing clothes that make your heart sing. If you need help, refer back to the visualization we did back at the end of Chapter 1 in "How Do You Add Beauty to Your Wardrobe?" Remember, you do not have to see a specific outfit. It's more the *feeling* that that outfit elicits that you are going for. Imagine looking in the mirror and saying to yourself, "Wow, I look stunning!" If *stunning* is too big a word to start, choose something that feels doable to you right now. Try *pretty*, *darned good* or *even so much better*. The universe will say, "Hey, she wants more of that," and that is what you will get. It might be in small doses and surprising ways, but you will get it.

9. **Start small.** You don't want to scare yourself by completely overhauling your style overnight. It probably took you years to get in a style rut, so give yourself a break and start small. If you've been wearing mostly neutrals, add a new color in a top, scarf or pair of shoes. Do not buy an entire outfit in shocking pink if you usually wear all black! Get a great new hairstyle or hair color to reflect the image you want to project. Hint: If you do that, you might find you need to make another change fairly soon to keep up with your new hairdo! Or maybe buy a handbag in a color you've been admiring, and use it every day for a week. See what happens!

10. **Buy it and wear it only if you love it.** As I have said before, do not settle for functional or feeling like something will get you by. If you don't love it, don't buy it! There are no exceptions to this rule. You will learn more shopping tips in Chapter 4.

Now that you have some ideas about your preferences, it's time to get some expert guidance. The following will provide personalized, concrete information that can help you pare down your options when shopping or help you complete your look:

- **A personalized color palette** tells you exactly what colors are your best. You will need to find a qualified color consultant to help you with this portion of your transformation.

- **A style analysis** gives you insight into your body's proportions and what works best to balance your look. Again, an image consultant or fashion stylist can help give you specifics.

- **A great hairstylist or colorist** ensures your hair is as fabulous as your clothes. Nothing can undermine a great look quicker than a bad--or just uninspired--haircut or color.

- **Two or three favorite stores** allow you to focus your shopping efforts. No one needs to shop everywhere! Choose a few stores, large or small, that you love, and work them! It doesn't mean you cannot shop other places, but if you get to know the salespeople at your favorites, they will keep you posted on new inventory that they think you would like as well as special sales.

Before you shop for the first few times of this new adventure or if you are feeling frustrated, review all your notes from the exercises in the book up to this point. And when you are shopping, be sure you have the index cards you created to help you avoid "good enough" and to remember what you love about your current wardrobe. You might also want to revisit "Are You Dressing for You or Someone Else?" in Chapter 1.

Despite what you see on the TV makeover shows, creating a wardrobe is not a one-time proposition, and there is certainly no magic bullet. Like most women, you will still probably have to try on many things before you find the pieces you love, but at least you will feel more confident about your final selections. Building a wardrobe is a lifelong project and, ideally, an enjoyable one. The more you see your wardrobe taking shape, the more fun the journey is! As new and wonderful things come into your life, you will feel more comfortable letting go of more of what is cluttering your closet now. And, you will also find that your wardrobe is smaller than you expected. Surprisingly, it will not feel smaller, because you will wear everything. That's when you know you are right on target!

A final word of advice: Pay attention to detail. Remember that a signature style is all about consistency. You will get discouraged if you do it half-heartedly. For instance, if you have a fabulous elegant look and throw on your old running shoes with it, you are going to feel frustrated when it doesn't feel right to you. You want to feel great in everything you wear, and when you follow these guidelines you will.

Are You Bored with the Basics?

As we started going through Michelle's wardrobe, she pulled out item after item that she wears frequently and that still fits. One of the things Michelle was most proud of about her wardrobe is that she takes good care of her clothes and keeps them for a long time. She has typically been a classic dresser; she has lots of navy blue and black trousers, button down shirts, a few patterned vests, simple sweaters and cardigans and a selection of jackets mostly in neutral tones with a hint of color here or there.

"So," she asked, "why am I so frustrated every time I get dressed?"

What a perfect question! She had called me for help, so obviously something was feeling out of sorts for her. She admitted that she had tried and tried to figure it out on her own, but in the end she just felt like she was spending more money buying the same clothes and not feeling any better. As a result, instead of three pairs of black pants, she had six, and instead of nine button-down blouses, she had fourteen-- mostly white!.

When it comes to fashion, you can absolutely have too much of a good thing. A few polka dots are fun. Polka dots on everything are overpowering. You might like red, but wearing a red pantsuit, red shoes and a red necklace, let's not even think about a red handbag on top of all that, and you could end up looking like a walking Popsicle.

While many women describe their style as classic, it is so easy to get stuck in a rut. Having the basics that you can mix and match with ease is fabulous. Wearing everything in black, beige and navy with few, if any, prints or interesting details is just downright dull, as Michelle and many others can attest.

I am not, in any way, belittling a classic wardrobe or style. The problem arises when the classic pieces turn dull, inflexible or frumpy. A classic style might be the mainstay of your wardrobe, but what about the rest of you? How do you reflect that quietly radiant, luminous, colorful or sassy part of you?

Are you suffering from classicitis? You are if:

You are bored. Being sure you have the basics covered in your wardrobe is critical: a navy-blue cardigan you can easily toss on over a sleeveless top or pretty dress, a fitted dark-brown blazer you can wear when you need to meet with a client or go to a networking meeting, a great pair of black pumps and knee-high boots and the like. But, don't get carried away. If that's all there is, your eyes glaze over, and you feel like you blend in to the woodwork. It's your personality that makes your wardrobe interesting, so be absolutely positive your personality shines through! And, don't worry. If you're now thinking, "I know. That's what I want to do, but I don't know how," keep applying all the principles you've learned so far and keep reading. It's all here to help you.

You are color deprived. The point of something being classic and basic is that you can wear it with a lot of things and that it will stay in style for longer than the seasonal trends. So, it stands to reason that most of these items will be in neutral colors. But you don't want to be only pairing one neutral with another. For instance, when we surveyed Michelle's wardrobe we saw a sea of black, navy and white--with a smattering of taupe thrown in. No wonder she's bored!

Adding color doesn't mean you have to go for fluorescent pink to make a statement. If you are drawn to a classic style, it is likely that you will wear your colors in a way that is more understated and not the least bit overpowering. Depending on your natural coloring, you might look amazing in eggplant, a beautiful wine tone, periwinkle, forest green or a delicious teal. Whether your best colors are light, deep, bright or muted won't really matter since they will be perfect on you and never look overpowering or out of place. Wearing your best colors will bring out the best of you.

Your closet is overflowing. More often than not, the career classic dresser will keep buying things each season in an attempt to freshen things up. As with Michelle, that often means adding more of what she already owns. Then, with her closet filled to overflowing, she has no idea what's really in there, and she's still bored. It's the classic "closet full of clothes and nothing to wear" syndrome.

Don't worry if this is you. Your look can be classic; you just want to create a gorgeous, classic wardrobe with a personal twist. Here are a few tips:

Pat yourself on the back. Yes, you have mastered the art of a basic wardrobe—a feat that many have not achieved—so good for you!

Spice it up! It's absolutely critical that you add some of your personality into your wardrobe. Otherwise you will find yourself sitting on your bed wondering why you feel bored or seeing yourself in a photograph and wondering why you look so drab. That doesn't mean you have to be a slave to fashion trends. It can mean adding a striking necklace that you adore; a jacket in a color that makes you sparkle; a cardigan with lace, ruffles, interesting buttons, rosettes or an unusual shape; a wide belt; or maybe an elegant pair of platform pumps. This is the very personal part of creating a signature wardrobe, and the options are endless. See the next section, "How Do You Add Visual Interest to an Outfit?" The true delight is in allowing your beauty to shine through all those great basics!

Know when to retire. No matter how well you take care of your clothes, they will wear out if you wear them enough. It's important to mention here that the idea of something being classic is not to keep it forever—very few items are truly *that* timeless. Your lifestyle changes, your body changes and fashion changes (yes, even "classics" change from time to time)—often not all at the same time! Your best strategy is to buy beautiful pieces that you love so much that you wear them over and over until it is embarrassing to be seen in public in them. Then you can replace them. It's a win-win. You feel great every day, and you get your money's worth out of every article of clothing!

Are you wondering how to determine if you have all the elements of a basic classic wardrobe? Here are some guidelines. But, remember that it is still up to you to make the choices that feel the best and most authentic to you. There is no such thing as a one-size-fits-all wardrobe, and that is true even for a classic wardrobe.

A basic classic wardrobe is built around your neutral colors (generally black, navy, charcoal, brown, camel, ivory or white). Trousers, a blazer or two, a simple cardigan and a pencil or A-line skirt in your neutral color(s) will serve as the foundation for your look. Some women enjoy button-down shirts, so include those if they make you happy. Add to these a crisp pair of dark wash straight-leg or bootcut jeans. When it comes to adding color, do this with a good selection of camisoles in pretty colors that flatter you for wearing under jackets and blazers. Some classic wardrobes contain turtleneck and pullover sweaters, but these are a personal preference. A trench coat, casual peacoat and a well-constructed, simply designed knee-length winter coat will round out your wardrobe. If you worry about adding width to your body, choose a single-breasted coat. It is often more flattering than double-breasted because the double-breasted style adds visual width.

When considering accessories, a cleanly designed (not too much hardware or pattern) handbag in a neutral color will be the mainstay of your handbag collection. If you have this good basic one for everyday use, then add one with color if you like. Shoes can be anything from classic pumps to ballet flats, and, of course, you'll want knee-high boots to go with your skirts in the cooler months.

Jewelry is where you express your personality even more, so sticking to the expected single-strand pearls, gold chain necklaces and diamond stud earrings found in most classic wardrobes is limiting. There are so many options that can add beauty and personal expression to your wardrobe that it is impossible to go into everything here. You can use all the supporting information in this book (especially Chapter 5 on accessories) as a guide to help you know those distinctive pieces that will work in your classic wardrobe when you see them.

As mentioned earlier, these are simply guidelines. There is no one way to put together a beautiful basic wardrobe. And, remember, once you have classic down, the key is to add your personality. To help with that, read the next section, "How Do You Add Visual Interest to an Outfit?," and make your wardrobe sing!

How Do You Add Visual Interest to an Outfit?

Now THAT YOU KNOW that super duper basic outfit isn't doing anything for you, you can take a baby step and add a touch of pizzazz. There are countless ways to do this, and they don't have to involve the latest trends or humungous jewelry—unless this suits your personality and lifestyle. It's about being a little adventurous, testing the waters a bit and, above all, being absolutely true to yourself.

Evaluate your outfit for the elements below and choose at least one to increase the visual interest on an existing "boring" outfit:

Texture

When you pair smooth with smooth with smooth, there is nothing to catch the eye (and this is especially true when it is all in neutral colors). One way to add visual interest is to add one piece with texture. Maybe it is nubby, crinkled, looped, ribbed, fuzzy or sparkly. It could have cutouts, ruffles, lace, crochet, pleats or ruching. The list is endless. When you combine texture and a color suits you, you have visual interest that is simple and fun!

Prints

I generally recommend that your wardrobe include about 20–35% prints. You can have more (or less, if you choose), but that's a reasonable amount to add interest and still allow you to be able to mix and match well. The prints available vary with each season and can include florals, watercolors, techy digital prints, animal print, geometrics, tribal, stripes, and much more. While I often discourage women from wearing a print head to toe, as it can be overwhelming, a little bit of a print can be just the antidote for a dull wardrobe.

Here are three tips for choosing a print that works for you:

1. **Be sure that the predominant color is one of your best colors.** Do not choose a print with lots of beige and yellow if you don't look good in those colors even if it does have a touch of your perfect pink. The yellow and beige will overwhelm you, and you'll have a hard time matching it to something in your wardrobe.

2. **Love it!** You must love the print because even when it is the perfect print for you in terms of color and the style is right, it will still take focus away from you. You want to be sure it is worth the attention it will get.

3. **Be sure the contrast of colors within the print echoes your natural coloring.** Wearing black and white together is the highest contrast you can wear, whereas wearing black and navy blue or off-white and a soft taupe is low contrast because both of the colors are dark and light, respectively. If you have light skin and dark hair, you can wear a higher contrast in your color combinations or prints than someone with blonde hair and pale skin; high contrast will overpower her and conflict with the nature softness of her coloring. To give another example, someone with dark hair and dark skin generally looks better in low contrast unless the whites of her eyes are very white. If this is the case, she has a higher contrast level because the whites of her eyes will be so noticeable against her skin.

One more thing about contrast: If your natural coloring is soft or light and relatively low contrast, you will generally look better in outfits that are monochromatic or tone on tone (close variations of one color). This way you are not overshadowed by too many colors on your body.

There is more to the concept of contrast, but these are some very general guidelines when it comes to adding color to your wardrobe. If you want to know more, *A Triumph of Individual Style* by Carla Mathis and Helen Connor is a great resource.

Accessories

Accessories are a great way to add pizzazz without feeling over the top. Check out these ideas.

Jewelry: The world of necklaces is huge! You can have a selection of fine jewelry, bridge jewelry (semi-precious stones) and costume jewelry. It's all beautiful and fun.

Scarf: This is a beautiful way to add visual interest and take a look from ho-hum to beautiful. Pay close attention to the print you choose. It is a convenient opportunity to express your personality and stay warm at the same time— the perfect blend of style and function. Be sure to learn a couple of interesting ways to tie a scarf so you aren't constantly fussing with it. You can easily find examples on YouTube including one that I made with my favorite scarf tie.

Handbags: Do you always carry the same basic handbag? How about shaking it up a bit by carrying a colored handbag when the feeling strikes? Try red! If red is too big a leap (or not one of your colors), try yellow, or find one with fun details or hardware in a classic style. There are plenty of other fabulous handbags out there to choose from. Do a little exploring, and see what you like. (Read "Do You Love Your Handbag?" in Chapter 5 for more ideas.)

Shoes: Your shoes do not have to match your outfit exactly despite what women did in the 1950s and even the 1980s. They just need to blend in a color or style that works with your natural coloring and the outfit you are wearing. For instance, let's say you are wearing a dark brown dress. How about pairing it with a pair of two-toned shoes— maybe brown and tan. Or get a little more daring and wear a pair of burgundy or aubergine shoes. Play with color and see what fun combinations you create.

The important thing is that the colors all stay within your color palette. Read the next section, "How Do You Find Your Best Colors?" to get you started, and consider having your colors done professionally if you can. Don't worry if this feels overwhelming at first. This is an opportunity to explore, and you will get more ideas as you progress through this book.

How Do You Find Your Best Colors?

SOME THINGS IN THE fashion world are slow to change, and views about color fall into this category. So many designers still believe that black looks good on everyone and, worse, that gray is a good alternative (it's usually not—especially light gray). I suspect that is because they are mostly designing for models in their early twenties who can often wear a burlap sack and look good. I have spent many seasons shaking my head as I walk through a sea of black and gray in every department store. Not to mention the number of closets I have been in where more than half of the wardrobe (and sometimes as high as 90%) is black or gray.

Here is the biggest question of all: Even if you believe you can look pretty good or OK in black, why settle? Why not go for great and fabulous instead of OK and good? I know. I know. It's easy. It goes with everything. There is lots of it. It feels slimming. It doesn't show dirt. You name it; I've heard it. And, while there is some truth to all of it, the fact remains that it is limiting and rarely—yes, you read that right—shows you off to your best.

Assuming you want to add color to your wardrobe, how do you know what to choose and how much color to wear? It's more than simply deciding that red looks good on you. What shade of red? Primary red? Or, perhaps a red that is closer to raspberry, russett, magenta or burgundy? How do you choose?

There is no quick and easy answer to this. The best way to know is to have your colors analyzed by an experienced color consultant. To get you started, here are some tips that can help you move out of the black hole:

Look in the mirror (preferably in daylight). What color are your hair, your skin (including the pink in your skin), and your eyes (remember to look at the ring around your iris if you have one)? Replay those colors in your wardrobe. To be honest, most people can't go beyond that without a little guidance. It's the subtleties that make the difference. A color can be classified as cool or warm, bright or light, and deep or clear, and many women get caught up in worrying about which color categories best suit them. That concern with labeling your colors as cool or warm, for instance, is unimportant in the grand scheme of things. Yes, you might fall into one category or the other or more likely a combination of the two, but once you know what colors look good on you, it's not as important whether they are cool or warm. You just match them to what you find in the stores.

To start finding your most flattering colors, all you have to do is match your natural colors—your hair, eyes, skin and the pink in your cheeks. That said, here are three colors that work pretty well on many people: deep teal, watermelon and periwinkle blue. Sure, the specific tones of each color will vary, but they tend to be flattering colors in general.

Consider your personality. Are you outgoing, energetic and playful, or serene, introspective, and gentle? Your personality, in addition to your natural coloring, affects the intensity (brightness) of the colors you wear. Lynn is a petite blond with brown eyes and translucent ivory skin. Her coloring alone dictates soft, understated colors. But let her loose for a few minutes, and you know you are dealing with a fireball. If the colors she wears do not reflect some of this intensity, she will terrify people when she first meets them. Her colors need to correspond to her personality as well as her natural coloring, and then the results are magnificent!

Walk. How you move affects your colors, too. Do you have bounce in your step, or is your gait smooth and effortless? The former might indicate that your colors should have a lively tone, and the latter might require more sophistication. One is not better than the other. They are just different.

Speak. Do you have a lilting laugh or a deep, resonant voice? If your coloring is deep and rich and your voice is light and airy, you'll want to add softness and feminine touches. You might choose a supple fabric, details such as ruffles or a touch of lace or bring in the feminine feel by way of your softest colors—maybe choose a color that resembles the lightest pink in your cheeks, especially around your face. The colors you wear speak volumes, especially when they are in sync with who you are.

Let me also address a very common question about color: "Does it really matter what color you wear on the bottom if you are wearing one of your best colors near your face?" The answer is yes. Let's say you have red hair, and the top you are wearing is a gorgeous shade of rich olive green. It shows off your eyes, makes your skin look smooth and makes your hair shine. Terrific! Then you pair it with light-gray pants. Oh no! "But it's not near my face," you say. That's true. But, the viewer's eye will always go to something that looks out of place or doesn't match the consistency of everything else. So, if you are wearing beautiful warm colors that enhance your natural coloring on top and cool gray pants on the bottom, someone's eye will automatically be drawn to the gray because it doesn't belong. Is it better than wearing an outfit all in light gray? Yes, of course. Ideally, however, if you were to pair that olive-green top with deep-brown or maybe warm camel-colored pants, the colors would all be in your palette, and someone's gaze would easily travel up to your face.

The next time you get dressed, look in the mirror. Reflect on what you see. Walk toward your image. Smile, and speak to yourself. Does it work, or is something missing? Perhaps you need to add bright earrings to bring focus to the whites of your eyes. Anything that brings focus to your eyes—either the iris or the whites—helps bring focus to your face, and that is generally where you want people to look. Maybe you want to change your pants from black to navy to soften everything and match the ring around the iris of your eye. Again, it will bring focus up to your face and make your eye color pop. Play, experiment, and experience the power of color.

What's Under There?

MY CATS LOVE TO hide. Their disappearing acts are a constant source of amusement. Invariably, a tail is sticking out—sometimes even a whole back end. It's the cutest thing! It's just not particularly effective! I think they think that if they can't see me, then I must not be able to see them.

I think women sometimes perceive their undergarments the same way. If they can't see them, then no one else can, either. As a result, we often see more than we care to and wonder why the person isn't aware of what's so obvious to the rest of us.

Undergarments are the basis on which a look is created. There is a reason they are called foundation garments. An ill-fitting bra, improper support, or things sticking out in unusual places can totally undermine an otherwise beautiful look. Just as you would not ask a plumber to do an electrician's job, you cannot ask a sports bra to do the job of a convertible bra or enlist a thong when support wear is called for.

Here are four common issues:

1. **Wayward bra straps:** There's a disturbing fashion trend out there of purposely visible bra straps. It befuddles me not because it's obscene, but mostly because it's unattractive. Not all bra straps are created equal. Here's a rule of thumb: If your bra straps look like bra straps, which most of them do, keep them hidden, even if they are in a pretty color. If you have a bra that matches your top perfectly and the straps are delicate and pretty so that you cannot tell the bra strap from the cami straps (maybe get some other input here because you cannot see your back or be as objective as well as someone else), then maybe a slight peek of bra strap every now and then is OK, *but* only for ultra-casual settings—never, ever at the office. You can also get

some really pretty sparkly straps to put on your convertible bra for evenings out.

2. **Visible panty lines:** Let's end this problem forever. Before you leave the house, always take a look at yourself from behind. It's that simple. Twist, turn, bend, and move. Can you see a panty line? If so, there are many options out there that make panty lines disappear. Two great options are thongs or laser-cut panties. The laser cut allows the edges to lay totally smooth against your body and leave no telltale signs behind on your behind.

3. **Visible thong:** One day I was grocery shopping and was waiting in line to check out. The woman in front of me wanted to get a closer look at a product on a nearby bottom rack. She squatted down and when she did, she exposed her underwear and much more. Yikes! I wondered if she could feel a draft!

    Although it seems to be fashion gone awry with young men, the idea of exposing one's underwear while wearing low-rise pants is downright unattractive on anyone. Again, check your rear view, and don't just stand there. Bend over and move around. Get a glimpse at what the rest of the world sees. Underwear is meant to be just that: under wear!

4. **Ill-fitting bra:** I saved the best for last. An ill-fitting bra can ruin an outfit, and the number of women wearing the wrong size bra for their bodies is mind-boggling. When your bra fits well, clothing hangs better, darts fall in the right place, and everything looks more balanced. If you're not sure, get fitted by someone who knows what she is doing. Even if you think you are sure, go for a fitting. It will either surprise you or validate that you are in the right size already. Just ask Leslie. When she went for a bra fitting, she was wearing a 36C. Imagine her surprise when the bra specialist handed her a 32DD and it fit! She could immediately see the difference: She was now well covered and supported.

So what do you think? Do you suspect you are wearing the wrong size bra or are yours just worn out and no longer offering the support they are meant to? Either way, having a professional bra fitting will give you a renewed appreciation of the value of undergarments.

The first step is awareness. Ask yourself these questions:

- Have you been taking your undergarments for granted?

- Do you buy a new bra and then don't replace it until it is so ragged and lifeless that it practically falls apart in the laundry?

- Do you figure that if it's covered up, no one else will know that your underwear desperately needs a makeover?

The truth is that only you see well-fitting, appropriate undergarments. Ill-fitting, inappropriate undies are "visible" to everyone. With a little forethought, it's an easy problem to remedy, and the results are immediate and fabulous.

Do Fashion Trends Fit Into Your Wardrobe?

BUYER, BEWARE. SOMETIMES I think this is what the stores should have on their doors as you enter to buy your seasonal wardrobe. We generally all want or need to add at least a few new pieces each season to freshen up our wardrobes or fill in when a key piece is worn out. There are times, and it is more common in spring/summer than fall/winter, when the trends are out of control. Peasant blouses, patchwork shirts, cropped tops, brightly color skinny jeans, baby doll tops and hip-hugging bellbottoms are just a few that have come and gone--or come and stayed too long--over the years.

Here's the question each season: Can you incorporate the season's latest fashions without appearing too trendy, looking inappropriate or wasting your money on something that will be passé a season from now? The answer depends on the trend. But, you won't go wrong if you follow these guidelines:

1. **Try it on.** Don't immediately dismiss something just because it's different. It never hurts to try it on. There's always the chance you'll discover a new style, color or fabric that you like.

2. **If you don't love it, don't buy it.** There are no exceptions to this rule. It doesn't matter if it's "in." You are better off wearing things that are already in your closet than spending good money on things you do not feel great wearing.

3. **Don't overdo it.** A little bit of trendiness goes a long way. While sixteen-year-olds can pile on the trends and do it with flair, the rest of us are better off choosing one piece in a trend we love and wearing it sparingly mixed with our regular wardrobe. For instance, animal print is a trend that has been popular every year for the past twenty-five years. A touch of animal print in a top, scarf or coat is great, but recently I saw a woman who was wearing animal print in her skirt, shoes, handbag, scarf

and even her umbrella. It was all coordinated beautifully but was just way too much. Wearing an animal print top paired with great dark wash jeans will look terrific. Wearing the top with animal print jeans and an animal print scarf and adding an animal print handbag to the outfit, similar to the woman above, is going overboard.

4. **Be prudent.** If you love a trend, but suspect it won't last long, don't buy an entire closetful, and certainly don't spend a lot of money on it. Spend your fashion dollars wisely, and wear the trend a lot while it's in style. Then you won't feel bad letting the items go when the style passes.

5. **Know where to shop.** Look for smaller, less trend-oriented stores that cater to their particular clientele (make sure you fit into that description) and are less driven by fads. Do not judge the store by the window display or a pre-conceived notion about what it has to offer. Go in! The worst thing that can happen is it isn't the right store and you leave.

Clarissa shared that she was initially nervous to go into a "fancy" boutique. Her first thoughts were that it would be way out of her price range, everything would be too small, and that the sales women would not be friendly. None of this was based on previous experience. It was more a general worry she had that others would judge her. After working with me by way of my *Who Taught You How To Dress?* coaching program, she took a big step. She gathered up her courage and went into a small boutique in her town that she had only previously walked past. To say it changed her life is an understatement. She tried on lots of clothes and ultimately left with three complete outfits. Each one spoke to that bohemian part of her that she had never had the courage to express before. In her new clothes, she felt more like herself than in the entire rest of her wardrobe, and she did it in less time than she had ever spent shopping before. She used what she had been learning through the coaching program about inner beauty and personal style to choose the items the sales women suggested. Plus, and this was a big one for her, she had fun!

When all else fails, try these shopping tips and read Chapter 4 Shopping with Joy and Ease:

1. **Know yourself!** Stick to what you know works for you, and shop in stores that meet your needs.

2. **Shop in the higher end departments.** Buy less but be willing to pay more for what you buy. The higher quality designers often show a more polished look. Stay out of the junior department and stores where teens shop.

3. **Save time by previewing store selections online** if possible. Sometimes the online department store merchandise differs from what is in the brick and mortar store, but it can still give you a sense of what to expect. On the other hand, sometimes with the smaller boutique stores, their online presence is either minimal or it does not do them justice, so it's better just to make a trip to see firsthand what they have on their racks. One word of advice: Whenever possible, avoid shopping in February and July. This is the tail end of the season and not yet the beginning of the next one--at least in the northern hemisphere. The stores are full of sales racks at this time, and there will be fewer styles and sizes to choose from. This is particularly true in many smaller stores. Shopping at the height of the season or as soon as the sales start will give you the best selections.

4. **Consider your wardrobe needs.** Make sure you do your closet assessment so you know what you need to get before you go shopping. You are less likely to waste your time, spend money on things you don't need or find yourself unduly frustrated or influenced by others who profess to know better than you.

5. **Remember your shopping mantra.** This bears repeating once again: If you don't love it, don't buy it.

Is Your Cardigan Frumpy?

And now for an item that seemingly never goes out of style: the cardigan sweater. Whether the style is short, long, embellished, patterned, tailored, flowing, colorful or neutral, some style of cardigan is always available. How fabulous—or maybe not!

While cardigans are extremely functional, they are also dangerous. It doesn't take much for a cardigan to go from adorable and pretty to downright frumpy.

You often hear celebrity stylists say rather nonchalantly, "Oh, yes, just add a little cardigan over it, and you're all set!" Then they leave it at that with no direction. Yikes! So, you go out and buy a cardigan, toss it on over a blouse, tank or dress and take a look at yourself in the mirror. But who's staring back? It's not some trend-setting celebrity, but your elderly grandma or, worse, Mr. Rogers!

Cardigans might be tricky, but they are very doable and can be flattering, not to mention practical. You just need to learn some general cardigan don'ts. When choosing a cardigan, avoid:

- **Rounded, jewel necklines, especially on a boxy style**. If they are somewhat fitted or you have broad, square shoulders (which always helps when wearing something as unstructured as a cardigan), it could work for you. But, for someone like me with narrow sloped shoulders, cardigans with round necklines can make us look dowdy in an instant!

- **Boxy designs on a curvy body**—unless you want to look like … a box.

- **A band at the bottom,** unless the band is purely decorative and does not squeeze your hips or you are very slim in the hips and can handle added focus there.

- **Too long or flimsy or, even worse, belted.** You can easily look like you are wearing your bathrobe. Yes, even celebrities can—and do—look bad in this style! This is especially true when wearing a dress. If you are at all curvy, you will want a shorter cardigan that ends at about the waist. You might have to try several on to see which one works best with the neckline and cut of the dress as well as the color.

Also, never button the sweater all the way, or you risk looking like Lisa Lubner on Saturday Night Live (am I dating myself?). Leaving it slightly open at the top and bottom creates a diagonal line that is very flattering.

Now, go out and purchase wonderful, flattering cardigans in all your best colors. Grab these when you see them and you'll be glad you did. I've learned from past experience in the fashion world that many great styles are here today, gone tomorrow.

Why Wear a Jacket?

Jackets are arguably one of the most underrated garments in our wardrobe, in my opinion. For those of you on the fence or just curious about my fascination with this particular garment, here is why jackets are so fabulous:

1. **Jackets hide a multitude of sins (as my mom would say).** Isn't this just the best reason? Whatever is going on under a jacket is a mystery to everyone but you. Lumps, bumps, extra tummy, fuller hips, wiggly arms—no one else can see them!

2. **Jackets keep you warm.** This is a key component for me because I'm always cold. A jacket adds warmth without feeling like I'm the abominable snowman like I sometimes feel in bulky sweaters. And, for someone who runs hot and cold or goes from inside to outside a lot, a jacket is a must because it allows you to easily adjust to the temperature changes.

3. **Jackets add an extra ounce of authority.** Do you work in a male-dominated field or one where you are in a managerial or supervisory role? Wearing a jacket adds visual authority. Don't get me wrong. I'm not talking about authority as a way of being intimidating or abusing power. It's more about lending an air of self-confidence so you hold your head higher. It can add structure to an outfit and a feeling of purposefulness.

4. **Jackets add visual interest to an outfit.** Want to add spice to a simple blouse and pair of pants? Adding a fabulous jacket is one way of bringing a bit more personality and flair to the outfit. It doesn't have to be over the top (no pun intended!). Again, it's all about expressing who you are and what makes you happy.

5. **Jackets create illusion.** Have you ever put on a top and pants and thought, "Yikes, all I see is my belly." Or, perhaps you notice that you have a straight figure with no noticeable waist

definition. Maybe your shoulders are a bit narrow and sloped so all you see are your hips. Whatever the situation, a jacket is a miracle worker. There are days when I feel like I have all three of those situations happening on my body at once! A jacket can create curve where I want it and boost my shoulders when I need it. Whew! What a perfect garment.

My favorite illusion: If you do not have a well-defined waist, there is a way you can get the waist you lost or never had, especially if you have been avoiding belts. Wear a jacket and then belt the top underneath so all you see, when the jacket is unbuttoned, is the belt buckle and a little bit of the belt on either side. No one else can tell if your waist is big, little, thick or thin. They just know you have one because the belt gives the illusion of a waist. It's like magic!

Jackets do not have to be ho-hum or stiff. So many of them now come with stretch in them that it's almost impossible not to be comfy! Plus, you get to choose the right flavor for your personality and the occasion. Take Wendy Yellen of EideticLifeCoach.com, for example. She has been working with me through the *Who Taught You How to Dress?* coaching program and has discovered that jackets really can have a prominent place in her wardrobe. Here's what Wendy has to say:

"Before I met you, I felt embarrassed and ashamed of my wardrobe and awful about my ability to shop. 'Hate' isn't a word I use, but if I did, I would say I hated to shop. I hated to go into the dressing room. I hated walking into a store. I rarely shopped, and when I did, it was still disappointing and even still a bit traumatic. Jackets, for instance, were something that felt too conservative and conventional for me. But, I was also drawn to them and really got, from you, that they add a special something to looking pulled together. But I had always avoided them for fear of feeling uncomfortable and restricted.

Because of your encouragement, I actually now have a 'favorite store,' and, unbelievably, people regularly—and often—ask me where I shop and tell me how great I look. Even better, I FEEL great about how I look! My cousin, who knew of my shopping and dressing problems and how they discouraged me, recently said, 'You really got that clothing thing together, didn't you?!'

So, one day, inspired by your encouragement and guidance, I went shopping for a jacket. I can't believe how much fun it was and how absolutely clear and certain and HAPPY I felt in making a choice. I walked out of there with, yes, you guessed it, the best jacket of my life. It's sassy, it's fun, it's beautiful, it's very original, and—I LOVE it."

The next time you are out shopping, be like Wendy and think about a jacket. Think beyond the traditional blazer to jackets that work for different aspects of your life. Try pairing one with jeans or a skirt or over a dress. There is something out there for everyone. Just keep in mind your coloring, body shape, lifestyle and personality, and have fun.

How Can You Dress to Look Slimmer?

WHAT IS THE No. 1 fashion rule that women embrace when they want to look slimmer? All together now: Wear black! This is a fashion mantra for many, and it results in closets that are seas of darkness. On the other hand, what's the top style women avoid if they don't want to appear heavier than they are? I bet you can guess it—horizontal stripes.

Let's explore whether there is truth to these two widespread beliefs and the rules for how to dress to look slimmer and keep your body in balance. Roberta's story is a perfect example.

Roberta epitomizes the average woman's body shape. She stands about 5 feet 4 inches, and her weight fluctuates between 140 and 150 pounds. When I first met her, she was wearing an oversized gray belted cardigan—a style that was very current at the time—and black cropped pants. Roberta shared that she had chosen the gray because it felt like a change from her usual: black. Black was her failsafe choice for pants, and to add some variety to her options, she sometimes wore cropped pants, as she had that day. She finished the outfit with her standby black clogs (they were comfortable and safe).

I could see that Roberta was trying so hard to figure out what would make her feel good about how she looked, but she made it clear from the outset that she was not having much success on her own. Her discomfort was also evident by the way she held her body slightly hunched forward as if she were trying to be as small and invisible as possible. She expressed more than once that she was tired of feeling so much anxiety around how she looked, and so with pencil in hand, she was ready to make a fresh start and learn some tips for avoiding the illusion of extra pounds. Here's what I shared with Roberta.

1. **Black is slimming.** Yes, there is truth to this often-repeated style tip. Black is slimming because it does not reflect light, so we do not notice shadows that are created as the material flows

over our curves. Please note that if the fabric is shiny, the benefits of wearing black are lessened because the light *does* reflect and create shadows. Then the overall effect is less forgiving. So, yes, black can be slimming, but when worn excessively, it can feel heavy, lackluster and overwhelming, especially on someone with light, delicate coloring. Another potential drawback for black is that it can create harsh shadows on your face thereby accentuating lines and wrinkles. This might not make you look heavier, but it will make you look older!

Did Roberta wear black because it looked great on her? No. She chose black because it felt safe and slimming, and she added gray because it felt like a change from black. Unfortunately, neither of those colors made her look radiant and energized. So we changed her sweater to a deep teal, and her face lit up. It was such an easy change, yet there was such a big pay off.

Luckily, there are other dark colors that can have a similar slimming effect without the barren quality that black can sometimes have. These colors might actually be more flattering with your natural coloring and will give you some relief from the endless parade of black in your closet. Mix it up a bit. Try aubergine, dark forest green, mahogany, midnight blue or a very deep maroon.

2. **Good fit is essential to looking sleek and slim.** When you wear your clothes too tight, you draw attention to every lump and bump, which makes you look like you are too big for the outfit you are wearing. Conversely, when your clothes are too big, as Roberta's were, you get lost underneath all the fabric, and it is easy for others to assume that your body is as big as the clothes you are wearing. The best way to show off your figure in a flattering way is to wear clothes that skim your body. They don't squeeze you, but they don't overwhelm you either.

3. **Cropped pants make everyone look shorter and wider.** Because the eye stops when the pant leg stops, cropped pants

give the illusion that the wearer's legs end there, too. If you are 5 feet 10 inches with long legs (compared to your torso), this is less of an issue for you than if, like Roberta, you are 5 feet 4 inches or less and have short legs. You can circumvent this a bit if your cropped pants are slim, which means they don't add extra width at the hemline, and are a soft color that blends with, or is the same as, your skin. This creates a long continuous line, and if you also wear shoes to match, the line continues all the way to your toes. This look is more lengthening than wearing contrasting colors, but a full-length pant will always make your legs look longer and your body taller in comparison.

4. **Beware of shoes that draw focus to your ankles.** Ankle straps are often considered an alluring style, but they really don't flatter everyone's legs and ankles. As with cropped pants, they make your legs look shorter because the eye stops at the strap instead of continuing down along the top of your foot. You have heard me talk about how my legs are not my favorite feature, and part of that, aside from being knock-kneed, is because my ankles are not as slim I would like them to be. I avoid ankle straps because they draw attention to my ankles, in general, and the thin strap makes my ankles look larger in contrast. If somewhat heavier ankles are a concern for you, too, keep the top of your foot as open and clear as possible so as to allow someone's gaze to flow easily past your ankles rather than lingering there.

If you think about the past two tips concerning looks that make your legs seem shorter, you will see that Roberta's combination of cropped pants and clogs was disastrous. To make matters worse, not only was she wearing cropped pants, but also the vamp (the part of your shoe that covers the top of your foot) of the clogs came up high on her foot. This added to the shortening and widening effect by encouraging the eye to stop where the shoe began.

All of this doesn't mean Roberta has to get rid of these two pieces. She's just better off pairing them with other garments.

For instance, if she wears her cropped pants with a ballet flat or perhaps a sling-back wedge sandal that is open on the top of her foot, her legs will look longer. She can further add to the lengthening effect by choosing shoes in a nude tone (close to her skin tone) or a metallic color. Unlike black clogs, where the dark contrast to her skin tone stops the eye as soon as it reaches her shoes, the lighter color will help to keep the eye moving because her shoes will blend in with her skin tone.

If you are a fan of clogs, don't worry. Roberta (and you) can still wear them with jeans or long pants. Then high vamp will not be an issue because the pant leg will cover the top of the shoe.

5. **Stand up straight.** How many times did we hear this from our mothers? While we might have whined or even ignored them, the truth is they had a point. When you stand up straight with your shoulders back and your chest held high, some of the lumps and bumps smooth. You also have a more charismatic and engaging presence when you stand tall instead of slouched, and the position is better for your body. Of course, as with Roberta, when you don't feel good about how you look, it is easy to understand why you want to hide. But hunching or slouching only adds to the problem by making your clothes look bunchy and forcing the garments to hang funny. So, regardless of whether looking slimmer is an objective of yours, Mom's advice has merit. And, even if your wardrobe is not exactly where you want it to be yet, this is one tip you can put into practice now with instant results.

6. **Pockets can ruin a good outfit.** Roberta's gray cardigan had big patch pockets (a big square pocket sewn on the outside of a garment) at the hipline, and, as often happens in pockets on sweaters, they were sagging and gapping. While pockets can be a very handy addition to a coat or jacket, there are plenty of other situations when you have to wonder what the designer was thinking. Roberta's sweater was one of them. Patch pockets

are big offenders when it comes to adding physical and visual bulk, yet they appear on blouses at the bustline, on jackets and sweaters at the waist and on the hips of skirt and pants. If you are small busted, you can handle a pocket on your chest because you can afford to add volume, but if you are larger breasted, avoid it. It will just make you look bustier than you are and draw focus to that part of your body.

My recommendation is to avoid patch pockets anywhere on your body where you do not want to draw attention. So if you carry weight in your tummy, you certainly do not want to wear a jacket or sweater with pockets at your mid-section. And, if you have a few extra pounds on your hips and thighs, then patch pockets on your longer sweater, like Roberta's, or cargo pants with pockets on your legs will not do you any favors. Also, while we are on the topic of pockets, angled pockets that are often in women's dress trousers should be banished. For most women, these pockets just pull and gap and make you look and feel heavier than you are. This does not mean you have to pass up a pair of pants that has them. In most cases, you can apply an easy fix. Just have the pockets removed and sewn shut by your tailor, and the front of your trousers will be nice and smooth.

7. **Use color strategically.** By this, I mean use color placement to your advantage. One great way to use color well is with color blocking. This just means that instead of wearing all one color or a smaller pattern of colors, you wear large blocks of colors in one outfit. Dresses often demonstrate this idea well. For example, a slimming design is one that has dark side panels (often with the dark panel indenting at the waist to create an hour-glass shape) and a brighter color down the middle of your body. The eye automatically goes to the brighter pop of color, and the darker side panels recede, which appears to whittle your waistline.

You can do this with separates as well. Match your tank top to your skirt or pants, and then wear a long, sleek, dark neutral cardigan or coat jacket. Leave the sweater or jacket open, and you create a long central column of color with the outer jacket fading into the background. Of course, monochromatic dressing—wearing an outfit all in one color (or slightly varying tones of one color) from head to toe—will also have a slimming effect because the eye doesn't stop or is not drawn horizontally as it would when, for instance, the hem of your yellow sweater contrasts with the brown of your pants.

8. **Gathers or pleats around the waist are no one's best look.** While there are exceptions to every fashion rule, very few women can pull off gathers around the waist. This is something we sometimes see in skirts that have an elasticized waistband and tiny folds of fabric pulled together (the gathers). This extra fabric adds width and fullness at the waistline. Pleated pants and skirts also add volume at your tummy and hip area and will automatically make you look heavier than you are. Sleek, flat front pants and skirts are always more becoming.

9. **An ill-fitting bra adds pounds.** This is not the only time I address wearing a bra that fits you properly, and that's because it is so important in creating a flattering silhouette. When your bra fits you well, your breasts are supported and lifted, and there is more space between your bustline and your waist. And, back fat is reduced when your bra fits your body. It's a winning solution all around.

10. **Accessories can add pounds, too.** We will address the topic of accessories more fully in Chapter 5, but for now let's look at one that is a little less user-friendly: the choker necklace. Thankfully, chokers are not often a popular fashion accessory, but they do come into style now and again. When they do, choose wisely as they are not always the most flattering embellishment. Wearing a choker is not a big problem if you have a long thin smooth neck—in which case you can wear a thick or thin choker if it really makes you happy. But, in general, if your neck is short or full, the choker will just make your neck look shorter and wider,

and, as you get older, it can draw attention to a softening jawline. Chokers can also have a somewhat unsettling effect—dare I say wearers look beheaded?—which is not usually a fashion statement anyone chooses on purpose.

Did you notice that something was missing in the list of looks that add pounds? I've saved horizontal stripes for last.

It has been ingrained in women from a young age that horizontal stripes are universally unflattering and make every woman look heavier than she is. As a result, women everywhere avoid them like the plague. And, this isn't always necessary. One general rule: the wider the stripe, the heavier it will make you look, and the thinner the stripe, the more slimming it is. You can also go one step further. If you want to wear horizontal stripes but worry about looking heavier, choose a thin stripe in related colors, such as medium blue with navy, and the effect will be softer and more forgiving (than black and white, for example). You can also experiment with stripes that are wiggly or with patterns where the lines are diffused. These will also have a softer effect. That said, it is not all lollipops and roses when it comes to donning a striped garment. As stripes—which are traditionally straight—navigate over your curves, they can look distorted and draw attention to the parts of the body they cover.

Believe it or not, for some women horizontal stripes are a blessing. Women who are tall and thin and feel a bit on the lanky side can use horizontal stripes strategically to add width and break up the vertical line. The point here is that you might not want to dismiss stripes so readily—unless you just don't like them—and allow for the possibility that you might one day find a beautiful horizontal stripe that looks great and that you enjoy wearing.

Roberta took all of this to heart, and we immediately began experimenting with alternative looks. Since her cropped pants fit her well and she liked them, we built the outfit around them. We added a shorter deep-teal cardigan that exposed more of her leg thereby elongating the line of her legs. The sweater did not have a belt—since the belt on her original cardigan just made her look like she was wearing a bathrobe—and we added a pretty black, teal and white patterned tank under it. So far, so good. We were bringing the focus up and elongating her legs all at the same time. Roberta smiled and automatically stood taller as she realized she liked this look so much better.

We weren't done yet. Because she was wearing cropped pants, her shoes were very important in completing the outfit and in extending the vertical line. She changed her shoes to a pair of fun pewter-colored ballet flats that had a low vamp to keep the top of her foot open and elongate her legs. Accessories would come later (you can be sure a choker necklace was not on the list!), but already, with just a few tweaks, she felt lighter and happier in her new look.

Roberta is not alone. I have yet to meet one woman who wants her wardrobe to make her look heavier and wider than she is. Whether you are mixing and matching from your existing wardrobe or out shopping for new items, this is a handy checklist to use to make adjustments to each outfit you put together. In fact, here's a distilled version of the list so you can refer to it often:

1. Expand your dark (a.k.a., slimming) color repertoire. Black is not the only option.

2. Choose clothes that skim your body—not too big or too small.

3. Pair slim cropped pants with shoes with a low vamp to elongate your legs.

4. Ankle straps and high vamp shoes shorten your legs, so be careful what you pair them with.

5. Keep your posture tall and straight.

6. Notice the pockets on the garment, and make sure they do not detract or add bulk.

7. Use vertical columns of color to create a slimming effect.

8. Avoid gathers or pleats around the waist or hips.

9. Wear a bra that fits perfectly.

10. Avoid wearing a choker necklace unless you are sure it is flattering.

Practice applying these ten powerful tips, and watch how those changes make you instantly appear taller and slimmer.

Are You Ready for Your Close-up?

THIS CHAPTER HAS GIVEN you a lot to think about. Now you can apply some of the principles. Yes, it's time to practice! One way to analyze what you've been doing and to determine if your changes are working is to look at candid photos.

In Chapter 2, I suggested you take pictures of yourself. Now it's time to get perspective on your style from a photo you didn't take specifically for that purpose. Flip through recent candid shots on your phone or camera that you or someone else took. If you are on Facebook, look at what's in your photo album there.

I know that some of you are shaking your heads. This exercise is not meant as a form of torture, I promise. It is meant to give you a fresh view of yourself now that you are thinking about your wardrobe and personal style in new ways.

So, what will you be looking for in the pictures? Two things: Whether your inner essence is shining through and whatever information you can garner about an item or your outfit that you might not have seen before (e.g., Do you like the fit, the color, the style? Does it mix and match well? Do your shoes enhance or detract? You get the idea.)

Have you ever seen a picture of yourself, for example, when you are thoroughly enjoying the experience of whatever you are doing and the joy just radiates through you? That's what I am talking about. Some of the women who have worked with me privately or who have been through one of my workshops can readily identify their inner essence with phrases such as *powerfully centered, engagingly unconventional* or *joyously unrestrained.* Maybe they can see that they are *centered in grace* or *quietly joyful.* The description is different for everyone, but the effect is the same: When your clothes express your inner beauty, you feel great and are more inclined to like the way you look.

The point is that these descriptive words are what you want your clothes to say about you, and a good way to evaluate your total look is through pictures.

I know that looking at pictures of ourselves is not always something we enjoy doing. But keep these ideas in mind:

You have not been airbrushed or Photoshopped—nor should you be! Part of your beauty is in being yourself and not looking like you've been plasticized like so many celebrities do on the covers of magazines.

The lighting might not be perfect. In fact, chances are good it isn't. Do you have any idea how long it takes to set up the lighting in a photo shoot? And, with good reason. Good lighting is flattering. It does not cast heavy shadows and can even diffuse certain features you might want to gloss over. Lighten up, so to speak, about it.

You are not posing in ridiculous, unnatural positions. If you've ever been part of a photo shoot (or seen an episode of *America's Next Top Model*), you will know why each body part is strategically placed in a photo. Certain stances can make your legs or neck look longer or your body curvier. The list of tricks is long. The point is that most pictures are not perfectly posed, so give yourself a break.

That said, let me give you a few quick tips for how to pose in a picture so you are more likely to appreciate the photo:

Angle your body slightly. Never face the camera straight on with your feet firmly planted. It will always make every part of you (including your nose) look wider. Instead, stand facing forward, then move your right foot back so the heel of your left foot is pointing at the arch of your right foot. Your right foot should be 8–12 inches from your left heel. Keep your weight on your back foot. As you do this, your body will automatically angle to the right. So your head will be facing forward, but your body will not. Now place your right hand on your hip. This keeps your arm from squishing against your body (which also makes you look wider) and gives your body some angles. Try it a couple of times before you're in front of the camera so it doesn't feel awkward when you do it. Of course, even if you do it and it's not quite perfect, you will still look better than if you faced the camera directly.

Stick your neck out. Some people pull their chins in toward their necks when they smile, which gives the impression of many chins. Putting the chin slightly forward is an old photographer's trick that will let you avoid the look of a double chin and smooth any lines in your neck. You don't want to look unnatural, so move your chin out just enough to elongate your neck and smooth the skin. This might take a little practice, so if you aren't ready, skip it!

Stand up straight. OK, we have talked about this befoe, but if you've ever been caught in a picture where you are slumping, you know it's important.

Smile! You always look and feel better when you smile. And be sure to do it with your eyes as well as your mouth. Here's another trick: Instead of saying "cheese," say "eyes"! This relaxes you and keeps your mouth in a natural smiling shape. I learned this many years ago from Boston photographer, Lynn McCann.

Looking at yourself and your clothes from a new perspective gives you one more opportunity to refine your look and create one more thing to smile about. You might even begin to love the camera!

— —

As you can see, there is no one way to create a dream wardrobe. This chapter has given you the tools to begin developing your strategy, which will evolve into *your* personal style. That's where the true beauty comes in.

You're not finished! The next step is to put your strategy into action and hit the stores. But, don't worry. You are not alone. There's an entire chapter here to help you. So let's go.

Chapter 4

Shopping with Joy and Ease

You now have a new mindset, a cleared and orderly closet and some ideas for what you want in your wardrobe. It's time to shop!

For so many women this is a dreaded experience. Every time I poll groups of women to find out who likes to shop and who doesn't, somewhere between one-third and half admit they hate it. If you add to that the number of women who like to shop but don't have time to, the percentage soars to almost two-thirds!

Perhaps you can relate to Amy's experience. At first, as I walked around a department store with Amy, we were not finding her colors very easily. This was back at the beginning of a spring shopping season when everything seemed to be beige!

After about fifteen or twenty minutes she turned to me and said, "If I had been on my own I would have left the store by now and gone home empty handed and frustrated."

I told her to take heart, take a deep breath, and relax. We would find what we wanted. Sure enough, by the end of our shopping time she had the two outfits we had been looking for so that she could feel absolutely confident making a presentation the following week. The colors were perfect, the styles suited her personality, and they were appropriate for a professional setting.

No matter what your previous shopping experiences have been like, you can make your next foray to the stores productive, efficient and, dare I say it, enjoyable. It won't take a lot of time; it's simply a matter of planning ahead and adhering to a few simple guidelines. Let's get started.

Are You Afraid to Shop?

I HAVE FOUND THAT whether they love shopping or hate it, many women are often frustrated by their shopping experiences because they find them inefficient and unproductive: You spend time you don't have wandering around stores that feel too big and leave with things you don't love but that will suffice. After all that, you go home worn out. There are no feelings of excitement about having new things to wear. You're just glad it's over.

Phew! It's completely understandable that you wouldn't want to repeat that experience anytime soon. So you keep the cycle going: You look in your closet day after day and think, "I have nothing to wear; I really need new clothes," and then convince yourself with seemingly valid excuses about why you can't or won't get new clothes any time soon.

Admit it. There's a sense of relief when you hear the reasons why you can't go shopping. You don't really want to do it anyway and having what feels like a valid excuse lets you stop worrying about it—at least for the moment. Instead you resign yourself to the daily stress of getting dressed and the familiar sense of longing for clothes that make you happy. You figure that some day the timing will be right, but it's not now.

What's your favorite excuse? Do you tell yourself you'll shop when:

- You have more time
- You have more money
- The stores have better choices
- You lose weight

What's behind each of these excuses? Fear. Fear that you will:

- waste time and come home with nothing worthwhile;

- waste money on things you will never wear. Often this piggybacks on an overriding belief that you have to spend a lot of money to have a great wardrobe (you don't!);

- discover that designers no longer make clothes that look good on you;

- buy new clothes and then lose weight and have to buy more new clothes; or

- buy clothes for your current (undesirable) weight and then feel complacent and not lose the weight you want to lose.

If you dislike shopping or you don't feel like you deserve a good wardrobe, then there's always something else that will come along to take up your time and money. And it's not surprising that you'd rather stay with what's familiar even if you're not happy with it than take a step that stirs up new feelings that support your deepest fears.

At the time, these reasons feel legitimate. The problem is that they are open-ended; you can go on forever. So what's the answer?

You must become a priority on your to-do list. And somehow shopping has to become a more enticing and rewarding experience, or it will be easy to keep putting it off.

Let's address some of the fears and then identify steps you can take to move in the direction you want to.

- **Time:** If you'd rather have a root canal than go clothes shopping, you will never set aside the time to do it until you're in pain, i.e., you don't have anything left to wear, or you need something for an event and *must* shop. Shopping when you are desperate is *never* a good use of your time and can severely deplete your energy. Nine times out of ten it just reinforces the time-wasting fear (and sometimes the rest of them, too!) and makes you even more reticent to shop again before you have to. Then there you have it—a vicious cycle of shopping only when you are desperate.

- **Money:** It's important to know your budget so that you can spend wisely, but you do not have to shop at the ritziest stores to have a great wardrobe. You can find great clothes at *any* price point. I have things in my closet from thrift stores, consignment stores, off-price stores, department stores, and boutiques. You name it; I've found clothes there. If you know how to make good choices, then you can shop anywhere. I know. I know. This is why you haven't been shopping—because you don't know how to make good choices. We'll get to that!

  One thing I need to point out is that bargain shopping sometimes takes more time and energy because thrift stores, consignment stores, and off-price stores are often more hit or miss, and you have to filter through more racks there than at department stores or a boutique that you (eventually) know carry lines of clothing that work for you. But when you know what you are looking for, it gets easier to either to find things or leave empty-handed but satisfied you didn't buy something just to buy something.

- **Better Choices:** Wouldn't it feel so much easier if fashion would just stay the same for a while? Maybe. The reality is that styles change, trends change, and your body change. Sometimes even your lifestyle changes, so your wardrobe is constantly evolving. There are always new choices to be made, and understanding how to make them for your body, lifestyle, and personality is key.

- **Weight:** This is by far the No. 1 reason women don't shop when they need to. Whether your body has shifted due to having children, menopause, health-related issues, or just getting older, it's easy to mourn the days when it used to feel easier to get dressed. Or maybe you've just become worn out as the years have passed. For some women, getting dressed has never been easy.

Whatever your weight, you deserve to feel good right now. This doesn't mean you have to go spend tons of money or buy massive amounts of clothes at your current weight if you are expecting it to change. Focus on basic colors and garments you can mix and match to leverage your purchases, and then add accessories to bring in personality. This will serve you much better than berating yourself for gaining weight or putting pressure on yourself to lose weight. Good self-care and kindness to yourself will ease the experience and help you achieve your goal with less angst.

So, what are you waiting for? Please don't just turn the page and say, "Yeah, yeah, I'll get to it soon." Make a commitment now! Get out your calendar, and schedule a time to shop, and stick to it. It is necessary self-care. Start visualizing the experience as being fun and easy.

Do You Know How to Shop Successfully?

As you know, shopping isn't fun if you're not finding things you love. The guidelines in the next four sections will help you transform your shopping experience. Remember, it's a step-by-step process, so celebrate every success and refer back to this chapter often to support you.

1. How to Navigate a Store with Ease—Some Dos and Don'ts

Do set an intention. Go in with the intention that you will find everything you want joyfully and effortlessly. If you go in as if you are waging a war, you will exhaust yourself and sure enough the going will be tough—just as you expected! I suggest creating a positive affirmation before you even start. For example, "Every time I shop I find clothes that I love and that look good on me." If that's too much of a stretch (you have to believe what you are saying—at least to some extent) then try something like, "More and more, as I'm learning what to look for, I am having enjoyable and successful shopping experiences."

Do set aside time. If you are used to dashing into Kohl's twenty minutes before you have to pick the kids of up at school, then you're setting yourself up for stress and frustration. Schedule in at least ninety minutes to shop. Put it in your calendar, or you will never do it. No matter what your schedule is, you can find the time somewhere if you really want to, even if you need to schedule it a month out. Go when you say you will, and don't let something else usurp that time. I know there will be a tendency to let that happen, especially if this isn't something you are looking forward to. Resist the temptation!

Do shop with a purpose. If you are shopping in a department store, walk directly to the specific department you need. Do not wander aimlessly around the store. Focus on your goal, and try not to get distracted from it. If this is difficult, ask for help from a shopping buddy or shop in smaller stores.

Do shop for one thing at a time, e.g., jeans, suit, outfit for a specific event. If you multitask and try to focus on three or more items at once, your mind and psyche will be overloaded. Go with a list—a short list—and stick to it so you can focus only on what you came into the store to buy. Keep it simple, and you are much more likely to feel happy with the outcome. Of course, if you have immediate success with your original objective and you have the desire and energy to keep going, then do so!

Do look for your best colors ONLY. Make this the first thing you look for once you find your department. Scan the racks, see what colors (your most flattering colors, of course) call out to you, and start there. It immediately limits the number of options you have and makes it easier and quicker to shop. For instance, if you are looking for a dress in your shades of green, teal or purple and all you see are gray and orange, then you're done. Move on to the next item on your list or to the next store. Do not try to make something work just because you're there. That's how wardrobes get out of control!

Do keep breathing. If you start to get overwhelmed, stop, take a deep breath, recite one of your wonderful affirmations (you have one, right?), and then continue.

Don't shop when you are crabby. If shopping is generally not your most favorite activity in the world and you head to the stores when you are crabby, in a hurry or not feeling well, you are setting yourself up for a very unpleasant and unproductive experience. You will buy things you wouldn't normally buy and then wish you hadn't. Shop only when you are as relaxed and happy as possible. If you say, "But I'm never relaxed and happy to shop," then just keep applying the information you are learning here, and as your successes grow you will find shopping to be a more pleasant experience.

Do not indulge pushy sales women. There are two types of saleswomen you want to avoid. The first is saleswomen who insist you try things on that are clearly not of interest to you. If they bring in a piece here or there to expand your possibilities, that's fine, but an entire dressing room full of things you don't want is not OK. You also want to avoid saleswomen with frenetic energy. Both will exhaust and overwhelm you—and you are sure to buy things you don't like and will not wear!

2. How to Decide What to Try On and What to Ignore

Stick to your list. Do not go into the store unprepared. Keep your list simple—a dress for an event, pretty tops you can wear with jeans or a great pair of black pants—and use it to keep you focused. Exception: if you are having such a great time and something delightful calls out to you. Happy energy has a way of running rampant!

Make a list of things that are non-negotiable before you go. For example, unless you are positive they look good, pledge not to try on:

- Tops with a band at the hip line
- Unflattering colors
- Boxy styles unless you look good in boxy styles or you suspect it will look less boxy on your body
- Patterns that are too big, too small, bad colors, etc.
- Fabrics that cling unless you have no bumps or are willing to wear shapewear. Exception: If the fabric has texture or a pattern that keeps the eye moving, it is worth trying on to see if it works.
- _____ (add from your list of things you'll never wear)

Be adventurous. Look for things outside your comfort zone. Sure, some garments will make you roll your eyes and wonder what genius designer thought *that* look was a good idea, but there are always new options hiding on the racks just waiting for you to try them on. If it calls to you and intrigues you, try it on! You can always (and must!) put it back on the rack if it doesn't work. And, if it *is* dreadful, remember, it's the garment, not you. Laugh and take it off. Not everything works on every body and believe me, there are some things that work on almost no one! If it does work, you will have something exciting and new to spice up your wardrobe.

A word about trying things on in general: Do not leave the store without trying things on —unless you really will return everything that doesn't work before the return policy expires. I've seen too many closets full of clothes with tags on them. Even if your intentions are good, I do not recommend taking something home without trying it on unless you already have the exact same thing at home so you know you love it. It's too easy to find an excuse to keep it just so you don't have to make a trip back to the store to return it.

3. How to Determine if Something Really Works—or Could Work with a Little Tweaking

Evaluate each item thoroughly:

- Is the color flattering?

- Does it reflect your personality?

- Does it fit or could it work with some tailoring? (See "Is It Really Ready-to- Wear?" below.)

- Is the fabric one you are willing to care for? This includes ironing!

- Can you complete the outfit so you can wear it immediately? See No. 4 below.

- Where will you wear it? It is not useful to have an item of clothing if you have nowhere to wear it.

- Do you love it?

Give it a chance. How many times have I shopped with a woman who tries something on and immediately decides it does not work? Not so fast! Unless it is clearly wrong for one of the above reasons, give it a chance. For more on this see, "Do You Need to Step Out of Your Comfort Zone?" below.

4. Pledge to Complete the Outfit

Finish the outfit so you can evaluate it honestly. When you are trying on a garment in the store, be sure to "complete" the outfit as much as you can in the dressing room so you give the garment a fair shake. Too often, I see a woman put on something like a dress while she's wearing butterfly ankle socks and a sports bra and then say, "This doesn't work at all." Well, she's right, if she's going to wear it with those socks and that bra. But, perhaps if she put on a pair of shoes (or at least took off her socks) and went shopping with a proper bra, she could honestly evaluate the dress. Believe me, it really does make a difference. Sure, you might still not love the dress, but it is easier to dismiss something when you cannot see the final look.

Know what else you need. Completing the outfit also means only buying the dress if you know that you have the perfect sweater to go over it, shoes to go with it, the willingness to tailor it if needs that—whatever will complete the outfit to your satisfaction. A dress that will sit in your closet because you have no sweater or wrap to wear with it or because you can't bear to spend the money on the tailoring is a waste of money and space. It's better to leave it at the store for someone who will truly love it to purchase. If you complete the outfit as much as possible in the dressing room, you will know what you need to finish the look. If you don't have these things at home, you need to buy them. And if you are not willing to do that, leave the garment on the rack.

Be sure you have the following pieces with you to complete the outfit when you go to the register or know with absolute certainty that you have them at home:

- Top
- Bottom
- Shoes
- Stockings or tights (if needed)
- Jacket or sweater
- Jewelry (This can be found later as long as the outfit is not completely dependent on it to feel finished.)
- Belt (if needed)
- Undergarments
- Handbag

Lastly, if you get stuck at any point and need help, ask for it. If the next several months pass and you still have not gone shopping, you might need a jumpstart. Many of my clients shop with me two or three times a year so they can get it done as efficiently and productively (and with as much fun) as possible. They know that they don't like to shop alone, that it takes too long by themselves or that they make too many mistakes on their own. Having support makes it all a thousand times easier. And then they don't have to think about it again until the next time we shop. There is no embarrassment in needing help. In fact, it's a sign of strength and honoring yourself. Believe me, I have done it in other areas of my life and am thankful I have. Everyone (yes, everyone) enjoys a second opinion from time to time. Just be sure to look at the source of the opinion. After all, being sure your money is well spent and your heart is happy is what is most important.

These tips will help you clean up your shopping act and save you time, aggravation and money. Not everyone loves the experience of shopping, but everyone deserves the experience of looking great every day. And, with these techniques for shopping successfully, you leave open the possibility of it even being fun!

So, what are you waiting for? Please don't just turn the page and say, "I don't have time now. I'll get to it soon." Chances are good "soon" will never happen. Make a commitment now. Get out your calendar, and schedule a time to shop. Start making a list of what you need—just one to three things. Start visualizing the experience being fun and easy. Stick to the date. Make that commitment to yourself and your self-care. Each step you take is one more step toward having a wardrobe you love. Do it now!

Do You Need to Step Out of Your Comfort Zone?

ONE DAY WHEN I was shopping at Nordstrom Rack, I came across an Alberto Makali top that caught my eye. The colors were beautiful and the design was sparkly, ethereal and just plain pretty! But I hesitated— just for a split second—but I made note of the hesitation.

My momentary uncertainty intrigued me. What was keeping me from running right into the dressing room to try it on? Was I limiting my options or was it really not me?

There's a fine line between "knowing" yourself (for instance, feeling genuinely confident that harem pants are not for you) and "limiting" yourself and your style when it is not necessary—for instance, following some questionable fashion rule about horizontal stripes being a no-no.

Many women pigeonhole themselves into a prescribed way of dressing and thereby limit their options and often squelch their sense of delight. Their wardrobes become functional and one-dimensional—often devoid of any personal style—and their boredom level escalates.

I hear these from women all the time: "I can't wear that," "That doesn't work on my body," or "I've tried that before, and it just doesn't look good."

Of course, sometimes it is true, but honestly, more often than not such a broad statement is a self-imposed fashion rule. And, most fashion rules have an exception from time to time.

So what is at the root of a one-dimensional wardrobe? For some it is a fear of stepping out and being noticed (as discussed in Chapter 1). These women might feel more comfortable when they blend in, or they are trying to disappear.

Some women worry they will make a fashion mistake and look silly. It's understandable that someone would rather look and feel boring than silly, but it is rare that most women will push the envelope to the point of looking silly. Such a worry is generally unfounded. Unfortunately, often when a woman steps outside the norm of what she usually wears, it feels so foreign to her that she loses perspective on whether it is trendy, fashionable, cutting edge or none of the above. As a result, tried and true--or not so true but at least tried--wins out.

And some women are so bound and determined to "find their style" that they hyper focus on certain designs to the exclusion of all else. For instance, many women believe that they can't wear horizontal stripes so anything that even resembles a horizontal stripe is immediately dismissed. The truth is that almost everyone can wear horizontal stripes of some kind at least somewhere on their body. Perhaps the stripes need to be narrow, diffused, wavy, in high-contrast colors or tone-on-tone to soften their effect. Rarely is this design completely unwearable. Not to mention that as time goes along styles change, our bodies change and lifestyles change, so something that seemed unflattering a few years ago might be perfect today.

Some women try really hard, but can't quite seem to figure out how to make it all work and give up from sheer exhaustion and frustration. What goes with what, is that color really flattering, are those accessories too much or just right? The confused mind always says "no" so it's understandable why someone would retreat to what is safe and comfortable.

Let me go back to the Alberto Makali top that caught my eye. I was intrigued enough to try it. In general I am not the bohemian type, but I also know that it's all about how you interpret any given style, bohemian included.

The top was beautiful, and I bought it. What factors went into this decision?

- It fit me perfectly.
- The colors are beautiful and look great with my coloring.
- The top has that ethereal, slightly bohemian quality but is also *exquisite* and *elegantly beautiful*—my inner beauty

words that I use without exception when choosing what to buy.

- I wear it with more structured pants to keep me from feeling swallowed up by too much airy fabric.

- I wear it when my mood is more relaxed, sultry and quiet.

- And, I bought it at Nordstrom Rack so if I had made a mistake it would not have been an expensive one. It is better to make an occasional mistake than to feel restricted by too many self-imposed rules.

How can you recreate this experience for yourself?

Sometimes it is as simple as following some of the rules for shopping successfully outlined in the previous section (see No. 3 How to Determine If Something Really Works). You will notice that the reasons I bought the top correspond to "yes" answers to the questions you should ask to determine if something really works: fit, color, fabric, personality, complete outfit and a place to wear it. And, of course, I loved it!

For example, I was being adventurous when I took the top to the dressing room. I wasn't sure but gave it a try anyway because it intrigued me. Pay attention to what catches your eye. It never hurts to try something new.

A note about having a place to wear something: My "place" to wear it was a bit broad—relaxed summer occasions. Yes, you should always imagine where you will wear the garment and how it will fit into your wardrobe and lifestyle. But if it is something you absolutely love, be adventurous. Although mostly I wear the Alberto Makali top casually and socially, I might choose to wear it to a picnic or baseball game if I felt inspired to and it made me feel good. Who says I can't? You can be practical and listen to your heart at the same time.

And last, but never least, I completed the outfit. I tried on the top with a pair of white jeans, which is what I imagined I would wear it with once I brought it home. Since I was already wearing the sandals I like with white jeans, accessories were the only other question, and I knew I had plenty of earring options at home to wear with the outfit. So I was all set to purchase it. And, I allowed myself the luxury of saying that if I got home and tried it on and decided I didn't love it, I could return it.

Each time you get dressed, not only do you want to like the way you look, but also you want to express your personality in a heartfelt, authentic way. Sure, there are parameters determined by your body type, your age (sometimes) and the particular occasion, but *you* get to put the spin on how you express your own individuality. Don't let yourself get stuck in a rut or a hard-and-fast prescribed way of dressing. Exploring is part of what keeps it all interesting and fun!

Is It Really Ready-to-Wear?

How OFTEN CAN YOU take an entire outfit "off the rack" and have it fit perfectly? I mean, really? If you think about it, what percentage of time does this happen for you? Sometimes? Always? Never? If you answered always, either you are one lucky woman or you are wearing clothes that don't fit you properly.

One day when I was shopping at a fun consignment store near my house, I tried on a jacket. It fit perfectly. Wow! I had a moment when I thought, "Yay! It fits; I'll get it." Believe me, that moment was fleeting because I remembered that I needed to be sure the colors were good (check), I had other things to wear it with (check), and I loved it (the best part of all!). All systems were go, and I wore it that week on a cable TV show and felt great.

Is this a regular occurrence for me? No, believe it or not. A significant percentage of what I buy needs to be tailored in some way whether it is taken in, taken up, let out or redesigned in some way. It's really not as daunting as it sounds.

When you open up to the possibility of tailoring a garment, you expand your options considerably. Take something that once was so-so, apply a little well-placed nip and tuck or realigned detail, and there you have it—a garment that is made just for you. If you try to wear the same thing "as is" off the rack, you would end up looking like you were wearing someone else's clothes, which, in essence, you would be!

Somehow we have gotten it in our heads that we should be able to go shopping, try something on, and wear it out of the store that day looking great—and if we can't there is something wrong with us and with our bodies. Let me set the record straight. There is nothing wrong with you. Our bodies are individual. No two are exactly alike. We vary in height, weight, valleys, hills and all kinds of in between curves.

Imagine if we put ten women who are all 5'6" and wear a size 10 in a line and put them all in the same dress. That could easily be where the similarity ends. Some women might have sloped shoulders while others have broad straight shoulders. You would see small- breasted and large-breasted women as well as women with a small waist and bigger hips and those who have slim hips and a bigger tummy. There would be long legs with short torsos and the reverse. I could go on, but you get the idea. Chances are really good that most, if not all, of the women who looked good in the dress would have to tailor some part of it to customize it to their bodies.

So, how do you know when tailoring can help? Here's a checklist to follow once you find something that intrigues you:

- Take the garment into the dressing room and try it.

- Do whatever you need to do to make the outfit look as complete as possible. It will not help you make a decision if you try to evaluate a long sweater while you are wearing shorts and a pair of sneakers. The parts are incongruent and, as they say in sales and marketing, "A confused mind always says no." You are likely to say no while wearing shorts, but if you had tried it on with a pair of jeans, you might have loved it.

- Decide if you like the basic look. Then look for things that are not quite right. Here are a few common issues:

- Pants, skirts or sleeves are too long. This is an easy alteration. You can waste a lot of time trying to find something that fits perfectly and is the right length when a quick alteration can take care of it.

- Pants, skirts or sleeves are too short. Check to see if there is enough seam allowance to let it down. Do it before you wear it and wash it. You do not want to risk being able to see the telltale mark of the original hemline.

- A top hangs too low so the darts fall below where they are supposed to. If it has sleeves, this can be a tricky alteration.

If it has straps then it's often a super quick, inexpensive alteration to have the straps adjusted so it pulls the top up and fits in the right places.

- Your bra straps show. There are two options that could fix this. One is to add lingerie straps (these are little strings with snaps on the ends that go around your bra straps). They keep your bra straps snuggly secured to your top so that when you move, the top and bra strap move together. No more bra straps slipping out! Or, you might need to get a different bra with convertible straps or a design that is specific to the cut of the top. If the top has spaghetti straps, you will need to wear a strapless bra.

- Pants are too big at the waist. Often, women either have gapping at the waist or bagginess at the bum. A tailor can usually fix both of these problems. When buying a garment you want to fit the widest part of you first (whether this is your hips, waist, shoulders or bust) and then have the rest of the garment altered. Remember, it is usually easier to take something in than to let it out.

- A top is too long. Have it taken up—even if it is just a T-shirt. This is usually one of the easiest alterations and one that most people seem to overlook. It can take a garment from looking frumpy to fabulous with a quick flip of the hem.

- Pockets gap. I often ask myself why designers put pockets in women's trousers! More often than not they gap, especially diagonal pockets. And, other than a tissue, who stores anything there? It will just add width to the hip line, which most women do not want to do. If yours do not gap, you are lucky. If they do, the easiest alteration with a big positive payback is to have the pockets removed and sewn up. Easy and clean!

- Go immediately from the store to the tailor. If you take it home first, it will likely sit there for weeks or months waiting to go. I know, I've done it!

It is worth keeping the idea of tailoring in mind while you shop. If you immediately dismiss something because the fit is off, you will miss out on some really great clothing. Yes, sometimes, the alteration is just too big or cannot be done. Then you can let it go with confidence. But, you will be surprised at how often a minor tweak here or there can make a major difference in how something looks and fits.

This part is really important: Always allow for alterations in your clothing budget. If you can't afford to make the alteration, do not buy the garment. And, yes, this is absolutely true: If you are *not willing* to spend the money on the alteration, don't buy it. Sometimes people say, "Well, I only spent $19.99 on that top. I'm not going to spend $15 to alter it." First of all, there is no reason you can't spend an extra $15 to create a top you love and will wear a lot. And, if you don't spend the money, the top will never look right and isn't worth the initial $19.99 investment.

One more thing: If you don't have a great tailor, ask someone who does. This is really the best way to make sure you get someone who knows what they are doing. The last thing you want to do is entrust your garment to someone and then get it back and find it is unwearable. I have seen this happen more often than I'd care to; finding a tailor through a referral is the best way to avoid such mishaps.

Do You Want Your Dream Wardrobe? Dare to Be Picky!

DESPITE YOUR ORGANIZATION AND best efforts, there will be times when you want to throw your arms up in despair because you know what you want, or at least have a vague idea, but cannot find it anywhere in the stores. You scour the racks, ask the sales staff, and search online. No luck! So what do you do? There are three options:

1. Get the next best thing that works even though it doesn't give you that thrill.

2. Give up and go with what's there because you want something new in your closet.

3. Wait! You know what you love, and you're not settling for anything less.

Obviously, you can do whatever you want, but if you are looking to create the wardrobe you dream of, the *only* answer is No. 3: Wait! Settling for anything less than what you feel great wearing will only leave you feeling humdrum about your wardrobe and constantly on the prowl for something better. It's a vicious and expensive cycle.

"Giving up" totally bewilders me. It is kind of like voting for someone not because s/he is your candidate of choice but because you know s/he will win. I never understand that philosophy! It's a fleeting, hollow victory at best.

OK, I know what you're thinking: If I wait for what is perfect I'll never buy anything! With very rare exceptions, this is not true. It might just mean that the designers have taken temporary leave of their senses and you just have to be patient. If you already have things in your closet that you love to wear, this means you've been picky in the past, right? You might be disappointed, but you won't feel *desperate* to buy something new.

If you are prone to settling, make it a game to catch yourself. Try this: When you leave a store with bags of clothes, assess how you feel. You have bags of clothes, but do you also have a nagging sense something is lacking? Are you missing excitement/delight/joy over your new purchases? In this case, turn right around and return it all! You must love everything you buy and wear—no excuses, no arguments!

Sometimes you just need to be a little creative. Let me share a personal example. A few seasons ago I was looking to buy a couple of new jackets to add to my wardrobe. I certainly know how to do it, but despite all my best efforts I wasn't finding anything I totally loved. Rather than settle for anything less, I did the next best thing: I became proactive. I did a search on eBay for my favorite designer and guess what? A number of fabulous jackets showed up in my size. So, I bought two. I took one to the tailor to have the long sleeves shortened to 3/4 length and wore both endlessly that season.

Settling for less than the best always costs you more in time, aggravation and money in the long run. Being picky will pay off on a much grander scale: You will get to look and feel great every day!

Do You Know How to Shop the Sale Racks?

For some people, a sale is one of the hardest places to be picky. There you are in a sea of special savings signs and final sale racks, and some of you can't wait to dive right in thinking, "Oh, boy, I can get three things for the price of one!" It is so easy to throw caution to the wind and run home with that item that was 80% off the retail price. For others, you think you'd love to take advantage of the savings, but when you see racks and racks of sale items, you want to turn around and leave—quickly! They feel messy and disorganized and, generally speaking, most of the good stuff is gone. This is often why these things are on sale.

Whether you enjoy shopping or you would rather clean your garage than hit the stores on a holiday weekend, these five shopping strategies can help.

1. **Choose the right store.** When it's time to shop, many women automatically head for the nearest department or chain store. This is great if the clothes there are what you like. If, however, you find yourself tediously sorting through racks of clothing to find one piece worth buying, then it's time to look elsewhere. There are smaller, boutique-type stores that are reasonably priced and offer delightful alternatives to the traditional stores. Yes, they have great sales, too, but you want to be sure you get there early because they often have a very loyal following and the good things get snapped up in the first day or so. Consignment stores are another valuable resource. Again, don't be swayed by the price tag. Just because you can get it there for 30% of the original price does not make it a sure bet. You must still apply all your learning here before it comes home with you. And, as an aside for consignment stores, their inventory can change almost daily, so don't just go once and decide it isn't right for you. Check back a few times. Make it into a fun treasure hunt to find something beautiful to add to your wardrobe. All in

all, a little research about where to shop can save you a lot of aggravation and money in the long run.

2. **Sort by color.** When you are looking at a disorderly rainbow of items, focus on the colors you love and that you want to build your wardrobe around. Do not take it off the rack unless it's a color that works for you. This will make your selection process, and your wardrobe, more efficient.

3. **Use your senses—including your sixth sense.** Identify what draws you to an item. Is it the feel of the fabric, the way it moves when you walk? Yes, you should walk, sit and bend in everything you try on. Maybe it's the detailing of the design, or does it just feel "right?" If it's simply that it fits or the price is tempting, put it back on the rack.

I doubt there is a woman around who has not bought by price alone at least once. When you do this, there is nothing strategic about the purchase. It is based primarily on desire to find hidden treasures and a desire to get a great deal. Have you heard or said any of the following?

- It was originally ten times this price!
- I've always wanted something by this designer!
- "If I just lose five pounds, do more ab and butt exercises or hold my breath, it will fit perfectly!"
- "If I just wear a little more blush and a different lipstick, this beige blouse won't make me look so washed out."
- "But it's so cute, such a good price or feels so comfy – I'm sure I can find *something* to wear with it."

Remember, buy it only if you love it and can wear it right now (or after some tailoring)! While there is certainly nothing wrong with finding treasures and great deals, sadly, it is not a great deal if you never wear it or, worse, wear it and look frumpy! Which brings me to my next point …

4. **Consider its worth.** I'm talking about the price per wear, not the actual price. Consider these three things:

  • Do you have at least two things at home that go with it, or are you purchasing all the pieces you need to go with it now?

  • Can you picture yourself wearing it a lot in a specific outfit, or does it have the versatility to go with many outfits and further increase the price per wear? Can you dress it up or down?

  • Are you already imagining all the places you can wear it?

  If you can answer a resounding yes to all of these questions, then buy it! If not, step away from the rack!

5. **Look for love.** Functional, useful, serviceable, and classic alone are not satisfactory euphemisms. Life is too short to wear anything you don't enjoy wearing just because it "works." Remember, too, that with a few nips and tucks a tailor can often take something from serviceable to beautiful.

  One last thing: Be sure you love it as much as the friend you're shopping with or the salesperson does. Listen to their advice, and then decide for yourself. After all, you're the one who will be wearing it.

If, after following these steps, you are still shopping and not finding things you love, go back to No. 1 and begin again. Or just wait until new seasonal items come into the store so you don't have to weed through rack after rack of jumbled up discounted clothes.

It can be fun to find a great buy at a sale, but sometimes you just need to pass up what's there and wait for something that makes your heart sing (even if you have to pay a bit more at the outset). If you wear it a lot, it will still cost you less in the long run than a barely worn sale item.

Are the Shopping Rules Different for Dressy Clothes?

IF I HAD A nickel for every time a woman told me that she can only find a dressy dress when she doesn't need one, I could retire. Not that I am ready to, of course! These women always say that when they go shopping specifically for a dress, too often at the last minute, it becomes an elusive purchase.

When it comes to dressy clothes (especially if you do not have any), buy something when you see it. It takes much longer for dressy items to go out of style, and you will be thrilled the next time you are invited to an event and actually have something nice to wear. As a bonus, the universe has been known to reward you with fun invitations just because you have a beautiful outfit ready and waiting.

Here's the story of how a beautiful dress came into my wardrobe. It also gives some insight into how much even I have to pay attention to ensure I don't settle for something I don't love.

One day, I stopped into one of my favorite store—the Studio in Brookline, Massachusetts, to pick up something they were holding for me. Shopping in July is nothing short of hit or miss, but they had some inviting sales going on throughout the store, so I wanted to take a peek.

It had been an unseasonably hot summer! Very little rain, temperatures topping ninety degrees and humidity hovering around the miserable level. As a result, my sleeveless tops were seeing more action than they had in at least five years.

Hot, humid weather also makes wearing pants rather unappealing, so one of the things I was looking for was more casual skirts. The fashion world, however, had other ideas, and the pickings were slim. There were dresses but very few skirts.

As I perused the racks, I thought I'd see what, if anything, they had left for fun summer skirts. Two items caught my eye right away. One was a green/yellow/brown jersey skirt. The other was a dressy dress. Oops, not what I was looking for, but there it was—a gorgeous ombré (gradation of color from dark to light) design of blue floating down into a shimmery beige. I was intrigued enough to try on both of my finds.

The skirt was nice, but the dress was amazing! My first thought was, "Well, the skirt is practical, and the dress isn't. It's also comfortable and a great price. ..."

Then, I asked myself the most critical (and revealing) question of all, "Do I love the skirt? Am I excited to wear it?"

The answer was a resounding NO! Practical? Yes. Comfortable? Yes. Great price? Yes. Exquisite? No!

In my heart I knew that if I purchased the skirt, it would be OK. But as I've said again and again, OK is never good enough! If you settle for good enough often enough, you end up with an OK wardrobe. It's a slippery slope, so you have to be vigilant.

The dress, on the other hand, made me smile. It felt great (very comfortable) and was a great price. And I felt like Grace Kelly wearing it! I admit I even had to squelch the urge to wear it home.

Yes, I had no occasion to wear it to right then. But it's hanging in my closet right now. Come on, universe!

Can You Master the Art of Online Shopping?

SO FAR MOST OF this chapter has been about shopping that involves leaving your house. But I know that many women, especially those who hate to shop, often resort to online or catalog shopping. Their guiding philosophy is that the less they actually have to step foot in a store, the better.

Any woman who shops online because she is trying to avoid stores probably is not perusing the fashionista sites that highlight up-and-coming designers or sites that focus on special sales on designer brands (which are excellent ways to find things you love). She's generally not looking for the latest and greatest. She's looking for familiar, safe, reliable and easy. For the most part, she sticks to the basics (e.g., Talbots, J. Jill and Lands' End).

To this I say: If you are shopping online simply to avoid going into the stores and regularly find yourself settling for "not horrible" just to get it over with, chances are really good you will never have a wardrobe or personal style you can delight in.

I'm so sorry to say that, but it's true. You will keep getting the same unsatisfying (or passable) results over and over. But, it doesn't have to be that way. Really! Once you learn how to shop with this book as your guide, you can shop in stores or online with satisfying results. As Abbie, whom I've been working with for several years, recently said to me, "I now shop less and am more successful." It's because she has a better idea of what to look for when she does shop.

How often do you shop for clothes or accessories online? When you do, do you *love* what you get? Are you thrilled when the package arrives in the mail because you can't wait to wear it? That's what I thought. Sometimes you are, and sometimes you aren't.

I admit that I have mixed feelings about online shopping. Yes, it can make life so easy, at least up front, but it can also complicate things unmercifully when what you get doesn't live up to your expectations. Inaccurate color guides, nonstandard sizing and fabric that feels itchy instead of soft and alluring all lead to returns or exchanges. This often boils down to added frustration and discouragement. Not to mention that it can get costly. And your closet can end up looking like a strange confusion of styles that don't make any sense together, or it can feel like a collection of blah "basics." Neither is quite what most women are looking for.

Online shopping isn't all bad, though. Here are some tips to make your experience more successful and minimize the returns:

Find three or four designers you LOVE. This is important. I am not talking about clothes you like or that fit you, but clothes that you *love*. These are the stores/designers you want to follow. It doesn't matter if it's Talbots, Eileen Fisher, Jones New York, Liz Claiborne or Armani. What is important is that you feel great when you wear their clothes.

Know your measurements. Women's clothing sizes are far from standardized, so if you know your bust, hip, waist, and in-seam measurement, it will improve your success rate. And, when in doubt, buy more than one size and return the one that doesn't work. It will save you the effort of exchanging it and can actually work out better financially. The exception is shoes, where it won't matter because so many websites offer free shipping and free returns to offset that problem.

Keep your lifestyle and personality in mind. Websites and catalogs are created to make the clothes look appealing. The models stand a certain way, the clothes are adjusted so they photograph well, and the ultimate goal is to get you to buy whatever they are selling. Always keep that in mind and respond accordingly. Use the enlarge feature most store websites have so you can see the clothing at closer range. Look at different views, if possible, and be discerning.

Stay focused. How many times have you been seduced by an offer such as "spend $100 and get free shipping" only to find out that the things you want only amount to $76? So, what do you do? You find something that's "not horrible" to make up the other $24 so you can save $9 on shipping! Think about it! Does that make sense?

Know the return policy—the store's *and* yours. Do you have any idea how many times I've been in someone's closet helping them decide what to keep and what not to, only to find things that they have purchased online but never got around to returning? Yikes! Sometimes having the option of returning the purchase to the store rather than spending the money or energy to pack it up and take it to the post office makes it more appealing. Be honest with yourself about *your* return policy. Will you do it before the return policy expires?

Learn from others' experience. Many sites allow buyers to review their purchases, and these reviews can be invaluable information. Read several to get an overall viewpoint to help you assess if something would be a concern for you or if it's just one disgruntled person's rants. Reviews can help you determine if an item runs true to size or is uncomfortable or not as picture, useful information, to be sure.

Use customer service liberally. Do you have a question about the garment or the store's policies that is not answered online? Then, place a quick call or use the instant chat services that some stores offer to confer with customer service. You could save time and money in the long run.

As one of my clients pointed out, sometimes online is the only place you can find things like petite sizes, plus sizes or wide-width shoes.

All of this is in addition, of course, to knowing what colors look good on you and understanding your inner essence and lifestyle needs. Online shopping can be fruitful as long as your long-term motivation is to create a wardrobe and personal style you love and not just to "clothe" your body.

The bottom line is—as always—never, ever settle for anything less than what makes your heart sing!

Does Your Outfit Need a Dress Rehearsal?

WITH LAST FEW CHAPTERS, you have been busy. You have been clearing items out of your closet as your inner essence begins to take a front-row seat, and you are beginning to invite in pieces you love. A big part of this ongoing experience is planning how to mix and match your clothes and accessories to create new, exciting possibilities.

Before you debut a new outfit, however, I recommend you take precaution: Give your clothes a "dress" rehearsal.

Fashion magazines and stores are full of great ideas, but you have to translate an idea directly to your body to find out whether it's a hit or a miss. Something can look just perfect and inviting when you lay it out on the bed or see it hanging on the mannequin in the store, but it's another thing to actually put it on your body and see how it all works in real life.

Perhaps you can relate to Jackie's experience. She told me, "I can't tell you the number of times in the past I put on a new outfit at the last minute and canceled out of the date at the last minute because the outfit didn't work and there was no back-up ready. It's a horrible feeling!"

I also have a story to share from a trip to New York City: I had carefully planned my wardrobe for spending an entire day shopping with a client. I'm not a light packer, and I don't apologize for that. I always bring something extra just in case my mood changes, the weather doesn't cooperate, or I spill something. This trip was no exception, but what happened made me more aware of the importance of the dress rehearsal.

I was leisurely getting ready in my hotel room on the morning of the shopping trip. I put on my brown pants and a jacket. My makeup was on, and I was fully accessorized. The only things left to do were finish packing and put on my shoes. And, then it struck me. The shoes I had brought did not have a high enough heel for the pants I planned to wear. Sure enough, when I put my shoes on, the hem dragged on the ground—not a particularly elegant look and certainly not good for the pants.

I was so upset with myself. Thankfully, I was not completely stuck. I was able to wear the pants I had on the day before. They were the perfect color, and the heel height was right. I just wasn't as happy with the combination since the pants weren't quite as elegant as the pair I had planned to wear (although I'm probably the only one who noticed). I took a breath, made peace with the outfit and vowed to rehearse my outfits more carefully the next time. This was a new pair of pants, and I had not put it through the rehearsal process long enough to be sure what shoes would work best with them.

During a wardrobe consultation with Diane, I mentioned my dress rehearsal concept. She told me that she does a "staging" with her clothes. She chooses her outfit pieces ahead of time and then hangs them altogether on her closet door. She reviews the complete outfit several times to see if she likes it before she decides to wear it. This certainly sets the stage for a fun outfit, but she agreed that it isn't until she actually puts it on that she knows for sure whether it really works.

We are not one-dimensional, and we do not have mannequin bodies. It's easy to assume that the outfit will look the same on us as it does on the mannequin, but those assumptions contribute to our frustration when they prove incorrect. Your own private dress rehearsal will solve this problem.

Amy told me of an experience similar to my New York City mishap. She found out she was to be the recipient of an award from her company, and it was to be presented to her at a special dinner. It's no surprise that she wanted her outfit to be special. She found a dress she liked. It was sleeveless, so she bought a pretty cardigan to go over it in exactly the right color. Her shoes, jewelry and handbag completed the outfit. She had been staring at the combination for two weeks with anticipation, and finally the day of the event arrived.

She got dressed and realized that not only did the sweater make the neckline bunch up funny, but also when she tried to walk more than ten feet in her shoes, her heels slipped, and she nearly fell out of them. The shoes had been fine while she was standing looking in the mirror and moving ever so slightly, but as soon as she walked any distance, yikes, she walked right of them. All she could do was wish she had done a full dress rehearsal earlier.

She ended up pinning the neckline to the sweater, and it turned out the room was warm so (phew!) she didn't need the extra layer most of the time. She found some gel pads to stick in the front of her shoes so she could walk up on stage to receive her award. Unfortunately, the shoes made her feet hurt, but at least she wasn't leaving them four steps behind her when she walked. She had averted disaster and supreme frustration, but her experience was not as fun and elegant as she had planned for it to be.

The moral of the story is that even if you have worn each piece separately—even many times—it's important to see if the new combination you're considering really works. Your memory can do funny things, and it's easy to forget that something was particularly clingy or only looked good with a skinny pant. The proposed outfit hanging on the closet door lulls you into a false sense of security that is broken immediately when you put the clothes on.

Yes, you might feel like you have better things to do (aka things you'd *rather* do) than try your clothes on ahead of time. But, I promise that if you do this, you will be so happy you did. No more frantic, last-minute clothing changes complete with cursing, tears and threats of not going anywhere. You'll breath a sigh of relief as you get dressed with ease. And, if a practiced outfit doesn't work during a dress rehearsal, you have a chance to tweak it with less stress, and you can use all the other chapters of this book to help you figure out whether you can fix it or should let it go.

A director would never go right from selecting the cast and staging the space to opening night, and it's not advisable to do that with your wardrobe, either. A dress rehearsal is an invaluable step in your journey (whether it's done in your home or at the store if you purchase everything at the same time) to creating a wardrobe you love with ease and joy. A few extra minutes of practice can save you frustration and anxiety as the curtain goes up, and the next day there will be glowing reviews all around!

— —

Have you planned a shopping trip yet? Take the information you've learned so far while it is still fresh in your memory (in fact, bring the book with you for moral support!), and go shopping. Reading what to do is great, but putting it into practice is how you'll get the results that Sally did:

> "My wardrobe is spectacular now—it's such a different experience to put myself together in the morning now (it's actually enjoyable!). I have been venturing out to shop at lunch and have been picking up a few pieces here and there to supplement my growing wardrobe. The best part is that for the first time ever I'm enjoying shopping because I don't feel overwhelmed."

Tara has also been putting her learning into action: "You have taught me so much about shopping that I'm getting good at buying things I love and making complete outfits. It's so exciting and such a relief!"

Use their inspiration along with your newly acquired knowledge. Take it one step at a time, and you, too, will soon have a wardrobe full of beautiful, complete outfits that you love.

Chapter 5

Accessorizing: The Finishing Touches

IT'S THE LITTLE TOUCHES, the extra care taken to be sure something is "just so" that complete a look. Imagine presenting a simple report in a beautiful binder with an enticing cover page rather than simply handing it out stapled. Or consider how much a garnish of mint adds to the beauty of a dish of sorbet. Although the ordinary presentation is acceptable and gets the job accomplished, it's that extra touch that gives it interest and gets noticed with admiration. That finishing touch says you are mindful of the details that make a lasting impression.

It's the same with your personal presentation. Putting a simple, basic outfit together is one thing, and it certainly gets the job done. But going the extra mile to make sure the outfit is special, which does not mean that it has to be obvious, flamboyant or expensive, is the difference between good and great.

The right accessories can take your look to the next level. These little extras will, at the very least, get an appreciative glance and many times a compliment. The best part of all, of course, is that they will help you look and feel great!

Are You Having a Bad Hair Day?

SOME MORNINGS I LOOK in the mirror and feel like I look about one hundred years old. I have learned that frowning at myself or analyzing every inch of my face in a magnified mirror does not make things better, and a big smile always perks me up. As Jodi said, you are never fully dressed without a smile.

I also know that how my hair looks can bolster my self-esteem or deflate my ego in about five seconds. That could account for my lifelong love of changing hairstyles. Maybe it has to do with living in New England where the running joke is that if you don't like the weather wait five minutes, and it will change. The same is true for my hair—often in direct reaction to the weather!

I have to admit that if someone asks me what my favorite feature is, my hair is the first thing that comes to mind. I was blessed with thick red hair. Although the red gets some help from my trusty hair colorist these days, I enjoy changing my hairstyle frequently.

That said, I still have plenty of moments of frustration and dreaded bad hair days. And I'm not alone. At least three-quarters of the women who come to me for help with their personal style are somewhat disgruntled or discouraged by their hair. It doesn't matter if they are fifteen or sixty-five!

Speaking of age, the question of whether a style is age appropriate is a common one. In fact, I remember speaking to a group of MBA students a few years ago, and several of them told me about an article that appeared in *The New York Times* entitled, "Why Can't Middle-Aged Women Have Long Hair?" They wanted to know my opinion.

After a quick roll of my eyes, I told the audience of mostly twenty-somethings that I couldn't believe it was still something we worried about! Of course, there I was, a fifty-four-year-old woman in the process of letting her hair grow talking to women in their twenties—which gives you an idea of my thoughts on that topic.

Many years ago, I wrote an article called "Hair Length Has Nothing To Do With Age." I thought this issue was a done deal back then, but here it is nearly two decades later and *The New York* Times still considers it newsworthy!

So, can women of any age have long hair? Yes, absolutely. Should every woman wear long hair? No, absolutely not. Therein lies the challenge—finding the most beautiful and flattering style for YOU!

Here are some answers to important questions related to your hair:

What is the No. 1 thing you can do to refresh your style in general? Get an exquisite haircut, and be sure your color goes with your skin tone. Having these will make you smile every time you look in the mirror.

I remember seeing Sally Field in one of her commercials for some medication and was shocked to see that her hair was way too dark for her skin. As a result, it looked harsh on her and definitely not flattering. Add to that the fact that her hair looked messy most of the time. I know they were shooting for casual and carefree, but for someone with as much spirit as she has, it just was not working. She ended up looking a tad haggard!

So if Sally Field, a celebrity, can't get a haircut and color that flatter her, how can you? No worries! There are exceptional hairstylists everywhere. If yours isn't giving you something that works for you, keep looking. Ask someone whose hairstyle or color you admire where she gets it done, and go there.

Can everyone have a "wash-and-wear" look? Don't I wish! Your hairstylist can only do so much to make your hair wash and go, and not everyone can make it work for them—at least to their satisfaction. It all depends on your hair and your expectations. Sometimes the two just don't go together. My hair (and my expectations) are a perfect example of this.

I have come to accept, albeit some days better than others, that it takes me a long time to blow dry my hair because letting my hair air dry just doesn't make me happy. I'm not an easy, breezy laid-back kind of gal, and my hair doesn't cooperate without a little TLC. It has a tendency to lay flat on my head and bend (not wave or curl but bend) in funny ways. I always feel messy when my hair looks like this. Honestly, this is a big part of why I wear my hair short more than long. It cuts my blow drying time in half, and I can more easily get the results I want!

Remember, it is not the hairstylist's fault if you want long wavy hair, and yours is pin straight or kinky curly by nature. It's just not going to work without at least a little intervention no matter how he or she cuts it.

Does your hair have personality? Understanding your personal style (your essence) affects *every* part of your image, and your hair is no exception. Are you sweet, bubbly, dramatic or direct? Whatever is true for you, your hair *must* reflect your personality.

For me, I like a little drama, glamour or sophistication. I greatly admire, and am often envious of, pretty, uncomplicated looks on others, but I have come to realize that they often do not translate well to my hair and personality!

Remember, too, that while others might compliment your hairstyle, the most important person to make happy is *you*.

Does hair upkeep have to be so expensive? Consider this: Your hair is your constant accessory. It is hard to hide, short of shaving your head or always wearing a hat. This is not a place to cut corners, or you will be miserable every time you look in the mirror. Yes, coloring your hair can get costly and can make the idea of gray hair appealing. But even going gray requires you to have an absolutely terrific haircut and clothes in your perfect colors, or you risk looking frumpy and, sometimes older than you are. Refer to "Are You Graying Gracefully?" in Chapter 9 for more on that topic.

The majority of women will admit that they want to look reasonably youthful as long as possible; old is not a look most of us want. Remember, attitude is everything, and your hair must have attitude—in keeping with your inner essence, of course.

Beware of do-it-yourself hair color or having a friend help you unless you are absolutely sure the color is absolutely perfect for your skin tone. My sister-in-law once shared a hysterical story about her adventures with hair dye and her desperate calls to the manufacturer's customer service department! It turned out fine, but there were moments when she wasn't so sure it would.

I can also attest to the fact that once you get enough white or gray hairs it becomes more challenging to use over-the-counter hair dyes successfully. My hair likes to turn pink if the shade is off even a little! And ending up with a color that doesn't go with your skin tone is a million times worse than being gray!

Since every time you look in the mirror you see your hair, it directly influences how you feel about the way you look. As a result, taking good care of your hair is important, and, yes, there is a cost associated with that. This is not a place to skimp. I have my hair colored every three weeks because if I let it go a week longer I don't want to leave the house for that last week. Do I wish I could spend less? Sure. But is it worth the slightly additional expense to like the way my hair looks? Absolutely. Be sure you are investing in your hair so that you feel great every time you look in the mirror.

Here's your checklist:

- Do you love your haircut?
- Are you reasonably good at styling it?
- Does your hairstylist listen to you when you ask for something different?

- Do you love your hair color?
- Do your haircut and color reflect your personality?
- Do you feel good about how your hair looks most days?

If you answered no to any of those, then it's time for a change.

If you answered yes to all the questions, then you are having a good hair day. Enjoy!

Does Your Makeup Routine Need a Boost?

What happens when you open your makeup bag every morning? Do you think, "Yay, this is fun!" or do you think, "Why can't I get it to look like the pictures in the magazine?"

While there is not a one-size-fits-all way to apply makeup, there are a few techniques that can make a big difference when it comes to creating a finished look you like.

And, please, be kind to yourself. If you are forty, fifty or sixty-plus and especially if you have not had any cosmetic surgery, do not compare yourself to someone who is twenty. It's a whole different ballgame, but that is not to say you can't look equally as amazing!

One other thing: Have you ever noticed that most of the makeup directions out there are given on women under twenty-five years old? What's that about? Makeup does not look the same on mature skin, so many of those tips are useless.

Whatever your age, here are three steps that make a difference on everyone:

1. **Use concealer.** As you age the center of the face (the inner parts of your eyes near the bridge of your nose, under your eyes, and along your nostrils and the lines down to your mouth) can begin to get a tad dark and shadowy. If you lighten up that part of your face, you look instantly lighter, brighter and more youthful. Use a good concealer in these areas before applying your foundation.

   Hint: Apply a tiny bit of translucent powder over the concealer to set it.

2. **Maintain your eyebrows.** Your eyebrows frame your eyes and give added dimension to your face. Take a candid look at your brows. Are they one part of your face that you tend to neglect

or just plain ignore? Have you noticed that as you have gotten older, they have become a bit more sparse or short? Shaping them, even when they are sparse, short or light-colored, can have a dramatic effect. Unless you are unusually handy with the tweezers, have your brows professionally shaped. The difference will surprise and delight you and they'll get all those little tiny hairs, too!

If your eyebrows are sparse or have turned a little white or gray, use a powder or pencil in a shade that complements your hair and skin tone. I am a fan of powder because it tends to look very natural and is easy to apply, but if you prefer a pencil and are good at making it look natural, then go for it. Either way, when applied lightly, the color will accentuate your eyebrows, and no one will be know you are wearing it.

Hint: If you have done very little to your brows until now, allow a little time to adjust. Changing them (especially adding color) can be a bit disconcerting, but stick with the change for at least a week. By then, it will most likely feel just right.

3. **Line and define.** Want to draw focus to your eyes? You can skip the eyeshadow, but always apply eyeliner. And, here's the clincher: You must apply it to the top lid. I know it's harder to do, but practicing will help. Lining the bottom lash line is optional (and it often depends on factors such as under-eye circles, the size of your eye, how comfortable you are with a little extra makeup). Never, I repeat, never, line only the bottom lash line. With rare exceptions, this will just make your eyes look bottom heavy rather than give a lift to your face and draw focus to the beauty of your eye color. This is the ultimate goal of eyeliner, of course.

Hint: Similar to adding color for your brows, I recommend using a powder liner for the most natural look, and it is also the easiest to learn to apply. You can also use an eyeliner pencil (natural colors only, please). And, liquid liner often looks hard and overpowering, so I recommend avoiding it!

Lastly, your makeup can only look as good as the skin you are putting it on, so be sure you are taking very, very good care of your face before you pick up a makeup brush. Forget the excuses; a good skin care routine does not have to take more than three minutes. And when done diligently—yes, that means every day—it will make a world of difference.

Do Your Eyeglasses Reflect Who You Are?

EYEGLASSES ARE ONE OF those things that once they are on your face, you forget about them. The truth is that they are an accessory, so you need to think about them as such.

The first place people look when they meet you is your face. Your eyes, your smile, your teeth, your hair—they all say something about who you are and the image you want to project. In fact, anything on your face becomes a focal point and that includes your eyeglasses. Many people who wear glasses own only one pair and wear them every day. Depending on the glasses or your personality, this can be good or bad.

As we've seen in the movies, glasses can figure prominently in creating a character. The main difference between Clark Kent and Superman—other than the obvious costume—is the glasses Clark wears. They help him present a reserved, bookish character in contrast to the worldly, heroic Superman. Want to look like a nerd? Choose the appropriate glasses, and you're done. Want to look cool? Choose a pair of sunglasses that scream trendy and you're there. It's truly amazing that something as seemingly benign as some wire or plastic and glass can so significantly alter how someone looks. But it can and does.

Remember Sarah Palin in the 2008 presidential race? She became known almost as much for her trendy eyeglasses as for her political views. The Jonas Brothers popularized wearing obvious nerd glasses! Every young person who idolized the Jonas Brothers wanted a pair, so thick-rimmed plastic glasses in almost every color were everywhere.

Glasses can be a wonderful accessory, but be careful. They can change your look immensely, for better or worse. The right glasses are a wonderful expression of who you are. Once you know what your prescription requires, here are a few tips to help you get the style right:

- **Consider the lifespan**. How often do you replace your eyeglass frames? Is it every year or two or more like every five to ten years (hopefully not!)? Obviously something trendy will not stand the test of time; a more classic look may serve you better. But even classic styles change as the years pass.

- **Get a second opinion**. Take someone with you whose opinion you value, especially if you can't see how you look when you're trying the glasses on.

- **Choose the store wisely**. Go to a store that has lots of choices so you can really get an idea of what looks and feels good to you. Then you will not feel forced to choose "good enough" from a limited selection.

- **Consider your style**. Glasses should complement your face, bone structure and coloring. In addition, they must express your personality. If you want something elegant and understated, perhaps a pair of rimless glasses with arms in a beautiful soft color will do the trick. Or maybe you want them to have a touch of pizzazz and would love a few sparkles on the arms. Some have iridescence or a contrasting color inside that just peeks out when you move. Vintage styles are constantly coming back, and laser-cut designs are all the rage. You get to decide what speaks to your personality. If you are only going to own one pair, be sure it does not overpower your features and the style is not so over the top that you can't easily wear them with your entire wardrobe. If you want more than one pair, then you can add "statement" glasses that are fun, quirky or creative—in other words, glasses that make a more obvious statement about who you are.

- **Check the fit.** The top of the frame should cover your eyebrows or be slightly lower—never above your brows—or you will look like you have two sets of eyebrows. I know this seems obvious to some, but there are still a few people who are stuck in the 1980s. The only exception is sunglasses. They can be as big as you want them to be. Lastly, your pupils should be centered in the lens of the eyeglasses.

- **Get rid of the glare.** Non-reflective antiglare lenses are a must. No exceptions, though I did once hear a story about one woman who refused to get non-reflective lenses because she was hoping the glare would detract from the wrinkles around her eyes! It didn't. They allow people to see your eyes more clearly when they talk with you, and they reduce the glare so you can see more clearly when you are driving at night. This is not a place to cut costs!

- **Avoid tint.** No tinting unless you have more than one pair of glasses. It obscures your eyes.

- **Do not settle.** This is not a time to let style, comfort or durability suffer in order to reduce the cost. If it means going to several optical stores to find the perfect pair in your price range, then so be it.

Think about it: You wear your glasses every day for the world, and you, to see. Use these guidelines to make sure you love the look reflected back to you in the mirror.

Do You Know How to Wear a Belt?

WHEN BELTS WENT OUT of fashion in the 1990s, no one was happier than I was to see them go. In fact, up until recently, that was the last time I had worn one!

I have to admit that I was reluctant to invite them back into my wardrobe. I always found them uncomfortable and could not imagine that would change. Since I was a child I have been totally intolerant of anything tight around my waist. Ridding my wardrobe of all belts was a very liberating experience, and I was loath to go back. That said, I'm also a believer in trying new things and never saying never! So, imagine my absolute delight when I discovered fashionable stretchy, comfortable belts. I am a convert!

The interesting thing about belts: Few things can change the look of an outfit and your body--for better or worse--than a belt. It's really remarkable, and it opens up possibilities that didn't exist before. Let me share my newfound enthusiasm with a few tips on belts:

Choose something beautiful! There are plenty of basic, boring belts out there. Ignore those. Be selective. Choose something with a gorgeous buckle or clasp or with an interesting design or texture. While they can be useful, do not limit yourself to the standard plain belt with a simple buckle.

Match your outfit. Choosing a belt that matches the color of your top or bottom garment will do a couple of things. It will elongate the garment it matches, which makes your body look longer in that area. If you have short legs, this is a great way to make them look longer and it draws attention to your waist but in a gentle, rather than a screaming, way. Wearing a contrasting or brightly colored belt will draw the eye immediately to your waist. That is fine as long as that's what you want to have happen and as long as the color of the belt blends well with both the outfit and you.

Rework an outfit. A belt is a great way to play with new ways of wearing an old favorite outfit or an outfit you just can't seem to make work. Are you having trouble finding a top to go with a favorite skirt? Does everything feel shapeless and dull? Try tucking the top into the skirt and adding a belt at the waist. You might be surprised at how fashionable and comfortable the outfit is now. Do you have a dress that could use a little updating? Try adding a fun belt, and see what happens. Belts can work over dresses, with skirts and pants, and even over long tunics and leggings. Explore!

Be comfortable. Stretch is my favorite invention ever. I will not buy a belt unless it has stretch in it. It is comfortable, stays put and even fits after I've eaten dinner!

Claim your 6-inch waist. So many women bemoan the fact that their waist isn't as small as it used to be when they were younger. That's OK. You can still wear a belt. A belt, strategically placed, can actually give your body more definition and an hourglass shape. At the very least, you can try the belt and jacket trick I explained in Chapter 3. If you wear a belt over a sweater or top and then wear a jacket or cardigan over that, all you see is about 6 inches of belt peeking through. No one can tell how big or small your waist is. All they know is that you have one. Ah, the deliciousness of illusion!

A word of advice about the best width to choose: I generally recommend removing most of the skinny (quarter- or half-inch belts) that come with dresses or sweaters. They often make your waist look wide in comparison to their narrowness. Wide belts of three inches or more, on the other hand, are great but can overwhelm some women. Try different belts on to see what feels best to you. When in doubt, choose a belt that runs between 1 and 2 inches. Those widths work on a lot of women's bodies. The Fashion Fit Formula (www.fashionfitformula.com) is a great resource for determining the exact width(s) of belts for your specific body.

As with everything, be open-minded and experiment. You never know what treasures you will find that will add some fun and adventure to your wardrobe. Maybe this season it's a belt!

Do You Love Your Handbag?

BEFORE YOU READ THIS, take a good look at your handbag. Have you been carrying the same one every day for years? Do you even "see" it anymore, or do you grab it and run out the door? Is one handbag enough, or would you love to have more but cannot figure out how to transition easily?

One of the most perplexing questions to many women is "what handbag will you carry with that?" Think about it: The outfit is a winner. You've even aced the shoes, but the handbag? Hmm. Frustration sets in. Your everyday bag feels too big and clunky, and the other bags in your closet include a quilted diaper bag, a well-worn tote, and a lovely evening bag that holds a credit card and maybe a lipstick. Where's the fun and pizzazz? Try this:

Take Inventory of Your Handbag Collection: Do you have at least two everyday bags, one tote, two fun handbags, and an evening bag? If not, it is time to shop.

Take a Fresh Look: Look at each bag you own as if you had never seen it before. Does it look sharp and fresh or a little tired? Do the edges or handle look worn? Does it go with most of your wardrobe? Is it a lovely reflection of you? Your answers to these questions will clearly let you know if your handbag needs a little TLC or if you need to get rid of it and find something wonderful and new to take its place.

Replenish: When you are in the market for something new, consider your wardrobe and your style. Do you wear a lot of black, or do you alternate it with another basic color? Do you want a bag(s) that can stand the test of time, or do you like a new, trendier style every year? What size handbag fits your body shape and size and your lifestyle?

If you are going to have only one basic handbag, keep it simple. Whether you choose an elegant shoulder bag, doctor's bag, hobo bag, bucket bag, compartment bag, satchel or messenger bag, just to name a few styles, choose a color that goes with most of your wardrobe and keep the hardware (buckles, grommets, and metal detail) to a minimum. The key to a useful handbag is to blend purpose, beauty and personality.

I love handbags, and I enjoy changing them to enhance my outfit and suit my mood. Changing them regularly also has the extra benefit of forcing me to streamline what I carry with me so I don't have to move too much stuff! I have to admit I change my handbag more frequently in the summer than in the winter, but I love my collection nonetheless. **Special note:** Don't have more than you can easily store so you can see them. Otherwise, you run the risk of out of sight, out of mind, or it just becomes too much trouble to make the switch. Oh, and to make that switch easy, consider using a purse organizer—a purse insert with pockets and compartments to store all your essentials that you can easily move from handbag to handbag.

Here's something else to consider. Where does your handbag spend most of its time? If you are like most women, it's everywhere: your shoulder, the car seat, your desk drawer, the restaurant bathroom counter and the floor or the back of your chair while you're eating lunch. As a result, your handbag can be laden with more germs than—oh, let's not go there. Think carefully about where you put your bag. The last thing you want to do is have it on the floor of a public bathroom—or any bathroom for that matter—and a few minutes later on your kitchen table. One solution for restaurants is a handbag holder. It hooks on the table and allows your handbag to hang freely under the table without touching the floor. It stays germ-free and close to you so it can't be easily stolen.

Your handbag, like most accessories, is a reflection of you. Forget about purely functional. There are so many styles available right now that no one needs to settle for something they do not enjoy using. So, go back and take a look at your handbag again right now. Is it perfect, or do you need to make some changes? And, before buying a handbag that is purely functional, always ask yourself this question: Do I love it, and will I look forward to carrying it?

Are You Missing Some Sparkle?

JEWELRY IS THE ELEMENT of a woman's wardrobe that can feel overwhelming. How do you know what works? What texture, size, color and how many pieces do you wear? No wonder many women skip this step. But if you do, you are missing out! One client--and she's certainly not alone--recently said to me that she had no idea how much she needed jewelry to complete her outfits until we found her some that worked with her wardrobe. Once you venture out with success, you'll never go back to being unadorned! It is such a fun way to add an extra bit of personal expression to your wardrobe.

Let me be very clear that this does not mean that you have to wear lots of jewelry or really large pieces. The jewelry you choose to wear should speak to your personal essence (refer to "What's Your Signature Style?" in Chapter 3) and also be dictated by your outfit and the occasion. But, you won't know what works for you or makes your heart sing until you try.

The next time you go shopping, wear the outfit you want to accessorize, and play. See what you like. It is very hard to determine what will look good with an outfit if the outfit is at home and you're at the store. You need to try things on with the outfit to see what balance among texture, weight, and color will work with it and you.

Every time you change your jewelry, even when you are wearing the same basic outfit, you change the mood of the outfit and create an entirely new feel to what you are wearing.

Start slow. If this is new, play with one concept at a time and add it to your basic wardrobe. You will be amazed at how the right jewelry can inspire you each morning as you get dressed and, as with any new habit, the more you do it, the more it will feel familiar and natural.

Most of all, have fun!

Are Your Buttons Beautiful?

BUTTONS ARE ONE OF those details that can dramatically affect the overall tone of an outfit. But most of the time, we take them for granted and ignore them entirely except when buttoning up for comfort or propriety. When you take a good look, however, you will notice that they contribute significantly, or sometimes detract considerably, from the overall look of an outfit.

Now that I have made you hyperaware of every button anyone is wearing within a quarter mile of you, I apologize. But attention to this seemingly insignificant, functional detail can set you apart from the masses and open up possibilities you didn't know existed. I'm not exaggerating!

When evaluating the buttons on an outfit, consider:

- **Color.** Do the buttons blend or contrast with the outfit? Generally speaking, most buttons, even on expensive items of clothing, are pretty ordinary at best. It is one place that many designers do not spend money! If, for example, you buy a navy-blue jacket that has bright-white buttons, change them to a subtle navy. Generally you want your buttons to blend in terms of color, texture and brightness unless they are exquisite buttons and worth drawing attention to (which is rarely the case). This will also give your outfit the most versatility. You rarely want the buttons on your clothes to be the first thing someone notices about you.

- **Size.** Are the buttons in proper proportion and balance to your body? An easy way to determine this is to keep them in relative scale to your facial features. Are you a 5'2" size 4 with small eyes and a delicate mouth? Keep the buttons small. Are you a 5'9" size 12 with big, bright eyes and full lips? Your buttons can be somewhat larger. And, sometimes someone who is a size 2 has large features, and someone who is a size 18 has tiny, delicate features.

- **Quantity.** Sometimes an outfit has many more buttons than are necessary. This makes it look cluttered and busy rather than simple and elegant. The excess can also make it very difficult to accessorize since the buttons act as an accessory all on their own. Don't be afraid to remove unnecessary buttons. You don't need them unless they are paired with a buttonhole. A perfect example of this is buttons on the sleeve. If this is the case, especially if you are going to change the buttons on the garment, remove them and don't replace them.

Recently, I was shopping with Marie, and she tried on a pretty blue cowl neck sweater. It had a subtle silver thread running through it. So far, so good, except that it had brown buttons running from the neck over the shoulder and part way down the arm—four on each side. Thankfully, there were no buttonholes associated with the buttons, so they could be easily removed so as to restore the elegant beauty of the sweater.

- **Placement.** If you are considering purchasing a one-button jacket, be sure that the button falls right at your waistline, not above and not below. If it doesn't, the jacket will look like it was made for someone else—and it probably was! In this case, do not buy it.

If you are in a quandary about the buttons on a particular outfit, try this exercise: Stand in front of a full-length mirror, about five feet away. Close your eyes for ten seconds, then open them and look at yourself. What do you see first when you open your eyes? If it's the buttons, you need to change them. Changing the buttons is also a great way to update an outfit so it feels fresh and new.

Much like wearing an outfit to the store to accessorize it, you will want to bring the garment that needs new buttons to the store with you. Yes, you can shop for buttons online, and I've had mixed success with doing that. Most fabric stores carry buttons as do craft stores. If you have a thrift store near you, check it out. You might find a garment that's the wrong size or style for you, but the buttons could be just what you are looking for.

— —

As you can see, accessories hold the key to adding personality, polish and pizzazz to a basic outfit. By building a personal collection of jewelry, scarves, handbags, shoes and belts you love, you can actually have fewer clothes but more outfits. Imagine that each time you wear a particular outfit you change the jewelry or add a scarf and a belt. You can change the focus of an outfit by pairing it with a professional tote or switching to a fun clutch for dinner after work. Maybe you have a jacket that you have grown tired of after wearing it for a couple of years. Simply change the buttons to ones that are more elaborate to stand out or to ones that blend in so the jacket is more versatile. You have breathed new life into an older piece! There is no limit to the ways you can change things up by varying your choice of trimmings. Your assignment, as always, is to explore the possibilities that speak to your lifestyle and heart and, of course, to have fun doing it.

Chapter 6

Casual Matters

I HAVE BEEN WATCHING reruns of "The Dick Van Dyke Show" from the 1960s. What a different world they lived in! When Rob and Laura Petrie invite Millie and Jerry, their closest friends and next-door neighbors, over for a relaxing evening of dinner and a card game, everyone is decked out in cocktail dresses and suits. Can you imagine that in today's world? There's rarely an expectation that you have to dress up to that degree when meeting friends for dinner, and you might even get funny looks or get teased if you showed up in a little black dress and heels. It is much more likely that you would put on a pair of nice jeans or leggings and a pretty sweater and feel well dressed for the situation. We are talking casual, after all.

Believe me, I am not trying to discourage you from dressing up, and I completely understand that everyone has a different definition of what casual looks like. But, in general, casual clothing has a much bigger place in our lives now than it did twenty-five or more years ago. While there are definitely various degrees of casual, the truth is that most of us wear some form of casual clothing to work, out with friends, for day-to-day errands and around the house. It's how you translate the concept of casual dress to fit each of those experiences that's important. Remember, it is not only about being appropriate, but also about feeling great about how you look.

No matter how hard you try, one basic casual look will not take you from lounging around the house to a fun dinner out with friends or your sweetie. In fact, it will only frustrate you if you try to make that work. You will either feel too dressed up at home or too underdressed going out. At least for the foreseeable future, your casual wardrobe is a staple in your life, and so it's time to talk about how to make dressing casually something that is easy and fun and that brings you happiness. Yes, how you dress casually matters, too!

Can You Have Comfort and Beauty?

REMEMBER THE OLD IDEA that you have to suffer for beauty? I don't buy it anymore! I wore my fair share of restrictive pantyhose and walked way too many miles in the 1980s in heels that were meant more for standing than moving, and, like so many women, I'm done. Comfort needs to be front and center in my wardrobe, especially my casual wardrobe.

When Sandra came to me, one of the first things she mentioned was that she felt pretty confident about choosing dressy clothes and could even feel presentable at work, but her casual wardrobe was virtually nonexistent. She had jeans and T-shirts, and beyond that she felt lost. She didn't know what to look for, what was appropriate or even where to find nice casual clothes. Above all, she wanted to be comfortable, but she felt she always had to sacrifice looking good for comfort, and she was tired of it. She needed a fresh start and new ideas.

If this is you, too, get ready to invite a new style of casual clothes into your closet. Yes, you might need to refine, revamp or overhaul your casual wardrobe to incorporate your own personal foundation of beauty, but you really can have it all. Follow these steps to begin figuring out how comfort and beauty can coexist for you:

Remember what is beautiful to you. This is sometimes one of the hardest steps for women to do because they often have no idea what the possibilities are, so don't feel upset with yourself if you need some review. It's perfectly natural. Remember, it's a matter of inviting your personality to be expressed in your clothing choices and identifying what makes you sparkle--yes, even in your casual clothes. Following these steps will take your casual wardrobe from dismal to delightful. Also remember that it's a practice and part of an adventure, so give yourself a break and have a little fun as you explore. If necessary, revisit "What Makes You Sparkle?" and "How Do You Add Beauty to Your Wardrobe?" in Chapter 1.

Set a new intention. If you always assume you won't find anything that feels fashionable and comfortable, then you won't. It's that simple. As Henry Ford said, "If you think you can do a thing or you think you can't do a thing, you're right." So, if you have been assuming the worst, flipping the switch in your mind can make all the difference. Create a new affirmation such as, "More and more I find beautiful, fun clothes that I feel good in when I'm running errands." Repeat it often, and watch for signs it's working. If you need to, try an affirmation about something simpler (like finding a parking space in a crowded parking lot) first. Your skills will then translate to your wardrobe aspirations. You will be amazed!

Give rejected styles another chance. I never, ever wore jeans until stretch was added to them a few years back. To me, regular jeans felt heavy, stiff and unforgiving at the waist. I never could understand why others found them so comfortable when I could not wait to get them off. Since the inclusion of stretch, I'm a jeans convert. I find them so much more user friendly now and have them in several styles and colors. If I had not given them another chance, I would never know. And stretch isn't just for jeans. My most favorite designer, Joseph Ribkoff, puts stretch in absolutely everything. I can be casual or totally dressed up and still super comfortable when I wear his clothes. And none of it—not even the jackets—needs to be dry-cleaned!

Shoes are another example. When I met Beverly, she wore only clogs. She was very clear about that from the beginning. She had been wearing them for years because everything else hurt. We didn't talk more about it for a bit, but when I eventually asked a few more questions, I discovered that she had not even tried anything else on in years. Her reluctance to wear heels was understandable. When she worked in corporate America, she had suffered through long days in high heels, and as a result, her feet always hurt. She vowed never to do that again. I assured her that I agreed that the health of her feet and her general well-being were very important. I also shared that not all shoes are created equal: Surprisingly, there are shoes now that have cushy built-in insoles, and sometimes a bit of a heel can actually be very comfy. She never would have believed that without feeling it for herself, and she might not have ventured there except that she wanted to wear dresses again and wasn't wild about the way they looked with flat shoes.

So, we explored. I'm not talking little pointy heels. I'm talking about an elegant but solid heel that supports the foot well and gives a little lift. She was skeptical but willing to try anything on at least once. Imagine her surprise when she discovered a pair of knee-high boots with a two-inch heel that felt dreamy. Not only that, but they also looked great on her legs, and she felt terrific wearing them with a skirt and tights.

Is there anything that you have been purposely overlooking because you cannot imagine it ever being comfortable? Give it another try. You just might surprise yourself, and the worst-case scenario is that you reaffirm your belief that it still does not feel good.

Embrace beauty at any cost. This is not what you think. I'm not suggesting that you spend lots of money on your casual clothes. Your budget for your clothes is up to you. I've learned that everyone has a different idea of what's a lot and what isn't. What I am talking about here is a little different.

Let me share Eve's experience with you. Eve grew up wearing her sister's hand-me-downs. She rarely spent money buying her own clothes, and when she did, it was usually for a special occasion. So, to her the idea of spending money on everyday clothes felt foreign. At thirty-five, she no longer got clothes from her sister. Instead, when she needed to run to the post office or take her daughter to piano lessons, she threw on a pair of shorts and a T-shirt she got from a 5K race she ran four years ago. No, she didn't feel special in it, but it got the job done and didn't cost her much.

OK, so that's one way of creating a casual wardrobe that's comfortable and inexpensive, but somehow the beauty part of it has gotten lost. Eve came to me when she realized she had nothing in her closet that made her happy. She felt too young to settle for such an uninspired wardrobe and figured that since she couldn't do it herself she needed help. I assured her that everyone deserves to look great and she was no exception.

If you are like Eve and equate beautiful clothes with high prices, let me assure you that you can be fashionable *and* frugal. With my help, Eve traded in her message T-shirts for a selection of cotton tops in pretty colors, neutral-colored shorts and capris and a couple of patterned skirts. We found them everywhere, including Target, Lord & Taylor, T.J. Maxx and a local consignment shop, and the best part was that she could mix and match all of it. She felt better when she went out, and she still had the comfort and ease of dressing that made her happy.

How do you translate that experience for yourself? Try this: Get a pretty summer dress at a lower price from a store such as Dress Barn. Scout the local thrift or consignment stores, and stop in regularly to see what goodies they have. Yes, you still want to apply everything you're learning in this book, but you can find some tremendous clothes and accessories at super-low prices. One summer, I found an Ann Taylor skirt at Savers (a nonprofit thrift store) for $5.99 and wore it for two summers. I often go to Nordstrom Rack and pick up some comfy jersey dresses in great colors that I wear around the house when it's hot. Who says you have to be in shorts and a T-shirt?

This approach to shopping is like a treasure hunt. With each fun new piece you find, you are adding beauty to your casual wardrobe—without breaking your budget.

Take one baby step at a time. If you are wondering where to start, then take a deep breath (or two or three), and do just one thing to get going. For instance, if you are a shorts-and-T-shirt gal right now, find a new T-shirt style. Buy just one and see how you feel. Read the section,

"T-Shirt: Friend or Foe," in this chapter for more on how to choose a flattering T-shirt. If you still want to wear your jeans and T-shirts, but are looking for a way to elevate the look of them, try adding a pretty--even sparkly--pair of earrings or a bracelet. Or, choose jeans that are a darker wash so they look dressier even though they are still comfy and casual. You don't have to overhaul your entire casual wardrobe. Just evaluate it outfit by outfit and make changes step by step.

What Do You Wear Around the House?

I HAVE LOST COUNT of the number of women who tell me their around-the-house clothes consist of old holey sweatpants or baggy jeans with an oversized T-shirt or an ill-fitting polar fleece in an unflattering color—or some variation thereof. When doing a wardrobe consultation with a client I frequently hear, "Oh, those are just my wear-at-home clothes. When I ask her if she feels great in them, she says, "They are comfortable." End of discussion. Eventually, the topic resurfaces as we continue to work together, and she realizes that maybe there are other options.

If this sounds familiar, here are six ideas to consider regarding your "at-home" wardrobe:

1. **Feeling yucky weighs on your psyche.** Have you ever caught a glimpse of yourself in a mirror at home and thought, "Yikes! I'm so glad no one can see me this way." Sure, your home should be your sanctuary, but it's also a place you go to feel happy, supported, relaxed and connected. You don not have to wear your fanciest finery, but you do want to feel content. Kudos to those of you who can feel grounded and happy no matter what you are wearing. For the rest of us, a little extra attention to this part of our lives makes a huge difference.

2. **You can manage the dirt factor.** So many women say to me, "But I cook/clean/ walk the dogs/do some gardening in my at-home clothes, so they can't cost a lot." Here's a radical thought: You do not have to discard something just because it gets dirty. Just buy washable clothes, or wear an apron. A third solution is to peruse the sales rack or off-price stores for options that you would never wear around the house if you paid full price for them (because you would be afraid of ruining them). Perhaps

you won't mind taking the chance when they are marked down.

3. **Fashion rules still apply.** Wait! Hear me out. The fashion rules I am talking about are those personal to *you*:

   - Choose colors that flatter you.

   - Don't forget about fit. You might think I'm crazy, but when I bought a too big zip-up polar fleece jacket in a gorgeous teal color from L.L. Bean (and there wasn't a smaller size), I took it to my tailor. No, I never wore this outside the house, but I needed to feel good in it. And I wore it so much I definitely got my money's worth, even with the additional tailoring costs.

   - Dress for your personality. Even when no one else will see you, do not settle. You won't believe how delicious it feels when you allow your inner beauty to resonate in your cozy clothes as much as in your out-and-about wardrobe.

4. **Repurpose your clothes.** Years ago, I was thrilled to find a polar fleece (yes, polar fleece!) jacket that had beautiful pleats along the lapel and tied on the side of the waist. I knew I shouldn't have bought it because it was black, but my enthusiasm got the better of me, and I thought, "Hey, if I purchase this, the designer will see that there's a market for pretty polar fleece jackets, and she'll make more of them." I am always cold in the winter, and it's my dream to have elegant jackets made out of polar fleece, so why not? OK, so it's probably not a realistic dream, but it's a dream.

   Not surprisingly (remember, it's black!), the jacket sat in my closet for at least a couple of years. One day I thought, "Hello, Ginger! You would tell a client that it's time to get rid of this, so what's up?" I realized I had fallen into the excuse of, "But I paid a lot for it. I can't just give it away." OK, I'll admit it was over $150.

I knew I had to do something with it, so I decided I would wear it—around the house. Yes, around the house! I could still enjoy it, and I would be cozy and comfy. So, that's what I did. I still have it because it was really well made, and there's no doubt I have gotten my money's worth from it.

So, if you find yourself saying, "It cost too much to wear around the house," stop and think about it for a minute. If something is just sitting in your closet waiting for the right time, you are really wasting your money. When donating it doesn't feel like the answer, if you wear it, no matter for what reason, you're getting value out of your purchase.

My jacket might be a somewhat extreme example, but you can see I practice what I preach. So, let's think about how the idea might apply to your wardrobe. Do you have a pretty casual sweater you used to wear to work but now doesn't look quite as crisp as it did a year ago? Instead of getting rid of it or feeling bad every time you pass it by in your closet, how about finding another way to wear it? It might be the perfect top to wear running errands. You know it looks great on you, and it's comfortable, right? So, you can still get use out of it even if it isn't quite smart enough to wear to the office. Think of it as your own personal hand-me-down. When it gets a few pills in it, relegate it to your around-the-house wardrobe, and you can still get use out of it. Chances are you will feel better wearing that than those oversized sweatshirts you used to wear.

Be sure to keep in mind Nos. 1–3 when deciding whether to keep something or donate it. I am not saying repurpose something that looks dreadful on you or that feels uncomfortable just to get your money's worth. If those are the case, then consigning or donating it is a much better idea. Repurpose if you love it but have not found a way to wear it that seems to work or if it is a tad too worn to wear the way you usually do. You will feel good on many levels.

5. **Try something new.** It is *so* easy to get set in your ways about what feels good and what doesn't. If you have been wearing the same at-home outfit for a while, it's time to explore new options. You might be surprised! For instance, if your go-to winter outfit includes sweatpants, try fleece-lined leggings instead. They are totally amazing! They don't bind at the waist (a pet peeve of mine), and they are soft, sleek and warm. Pair them with a longer sweater that is not too bulky or oversized, and you'll feel cozy. How about a cute maxi dress for the summer months? Some even have built-in bras for small-busted women or are bra friendly (i.e., the straps are wide enough to cover your bra straps) for those who are not, and most come in comfy cotton or soft jersey fabrics.

6. **What you wear at home stays at home.** My stay-at-home clothes are just that. I'm not embarrassed if friends come over, and I will run to the mailbox or shovel snow, but they are not what I wear when I'm out and about.

Remember, this is not about being a fashion plate at home, and it's really not so much about fashion rules. It's about what makes you feel happy and cozy. I have learned over the years that so many women feel drab, frumpy or messy at home and wish for a home "uniform" that is comfortable and makes them feel good. Apply these tips, and you'll see that this wish can come true.

Is Your Sleepwear a Dream or a Nightmare?

I HAVE FOUND THAT sleepwear tends to be another one of those wardrobe concerns that doesn't really register until you purposefully take a good, long look at what you are wearing for those eight (seven? six?) hours a day.

So, let's think about it now. What do you sleep in? Believe me, I totally understand that at no time is comfort more important than when you are sleeping. Would you agree? If you have ever been annoyed in the night by sleepwear that is binding, scratchy, stiff or aggravating in some way, then you know what I mean.

It's also true that very few people see you in your nightwear. But as you know, it's first and foremost about how *you* feel in what you wear. Not only that, but having stylish sleepwear is another way of honoring yourself and celebrating your own natural beauty.

Will we all agree on what is beautiful and comfortable to sleep in? I doubt it. Just one peek in the stores, and you'll see that the choices are quite extensive.

I'm a big believer in surrounding yourself with beauty (your personal definition of beauty) as much as possible, and what could be sweeter than to envelop yourself in something beautiful while you rejuvenate through sleep?

I love nightgowns. I want beautiful, elegant, soft, pretty nightgowns. Not baby dolls and not long-sleeved flannel gowns. I am sure there are people who love both of those, but I prefer flowing, sleeveless, knee-length or long (depending on the season) nightgowns. You wouldn't think they would be so hard to find, but it seems that everyone is wearing pajamas right now. But, here's the important part: I don't give up. I don't settle for something I don't love wearing. I keep looking and wear what I have in the meantime.

Here are five things to consider when you are selecting your sleepwear:

1. **Comfort:** Obviously, you don't want anything binding or stiff. It's also important to be wary of elastics or details that might be uncomfortable. For instance, I bought a beautiful nightgown that had adjustable straps in the back. It seemed like a great idea when I bought it, but the clip that made it adjustable kept hitting my shoulder blade and I'd wake up with a dent in my back! Not exactly cozy. I also once bought a nightgown that had lace around the neckline. I didn't realize until after the first night that the lace was stiff and scratchy. That was the last time I wore that nightgown!

2. **Fabric:** This is definitely a personal preference. Cotton is one of the most popular because it's a natural fiber and breathes. It's soft and comfortable and cool in the summer or, if you experience hot flashes, any time of the year. Plus, it's machine washable. There are also special moisture-wicking fabrics that work well for those who get too hot when they sleep. Flannel has the added advantage of breathing and keeping you warm, but obviously is not a good choice in the summer unless you sleep in heavy-duty air conditioning. I like the manmade fibers in the winter because they are warm and soft.

3. **Color:** Please tell me why designers of sleepwear think that, other than black and white, we only want to sleep in pale pink and blue with a smattering of soft yellow? We are not babies. I love my personal colors and am constantly looking for beautiful teal, green, orange and coral nightgowns. It takes me a while, but I find them. My point is that it should not be so hard to find a variety of colors. I, for one, want a color that looks good on me so that when I take that first look in the mirror in the morning when my hair is sticking out and I'm still half asleep, I don't look gray and washed out.

4. **Personality:** Do you feel like yourself or like an imposter when you wear your PJs? When I put on a baby doll nightgown, I don't feel even remotely sexy, although judging by most lingerie stores, you'd think this was the most alluring choice. Instead, I feel like I'm about twelve years old—not exactly the pretty look or feel I'm hoping to achieve. And, boy shorts with a little t-shirt don't do it for me either. Both of those are perfectly acceptable choices for sleeping, and many women wear them. They just don't resonate with me. It's important that *you* choose a style that *you* love that makes *you* feel authentic.

5. **Care instructions:** While this is not usually a big problem with sleepwear, it is important to check to be sure the garment is not so delicate or poorly made that one wash will destroy it.

One last thing: If your usual resources are not cooperating and you can't find something you like, try someplace new. Maybe look online at stores like Bare Necessities, Soft Surroundings and Garnet Hill. Or find out when the next "Last Call" sale is at Neiman Marcus, and get there the first day. You might find a gorgeous nightgown or robe at a fraction of its usual cost.

Whether you want to feel down-to-earth, cozy, sexy, sweet or a little exotic and no matter your budget, there's something out there for everyone. The important thing is that you love what you wear even when it's in the middle of the night. Your dreams will be sweeter!

The T-Shirt: Friend or Foe?

Now THAT WE HAVE talked about changing your mindset when it comes to casual dress, here are two sections that will help you outfit yourself casually yet beautifully regardless of the season.

In the warmer months, T-shirts reign. Everywhere you look there is a sea of crewneck, shapeless, dreary-colored T-shirts. I keep hoping I'll wake up and realize it was all a bad dream.

The T-shirt got its name because of the shape of the shirt, a "T" (which right there tells you it's shapeless) and evolved from being the top of a two-piece undergarment and a military undershirt to mainstream wear. Because T-shirts are so universally loved, they are touted as being versatile and basic, but to be honest, they are neither. Let me explain.

The average T-shirt is generally unflattering for most women because:

- A crew neck is not a good neckline for many women. A woman with a long neck who is small busted *might* look acceptable (notice I didn't say great?). In general, it makes your head look like it isn't attached to the rest of your body, accentuates sloped shoulders, magnifies a large bust and does nothing to elongate your neck. Why settle?

- The sleeves usually hit at a bad point on the arms and often stick out. This makes your body look wider than it is. You can have them altered to improve the look, but 99.99% of people don't. For more on sleeve length, see below.

- A T-shirt is boxy and shapeless—which describes exactly how you will look in one. It does absolutely nothing to flatter your figure mostly because you can't see your figure, and it *does not* make you appear smaller by hiding things. In fact, it does just the opposite.

- The color often fades within a few washings.

- The lightweight, flimsy cotton is very unforgiving. This totally undermines the intended effect of "let's hide this body."

Some manufacturers have tried to update the style to make it more appealing, and the results are mixed. Here are a few looks to avoid:

Cap sleeves: The cap is an unflattering sleeve length on many women. These sleeves often hit your arms at an unflattering place (the widest part of your arm), and the flimsy ones make sloped shoulders look even more sloped, so they do nothing to balance the hips. They can also give the illusion of abnormally long arms so the body looks oddly balanced. A few people with very toned arms can get away with (notice I didn't say really rock?) cap sleeves.

So, why are there so many cap sleeves out there? Because youth drives the market and because young people are the ones most likely to have slim, toned arms that look OK in a cap sleeve. Also, many women believe that a little bit of coverage on their arms is better than none. Not so! You will be shocked to hear that sleeveless is generally much more flattering than cap sleeves--yes, even on women who do not have the most toned arms. When you expose the shoulder you give structure to your body, and it just looks better.

V-necks: Usually a V-neck is more flattering, but T-shirt companies often make the "V" too short so the balance is all wrong. In general, if you measure the length of your head from hairline to chin and then repeat that length starting at your chin, you will find the best depth for your V-neck top.

Extreme fit: Instead of being too baggy, T-shirts are now skin tight, which can be equally unflattering when it exposes every bump.

Yes, T-shirts are cheap and easy, but are they worth it? Do not settle! This is not to say that you shouldn't wear T-shirts. Just be sure to look for the following before you add another one to your wardrobe:

Flattering necklines: Generally, use the directions above for how to find your best length and choose a V-neck or scoop neckline.

Sleeve lengths: You want a short sleeve that hits below the widest part of your arm and doesn't stick out. Or go with three-quarter length or sleeveless. Here's a tip: If you find a top you like with sleeves longer than you prefer, take it to your tailor and have the sleeves cut to the length you like.

Flattering fits: Look for something that skims your body rather than swallows it up or looks and feels like it's glued to you.

Patterns: If a solid color is not your best look, try a fabulous pattern to distract the eye. It works wonders!

Try Glima (www.glima.com), one world (www.oneworldapparel.com), or Before+Again (www.beforeandagain.com). These companies offer T-shirts made of nice cotton fabrics in pretty colors with beautiful necklines. I have several that I wear at home and to go to our neighborhood café.

What Is the Biggest Summer Fashion Faux Pas?

YAY! YOUR FEET SLIDE into sandals, you wiggle your toes, and you breathe a sigh of relief. Warm temperatures have arrived, your feet are free, and you are good to go, right? Well, maybe.

It is easy to forget about your feet. I mean, hey, they are way down there, and you don't see your heels and the bottoms of your feet unless you make a conscious effort to do so. So, unless they hurt for some reason, you are probably not thinking about your feet.

Here's the dilemma: Other people can, and do, see your feet—much more than you might think! And, while fashion and style preferences might be personal, good grooming is universal.

I remember one day when I was sitting at the little café next door drinking tea and writing. As I was thinking and mulling over some ideas, I casually glanced around the room taking in the scenery and the people enjoying their social time and lunch. I noticed several women sitting at a table nearby. All neatly dressed, they were chatting and having a lovely time.

As my eyes drifted down, I could not help but notice a row of dried, cracked heels staring back at me. Perhaps I am wrong, but I suspect that if they had been aware that their feet were in such a sad, neglected state or had realized someone could actually see the bottoms of their feet so easily, they would have run to their bathrooms to grab their pumice stones or gone for pedicures instead of lunch.

People who would never leave the house with dirty, unkempt fingernails are unwittingly walking around with heels and sometimes toes that clearly need some attention. Please know that I am not talking about bunions or more complicated feet issues—unless those feet could also benefit from some simple basic grooming.

And, I am not pointing this out to embarrass anyone. It's really more about awareness. Like I said, it is easy to overlook something you can't see. Even if you take a shower or bath every day, it doesn't mean your feet are getting as clean as you think. And during the summer when you walk around in sandals open to the dirt of the streets, your feet get twice as dirty twice as fast!

Take a peek and see whether your feet need some attention. If so, here are three quick steps to get your feet looking and feeling good:

1. Every day when you take a shower or wash up in the morning, take a look at your feet. It is easier to give them a little TLC once a day than to have to do a major intervention every week.

2. If they need some refreshing, give them a quick wash and then use a pumice stone to give them a once-over. It takes all of two minutes once you get out of the shower if you have everything at the ready.

3. Rub a little moisturizer into them. Now you're good to go!

If doing anything more than that feels overwhelming and you just keep putting it off, then find a nearby salon. Ask around to find one that you'll enjoy going to and that takes sanitation very seriously, and go for a pedicure once a month. It's good for your feet and is soothing and relaxing, so it's good for your soul, too.

Winter: Do You Know How to Stay Warm in Style?

As THE TEMPERATURES DROP it's easy to settle for something based solely on how warm it will keep you without figuring in the part of your wardrobe that touches your heart. Even when you are bundled up to your eyes, you want to feel good. Plan ahead, and you can actually find yourself smiling as you don your parka to head out for a winter walk with friends. Here are some tricks:

Buy warm undergarments. Hanro, Only Hearts, and Hanky Panky are three companies that make lightweight, formfitting undergarments that keep you warm but don't add bulk. I have a big selection and wear one every day when it's cold. Hint: If you have sloped shoulders and find that spaghetti straps fall off your shoulder, get ones with wider straps, and they will stay put.

Dress in layers. This seems obvious, but some of us have an aversion to too many layers. I like things that feel sleek and polished, so if I get too many layers going I just feel messy and overwhelmed (one of my clients calls this "bunchy"). If that resonates with you, try to keep your layers as unbulky as possible. That is where No. 1 above can help. Choose a sleek fabric so that anything you put over it will glide on easily and not give you that bunchy feeling.

A fabulous option is Recover Designs tops (www.recoverdesigns.com). They come in a variety of styles, feel warm with out adding bulk and come in an array of beautiful colors. They are very fashionable and cozy! They are one size fits all, and I have found that to be mostly true for women size 2 to 16 or so. You might have to shorten the sleeves or take them in at the wrist if you have small wrists, but that's easy to do. Otherwise, they are great layering pieces.

You can even layer a long-sleeve fitted top under a short-sleeve garment if you have a funky side to your personality. Hint: Make sure the transition between sleeves (the place where one sleeves ends and the other begins) blends nicely in terms of color and style, or all the focus will go to your forearms.

Wear scarves. Thankfully, scarves have made a comeback, and I hope it will be a long-lasting trend. I do not consider myself the most devoted scarf person on the planet, but I have grown to love them in my wardrobe and have learned a few fabulous scarf ties and even share one in a YouTube video (Search "Ginger scarf tying"). When the temperatures dip, scarves come in very handy for keeping you warm. A scarf is also versatile because if you are going from the car to outside to indoors and the temperature fluctuates, you can easily put it on and take it off as needed. Hint: Long rectangular scarves are much more versatile than square ones for tying in a variety of ways. Find one that is five or six feet long for the most versatility.

Wear boots. There are probably twelve pairs of boots in my closet. I have everything from booties to knee-high boots in both black and brown and with varying heel heights. I wear all of them, in case you're wondering. Essentially, each year I try to go from sandals directly into boots—that's where the booties come in—because I have trouble finding shoes that don't slip off my heels! The bottom line is that when your feet and ankles are toasty, the rest of you feels warmer, too, especially if you are also wearing a scarf. Hint: I buy my boots a half size too big and get cozy liners to put in the bottom. So nice!

Skip the black. The winter months are gray enough without filling your closet with more of the same. Resist the temptation to buy one more black item. Add color! How about a simple cozy cardigan in an exquisite color for you? Even your everyday winter coat can be in a beautiful color instead of a neutral tone. The color doesn't have to be bright. It should just be a color that looks great on you. That's what makes it special. Hint: Start small if you need to. Get a scarf, gloves, hat or handbag in a beautiful color, and add that to your neutrals for a fun pick-me-up. Don't be surprised if, as you experiment, you become addicted to color!

Add a touch of class with velvet. What is more delicious than velvet? Well, maybe polar fleece, but, hey, most fashionable looks are not made in polar fleece. Yet! Nearly every winter the designers offer us some jackets, jeans, scarves and even skirts and dresses in velvet. Depending on the styling they can look elegant or fun and they certainly add a wonderful sense of warmth. Hint: Remember, a little bit goes a long way, so you probably don't want to outfit yourself head to toe in velvet.

Keep your head warm. I'm as guilty of forgoing this as anyone! I generally don't wear hats, although I own at least four of them, because I can't stand "hat hair." But when I do choose to wear one, I want something pretty and fun—not to mention warm. Don't settle for something ho-hum, and be sure to shop for one before it gets cold so you don't end up buying one in desperation. That rarely makes you feel great. Hint: There are many different hat styles out there, but it might take some work to find the ones that look good and delight you. Try on everything—beanie, fedora, cloche, beret and bucket hat—to see what looks and feels the best to you.

Now you know what to do to stay warm, short of moving to the tropics. You can be toasty and pulled together whatever the occasion.

— —

Finding a casual look you love can feel daunting at first, but once you explore and use the tools here, you'll see that it actually can be fun! As I write this, I am sitting at my neighborhood café in a pair of comfy white jeans, sandals and a fabulous Glima T-shirt.

I look casual, comfortable and pulled together—I even have a cute pair of earrings on—and that's the look so many women struggle with. Now it's time for you to give it a try. Make a commitment to yourself to feel good whether you are going to work, running errands or hanging out at home. You will love how you feel!

Chapter 7

Making Your Work Wardrobe Work for You

As you know, how you look makes a difference, and nowhere is this truer than at the office. Whether you are job hunting or firmly ensconced in a job you love, how you look and carry yourself give people cues about who you are. People will often make judgments about who they think you are based on this information alone.

Remember from Chapter 1 that every time you enter a room you make a statement without saying a word. Are you aware of how others perceive you at work? If so, is it the perception you want to project? If you aren't sure, take a minute to look in the mirror, and imagine meeting yourself for the first time. What do you see first? Is that what you want people to see when they first meet you?

Too often people have a sense that no one notices or cares how they present themselves in the office, so they give little attention to it themselves. Or, they imagine that they have to dress a specific way in order to be taken seriously at work. Nadine fell into the latter category. She worked mostly with men in a high-powered job at a construction company. To convey her authority, she wore a lot of black suits, which felt easy, but they also left her feeling austere and limited. She wanted to expand her work wardrobe but was worried about looking too understated and feeling disempowered.

Nadine was dressing based on a notion of how she thought she *should* look and how she thought others expected her to look. When I asked her to describe herself, she shared that she had a sense of being someone who was approachable, impassioned, fun and purposeful. Her previous black work wardrobe was purposeful, but that was about it. There was no sense of passion or feeling of being approachable, and fun was missing altogether. She felt stuck when it came to understanding how to add touches of those elements without undermining her effectiveness in her position.

I showed her one possibility. We kept her black pants and added a beautiful deep-purple jacket. The color looked great on her and was dark enough to have a conservative feel. The design of the jacket was structured and crisp, so it was appropriate to her professional position. All in all, the outfit felt impassioned and beautiful to her without losing its sense of purpose. When she added a scarf that had a few subtle polka dots, she embraced that touch of fun without it being too much. (Polka dots have a playful feel to them and tend to make people smile.) Did she compromise her sense of authority? No. Did she become more approachable when she felt better and more authentic about how she looked? Absolutely.

Like Nadine, you can purposefully create the visual image you want to project while always being true to your authentic self, of course, and still meet the demands of your work environment. This will give you confidence and a more empowered presence, and it offers others valuable insight into your personality. One of the most decisive elements of a first impression is visual. Leaving that first or long-term impression to happenstance will only create confusion and distraction and disempower you.

Let the information in this chapter support you in creating a professional look that you love and that serves you well in the workplace. In work, like in all areas of your life, liking the way you look boosts your self-esteem, bolsters your confidence and draws people to you—all of which will help your career.

What Is Appropriate Dress in the Workplace?

UNFORTUNATELY, THE IMPORTANCE OF professional dress has taken a backseat to comfort over the years, and this has had far greater consequences for women than you might think. As dress codes have relaxed so have people's attention to how they look—or at least this is how it appears. Business casual has lured us into a false sense of security. As my mother would say, "We've been given just enough rope to hang ourselves!" We often hear about the more extreme office fashion faux pas such as Crocs, ripped jeans, tube tops, micro mini skirts, gym wear, hoodies, short shorts, leggings worn with a short top and anything wrinkled, stained or threadbare. What is often challenging, and seemingly less talked about, are the more subtle aspects of dressing appropriately for work—those that go beyond whether to wear jeans.

Recently, I have seen increased focus on improving the standard of dress at work. I doubt we'll ever go all the way back to formal business dress, but the trend is moving in that direction and not just in the more conservative professions. Why? Company leaders are unhappy with what they see. When it appears that people are not taking pride in how they look, this reflects directly on the company.

When you dress well, not only does it make the company look good, but it also helps you, too. For example, a client shared the following: "I wanted to let you know that I am up for a promotion at work (the position is mine if the price is right)! I really think my improved image had A LOT to do with being recognized—so, many, many thanks!"

Because it is so easy to get complacent about our work wardrobes, especially in offices that allow business casual dress, here are a few reminders:

Know the rules. Become familiar with the dress code. If your company does not have a dress code or it is so vague that it is useless, ask. If you have a question about whether something is acceptable, ask. Most supervisors will welcome questions and be impressed you asked. Believe me, they hate having to be the one to open a discussion about inappropriate dress! (See "Can You Give Fashion Advice in the Workplace?" later in this chapter.)

For instance, open-toed shoes, whether flip-flops or peep-toe heels, are a constant source of contention at work. Few dress codes are specific, which leaves employees to interpret this rule for themselves—sometimes with disastrous results.

Dress for the job you want, not the job you have. Dressing well, which does not have to mean flamboyant or overdressed, shows initiative and helps you stand out from the crowd. If you are looking to advance within the company, how you dress can set you apart and give you the competitive edge. Look at what your supervisor or those in the job you want are wearing. Hopefully, they are good role models.

Pay attention to detail. Things such as poorly maintained shoes, clothes that do not fit well, messy hair and badly groomed fingernails count. Look at your wardrobe objectively. Your clothes do not have to be expensive, your style doesn't have to be trendy, and you don't have to be a waif to look good in your clothes. Impeccable grooming is critical, however, and that goes beyond basic cleanliness. Are your nails clean and chip-free? Are your clothes pilled or fraying? Have you checked your clothes for dog or cat hair? You might think the stain that is mostly gone isn't noticeable, but I guarantee it is obvious to others.

A human resource professional once told me about two men who were being considered for a specific position at her company. They were both equally qualified and liked by the search committee. When looking for a reason to choose one candidate over the other, the committee members finally excluded one candidate because he was wearing scuffed shoes. It was a minor detail in the scheme of things, but in the end those doing the hiring wondered if he would pay as close attention to work details as the other man. Perhaps it seems silly. Clearly, they were being very picky. The point is that it mattered to them, and they needed to find some way to choose between the two candidates. Was he aware of the scuffs on his shoes? Perhaps. And perhaps he didn't think it was a big deal. That's fine. It probably saved him from being in a job that would have stifled him. The important point here is that small details can make a difference.

Most people will not say anything to you if they notice an issue but will store it away for future reference. When your manager is looking for someone to meet a potential client for dinner or needs a presenter for a conference, do you want your name to be the first one that comes to mind? Your visual presence can support you in your career, or it can undermine your effectiveness and leave you feeling invisible. Good grooming is a key component if you want to stand out from the crowd in a good way.

Never underestimate the power of a jacket. A jacket is the most versatile article of clothing you can have in your wardrobe. The nice thing is that there is a jacket style to suit any personal preference and the degree of casual or professional attire you need. As John T. Molloy writes in *New Women's Dress for Success*, "When men dress casually, they lose some of their authority. When women do the same, they lose most of theirs. The key to that authority, especially for women in male-dominated fields, is the jacket."

Too many women are walking around in the dark when it comes to the impact professional dress has on their careers. If career advancement is important to you, then this is no time to be complacent. I'm not talking the early 1980s here. There is still plenty of room for personal expression in the wardrobe choices you make. I am talking empowerment: Understanding the expectations and the unspoken rules gives you the advantage. When you have this knowledge and are aware of the potential consequences, you can choose whether to comply or disregard the rules. Either way, you are in control.

Are You Too Sexy for Your Job?

SOMETIMES IT SEEMS LIKE women can't win! When it comes to how to dress, the message is often inconsistent and demeaning, and the rules keep changing. Television makeover shows whisk women away to salons, boutiques and plastic surgeons to reinvent their images to something supposedly more socially acceptable. Scores of magazines and books are written to help women navigate the world of fashion, and overriding all of that is the media's insistence on sexualizing women and the clothing choices they make. Is it any wonder that women are confused?

A 2005 study in *Psychology of Women Quarterly* by researchers at Lawrence University in Wisconsin indicated that women managers, especially those in male-dominated fields, who dress too provocatively at work are often perceived as less intelligent and less well educated than women who dress conservatively. As a result, they may be undermining their career advancement without knowing it.

I doubt this is really news to many women, but for those unaware of the stigma associated with dressing provocatively at work, especially young women entering the workforce, this can be a very enlightening study. Because we have pushed the envelope so far in recent years, even knowing what is considered provocative eludes some.

No matter what your beliefs about how women should dress in the workplace, the fact remains that, unlike a man, a woman's dress is publicly scrutinized and does affect how others perceive her. Whether it's fair—which it is not—is not the issue here. What's important is that knowing that this double standard exists allows you to make educated decisions to empower yourself. Consider two guiding principles:

1. **Know where you draw the line.** The term *sexy* is misleading and highly subjective. One person's sexy is another person's boring or even someone else's cheap or tawdry. Self-confidence, a radiant smile and an enthusiastic attitude can all be sexy in

an appropriate way. On the other hand, necklines cut to the waist, tight tops and excessively short skirts are provocative and inappropriate any time at work.

2. **Know the rules and the consequences.** Understanding the rules about dress, both spoken and unspoken, allows you to make an educated decision about how to present yourself. How you respond to those rules is up to you. Understanding what the repercussions might be if you choose not to conform and feeling fully confident and authentic in the image you put forth are critical. Ultimately, you get to decide.

While overtly provocative dress is best kept out of the office, personal expression is important. Years ago, women modeled men's dress to succeed in a male-dominated workforce. We've been there, done that. Today, personal expression is encouraged. The key, however, is to understand the message you are communicating and use it to your advantage.

Can You Offer Fashion Advice in the Workplace?

As CHARM AND FINISHING schools have gone the way of rotary phones, young women often get little or no guidance in personal presentation. This leaves more experienced, more established women to serve this purpose. As I have said, how you present yourself is regularly scrutinized, and this is especially true if you are a woman who has already made it to a top rung of the corporate ladder because you are modeling for the women coming up. This is an incredible opportunity to demonstrate professionalism and advise by example.

You also might find yourself needing to do a little more than provide a good example. In fact, I once covered this in an interview with Fox News when I was asked: "Is there a way I can talk with a new hire in my office about how she dresses without being rude?"

As the reporter astutely presumed, in general it is not OK to comment on someone's dress without his or her permission. We each take our appearance very personally, and to have someone offer criticism, constructive or not, can have long-lasting negative ramifications that often outweigh any positive outcome. As evidenced in Chapter 1, women regularly internalize negative comments about their appearances, and these comments often still have painful repercussions twenty, thirty and even forty years later.

So when *can* you talk to someone about this? When you are her supervisor. Your staff members rely on you for information about proper attire, and you do them a disservice if you do not help them understand the obvious and less obvious rules.

I have heard from human resource professionals that a new hire's standard of dress can decline by thirty percent once she has the job. There seems to be a feeling that once people are hired they don't have to try so hard to look presentable. If true, this is a frightening statistic! If you are in a managerial position, be sure to review the dress code with a new staff member at the very beginning. This gives her an opportunity to ask questions and makes it easier for you to speak with her later if her dress fails to meet company standards. Unless you are sure that someone is dressing poorly out of defiance, you must assume that she is doing the best she can and just doesn't know how or that there are extenuating circumstances, e.g., a medical condition or severe financial constraints. No matter what, it is imperative that you approach the topic with sensitivity and grace.

Let me reiterate: Unless someone asks your opinion about how she looks, it is none of your business. It is also never OK to tease or joke about someone's appearance.

That said, you don't always have to stand around feeling helpless. If your connection with a subordinate continues outside of work, get together for a meal. While you are both feeling comfortable and relaxed, you can broach the topic of work wardrobes—yours! Only do this if you really do have something to talk about and can make the transition easily. You don't want it to look forced or like you are ambushing her. Chatting in an honest, open way about it might allow her to feel comfortable opening up. If she does, don't speak so frankly that it is unkind or use words to the effect of "it's for your own good." Ever.

Of course, there is always the chance that she has no clue that her wardrobe is not supporting her and again, unless she asks your opinion, it is best that you not say anything.

Let your intuition guide you. If it feels forced, stay away from the topic. If she asks your opinion, give it with kindness and grace.

Are Nude Stockings Posh or Passé?

STOCKINGS ARE AT THE crossroads of appropriateness and personal expression. Everyone has an opinion about them. Back in the 1980s, they were a mainstay of every workingwoman's wardrobe. It was unthinkable to go to the office without them if you were wearing a skirt. Well, that has certainly changed. Stockings are routinely snubbed, especially by those under thirty, and some women now forgo dresses altogether because they don't know how to navigate the controversial world of pantyhose!

You might remember that my legs are not my favorite feature. Since we all teach what we have to learn, I have spent time doing the inner work necessary so I can honestly say that I have come to love and appreciate them. Will they ever be the legs of my dreams? No. But am I thankful that they are relatively long and strong and take me where I need to go? Yes. And, part of my accepting them the way they are is knowing how to dress them in a way that makes them look pretty good. The magic of illusion is a wonderful thing!

That's where nude stockings come into play. I can hear a collective groan as I say that, but please don't stop reading. Trust me, I am not a fan of pantyhose either. Since I was a teenager I have not been able to stand anything tight around my waist, and I spent decades cutting the waistband of my pantyhose so I could breathe. You can still do this as long as you don't buy "sheer to waist" pantyhose and you don't cut them so much that they fall down. And certainly there was no chance that a pair of control-top pantyhose would come anywhere near my body!

Then, along came the current generation of young women who reject any suggestion that they wear nude stockings. In fact, they snicker at the idea that they should even consider wearing them! They see it as wearing fake legs and just the idea makes them kind of squeamish. In their opinion, bare legs are the only way to go. Obviously, this is a fashion topic that is highly polarized, and there doesn't seem to be much middle ground.

When worn well, nude stockings should not be obvious. They will just blend and smooth your skin in a subtle way. It's the *idea* of them that offends young women. Women felt the same about bras thirty-plus years ago!

I know I am not going to change your mind if you are firmly ensconced in the belief that bare legs are the only option. Let me just say that I believe strongly that in a conservative professional setting, what's appropriate is men wearing socks and women wearing stockings, tights or socks.

So, back to me since I suspect those of you who are still reading this section can identify with my experience. I am writing about this now because for years I did not wear many dresses. Just the idea of it felt complicated. But that has changed, and it is exactly the reason nude hosiery is on my mind.

Here are five reasons nude stockings have disappeared from so many women's wardrobes *and* five reasons to invite them back in to stay.

1. **They make you look like an "old lady!"** Any twenty-something woman will gasp at the mere suggestion that she wear nude stockings. To her, they are so not cool. As with most fashion trends, it's really just because she didn't grow up with them. Because they were never a part of her personal dressing experience, she sees them as something her mother wears and that feels old-fashioned. She wants to make her own fashion statement, and as with many generations in the past, this means going to the other extreme from what her mother wears. I mean, really, just look at those young men who wear their pants down below their butts with their boxers showing. You can't tell me it's not a fashion rebellion. The same is true for bare legs.

   Counterpoint: Nude tights don't have to look obvious or matronly. Just look at Kate Middleton. She wears nude stockings (oops, they are now called nude tights!) and has brought them back into favor. Sales have increased significantly since she entered the celebrity fashion scene. It is astonishing how many celebrities and rock stars, such as Beyoncé, Adele and Rihanna, are wearing nude stockings. You just can't tell because they are doing it so well, and that's the key.

2. **Pantyhose are uncomfortable.** I don't think that most people will debate this. This is arguably the No. 1 reason pantyhose fell out of favor with those of us who used to wear them.

I am the first to admit that they are not my favorite accessory. I wore them for years because they were an expected part of our wardrobes in the '80s and '90s. However, instead of embracing the bare leg fashion statement, I just covered my legs in a different, more comfortable way: pants.

With dresses being such a huge fashion trend now (after years of not being able to find anything other than a dressy dress), I was beginning to feel the pull to wear them. It was after one or two dresses sat in my closet for a year or more because I never felt right wearing them with bare legs that I finally decided I had to do something and solve my dilemma. And I have!

Counterpoint: Bear with me on this one. **The solution is thigh-high stockings** (just breathe and keep reading). They are comfortable with no waistband to squish you, *and* when you are wearing an A-line skirt or dress or one that just flows softly over your curves, no one can see the band on your thigh. More on brands coming up.

3. **They are *so* 1980s.**

Counterpoint: Half of the 1980s styles, such as bright-colored pants paired with other bright colors or black, peplums, and "Flashdance"-style shirts, have made a comeback, so shouldn't nude stockings, if worn well, feel right at home?

Bring the stockings into your current wardrobe with a pretty pair of platform shoes, for instance, or with a fabulous patterned dress to feel current and elegant.

4. **They are a huge expense.** They are expensive. I even bought them in bulk years ago to keep the cost down. Invariably, after just a wearing or two, I'd put my toe through a pair or catch it on something and have that unsightly "laddering" (the British term for runs).

   Counterpoint: A little laddering (if it happens in the middle of the day) won't be an issue if your stockings are the right shade. If your stockings are truly "nude," they should match your skin color and not change it noticeably. "Suntan" stockings should be outlawed or you run the risk of looking very dated. When nude stockings run, it is less noticeable because they blend in so well with your skin.

   Another reason to go with thigh-highs: When you get a run, you only have to discard one leg of the pair! My favorite brand of thigh-high stockings is VienneMilano. They are beautiful, do not snag easily and can be worn over and over.

5. **You can't wear stockings with sandals.** This was another reason I stopped wearing stockings for a while. No one wants webbed toes.

   Counterpoint: Enter one of my favorite kinds of stockings: toeless. Donna Karan makes a good brand, and you can even get the Berkshire brand for less. It is not as smooth and silky, but will do the job just as well, and Berkshire also makes a toeless thigh high so it's the best of both worlds. Yes, you have to play with the band around your toes to be sure you can't see it when you put on your sandals, but it's amazing how it turns invisible in many strappy sandals or peep-toe shoes. I recommend that you try these stockings on ahead of time with the sandals or shoes you want to wear to be sure this is true. Sometimes they are obvious, and that's worse than webbed toes.

Still unconvinced? Let's talk a little bit about going bare legged. Women with long, slender, evenly tanned legs are quick to encourage everyone to shed their stockings, but for the rest of us the answer isn't always so straightforward.

I'll just use my legs as an example. I've never had a tan in my entire life. Burns, yes. Tan, no. Being a redhead, this is not surprising. My red hair (which I wouldn't trade) is accompanied by super pale, translucent skin. You can see a mix of freckles, purple undertones, red and white, so my skin never looks smooth and even. And this has little to do with aging. This has been the case since I was a kid.

I could get a spray tan, but do I really want to commit to something that I have to do so often? It gets expensive and is time consuming. To be honest, having even slightly tanned legs looks very foreign on me. On top of that, I don't know exactly what is in those spray tans, and I'm not so keen on repeated applications of something of which I feel so unsure. I do enough "beauty treatments" without adding one more! But, that's just me. So, more than anything, what the stockings do is smooth out my skin tone and create a sleeker line (and, yay, they also smooth out any dimpling). My clients and friends who have borne children and now have the veins to prove it can attest to this benefit of stockings as well.

Of course you can still go bare legged despite having unevenly colored skin. It's certainly a personal preference, and, yes, I do go bare legged with skirts when I am being very casual, but I'm even more vigilant about the fit, length of the skirt and shoes I wear so that I feel good in them. That said, I also know that my legs will draw more focus when they are bare because they are not as smooth, and that is not my preferred place to have the eye go. No matter what you think of nude stockings, once it gets to be cold outside, bare legs look out of place—kind of like shorts in the office on a snowy day. If nude stockings are not your thing, then opaque tights, preferably a dark solid color for a more conservative business environment, will do the trick just as well.

The most important thing is to think about is this: What will serve you in feeling confident and professional as you advance in your career? No one will force you to wear nude stockings, but for those of you who have been wondering what your options are, now you know. If you are firmly entrenched in your no-nude-stocking beliefs, I'm sure this information has not changed your mind. But hopefully those of you on the fence found some support and enlightenment. Now you can make a decision based on everything you have read in this book and this chapter and feel like you are putting your best foot forward.

What Is a Work Wardrobe?

Now THAT YOU KNOW what not to wear to work and realize the importance of presenting a professional image you feel good about, let's talk about how to do that with intention. There seem to be so many options for women that knowing what to choose to wear to work can feel confusing. So, let's talk about how to create a streamlined, yet versatile, wardrobe that offers you ease of dressing with a variety of options because you can mix and match garments easily, and it is extremely cost effective because you can have fewer clothes but wear them more.

This type of wardrobe combines your best colors with accessories that express your personality to simplify your life in a way you didn't think possible. No matter who you are, the premise remains the same: You mix and match a few classic, basic garments with beautiful accent pieces to create a well-pulled-together look every day! With a little forethought and a well-outlined strategy, it's very doable. Here's how to get started:

Choose one neutral color. Although there are other choices, the best--the easiest to find with any consistency--neutrals are black, dark brown, charcoal gray, camel, taupe, off-white, white and navy. Eventually you can have more than one neutral in your wardrobe, but don't get too ambitious to start. Keep it simple, and choose the one that looks best on you. When in doubt, match your hair color or the darkest color of your eyes.

Buy the basics. In your chosen neutral, purchase two pairs of pants, one skirt and two tops, such as a turtleneck and a simple scoop neck or V-neck top in a nice fabric. Whether it's a man-made fabric or natural fiber is less important than that it looks crisp and wears well. It should not be too sheer or limp, and it should not easily pill, wrinkle or fade. Lastly, purchase a jacket and/or a cardigan sweater in your neutral color.

Don't get anything too busy or trendy so that it can mix cleanly with interesting tops and accessories.

Add color. Purchase two tops in your best color. This is your accent color. You can buy more later. This is just to get you started and help you understand the how it all works. Purchase a jacket in the same color.

Add personality. Choose two or three pieces of jewelry or scarves that combine your neutral color and your accent color. These pieces must be large enough to make a statement--no wimpy jewelry. You must love them, and they must feel special to you. Otherwise you will still feel frustrated when you get dressed in the morning. The spark comes from these pieces.

Put it all together. Wear two colors at a time--no more! There are many different ways you can mix and match. Here are two examples: Neutral pants, neutral jacket or sweater, and a top in your accent color. Or neutral pants with a top and jacket/sweater in your accent color. Then, add texture and personality with your jewelry or a scarf.

When you build your wardrobe with this kind of foundation, you can create beauty, elegance, a dash of funkiness, artistic flair or trendiness with less effort and more peace of mind! You will also have a solid foundation to which you can easily add a few unusual or fun pieces later. And, you will no longer dread opening your closet in the morning. Right away, you will find you have more outfits with fewer clothes. Mismatched pieces will no longer create chaos in your wardrobe!

Summer: Can You Keep Your Cool When It's Hot?

MANY OF US LOOK forward to the warm temperatures of spring and summer, but the heat can become unwelcome when it comes to figuring out what to wear to work. I can relate.

On one particularly scorching summer day, it was 92 degrees in my bedroom as I began to get ready to meet a client to shop. This meant I had to put on something other than the pretty teal sundress I wear around the house. I don't have air conditioning, so getting dressed when the temperature and humidity soar is not pretty. Not much feels good when you are hot and sticky.

Everything I considered wearing— lined pants, a lined jacket, a long-sleeve jacket—sounded stifling. I was running out of options. What was left? A dress. Well, that presented a host of other considerations.

At that time, very few people had seen me in a dress. It's not because I don't like dresses. It's the whole redhead with white freckly legs thing. A dress meant putting on stockings, and I prefer to avoid that whenever possible.

That said, I realized that a pair of stockings (toe-less so I could wear peep-toe shoes) was *far* preferable to pants and a jacket. So I put on a simple Joseph Ribkoff dress and pretty jewelry, grabbed a cardigan in case I needed it and headed out. I got a compliment right away heading into the bank on my way into Boston. The best part was that I felt summery and unencumbered—even wearing stockings! Thigh-high stockings really are amazing.

Here are some tips to help you feel the same when you have to be out in the heat.

Be prepared. About mid-February, it seems spring will never come, but it always does. And often it seems to catch us by surprise. You don't want to be without some good warm weather options when the heat hits. There are several reasons why starting early will make a difference.

You will have more choices. I agree that the retail shopping schedule is nutty. It is hard to think about buying sleeveless tops when the temperature outside is hovering around freezing, but you must. If you wait until the weather warms up to realize you need things, it could be too late. The stores go into serious sale season by late May!

It will save your sanity. Sometimes you can put together a seasonal wardrobe in the middle of that season. More often what happens is that there is little left to buy—at least in your size (or so it seems). You find a great skirt but no top to go with it, or you have a great pair of capris but can't find any good shoes in your size. Not only will your sanity suffer, but you will also waste time inside agonizing over how to put together a wardrobe when you could be outside enjoying the warm weather.

You will be ready for fickle weather. In New England (and maybe other places as well), you must be prepared for the possibility of either a cool summer or a brutally hot one. By the time you know for sure what the weather will be, fall clothes are in the stores. So be prepared either way, or you will be out of luck about mid-July if you guessed wrong!

Dress in layers. With layers, you can be cool walking around outside (or sitting in your car waiting for the air conditioning to cool it) but look and feel professional at the office. Here's a tip: Layers work only if you are willing to remove the outer layer. You are defeating the purpose if you wear a sleeveless top but refuse to show your arms or if your hot-pink bra shows through your white cami.

Skim your body. Wearing clothes that skim your body allows you to show your shape without having fabric glued to your skin. Air will be able to circulate and keep you feeling cooler and fresher longer.

Choose your fabrics wisely. Cotton and linen are great for cool dressing in the summer. In general, linen looks best when it is lined, which might make it less appealing on a hot day, or when it is blended with another fabric to help control the wrinkle-factor. Cotton is great, but again, it is often best when mixed with another fabric or stretch to help it hold its shape and color when you wash it. The simple jersey microfiber dresses are fabulous and virtually wrinkle-proof. For those of you who say you can't wear one because it clings and shows every lump and bump, you might need to go up a size--I have found that most women go up one size in dresses--or try a different style. Yes, shape wear is also an option, but when the idea is to stay cool, it defeats the purpose.

Lighten up your colors. Dark colors absorb heat, so wearing lighter or brighter colors can help make you feel cool both literally and emotionally since they are cheerier than dark colors on a bright, summer day.

Adjust sleeve length. Three-quarter-length sleeves are your friend. Somehow just baring that bit of forearm feels so much cooler than longer sleeves, yet it's still professional.

When the temperatures rise, it's natural to want to wear as little as possible. Now you have the keys to doing this and still looking and feeling appropriate and professional.

What Should You Wear for a Presentation?

We often obsess on many levels when we know we have to do any public speaking. The goal, of course, is to communicate your message effectively. The fewer distractions the better, and these include not only food in your teeth, but also clothing, hair and makeup distractions as well. You want to have a visual presentation that boosts your confidence and supports your message instead of distracting from it.

Whether you are presenting a new idea to your colleagues at a staff meeting, giving a lecture at a conference, interviewing for a new position or appearing on TV as a representative of your business, you want to represent yourself well.

Here are a few strategies for success:

Keep the focus on your face. Color is one way to do this. Color is powerful, and when well chosen, it can draw attention to your face and make your eyes sparkle. You can also bring the focus to your face with your makeup. Accentuate your eyes with eyeliner, and choose a lipstick color that makes your eyes shine. But keep it simple. You don't want to appear flashy or overdone.

Keep the noise down. For example, avoid wearing jingling bracelets, loud prints or colorful shoes that draw the eye away from your face. That doesn't mean you do not want to accessorize in a way that shows your personality and brings focus to your face. Just don't overdo it.

Be neat: Wear a fabric that doesn't wrinkle excessively and have a spare top handy in case of spills or wear a top that you can turn around if you should accidentally spill something.

Be comfortable: If you keep adjusting your collar or pulling your pants up or your skirt down, choose another outfit. Extraneous movement will be distracting. Wear something that fits well, that gives you ease of movement and that you enjoy wearing. Your audience will discern your comfort level, so it works to your advantage to like what you are wearing and to feel good while wearing it!

Be yourself: Although there are certainly rules of propriety and professionalism to which you want to adhere, the most important rule is to be yourself. While you do not want to wear something that is distracting, you also don't want to feel boring. Lauran Star (www.lauranstar.com) is a perfect example. There is absolutely nothing boring about Lauran. She radiates confidence and has an unstoppable personality. One of her signature talks is "Empowerment – From Boardroom to Bedroom," and during one of our shopping trips, we created an outfit for her to wear on stage. As Lauran says,

> "I am passionate about fostering talented and ambitious women and launching them toward even greater success, all while creating a balance between personal and professional growth. It is more than just the boardroom that affects leaders today; you need someone who also understands the bedroom (home life) and how they interchange, providing a balance."

As you can imagine, Lauran's stage presence certainly needs to be professional but must also reflect her inner beauty and her natural spiciness. A basic suit just wouldn't do it for her!

When you meet Lauran, you realize she already has a lot going on visually with obvious streaks of blonde and red in her hair. That's another example of her fieriness. So we had to be careful that her outfit didn't compete with her coloring or distract from her getting her message out. We settled on a deep-periwinkle flowy jacket over a sleek black pencil skirt. Remember earlier when I said to be careful of colorful shoes? In Lauran's situation, colorful shoes added that essential touch of spiciness to her outfit. Without them, she looked nice but too staid. With a pair of gorgeous coral high heels, she shined! On her the shoes seemed authentic, natural and empowering.

An audience is quick to pick up on authenticity or disingenuousness. You must be yourself. If Lauran had tried too hard to play it safe and fit in rather than to fully express herself, her audiences would feel that and be distracted or less connected to her. Being true to yourself is more likely to put your audience at ease than dressing in a prescribed way because you think you should.

Know your audience: Are you speaking to a conservative group or a group that expects and exudes creativity? You never want to sacrifice who you are to try to "fit in." We all have different sides of ourselves, so remember to be yourself and be comfortable. Choose which side you want to highlight most prominently according to the audience you are addressing.

Be prepared. If you are speaking to a larger group, be sure to wear something that has a lapel or a place to connect your microphone as well as a waistband, belt or pocket for the little black box that you will need to hook on to your clothing. If you wear a pantsuit or skirted suit, you can hide the black box and wire under your jacket. If you wear a dress without a belt, you will have to hold the box in your hand, which is awkward and leaves the wire visibly snaking around your torso. In addition, make sure you are not wearing something that will rub against the mic!

Make a quick visual check before going on stage. I remember the night I was the featured speaker at an annual dinner for the Massachusetts Association of Women Dentists. I had to laugh when they served the salad with poppy seed dressing! With visions of black specks dotting my otherwise very nice teeth, I made a quick trip to the ladies' room right before my presentation. That kind of distraction just wouldn't do! Whether you remove something from your teeth or simply fix a piece of hair that's askew, you'll feel better knowing everything is in place before you give your presentation. Lastly, do not drink a carbonated beverage before speaking for obvious reasons!

Beware of being too casual: I have one word when it comes to dressing casually for a presentation: Don't! Although you do not want to appear stuffy and unapproachable, you also want your message to be taken seriously. Unless you are absolutely sure that casual dress is the way to go (perhaps when speaking at a summer festival or to children), always dress it up a notch.

Now, go out there, and show them how brilliant you are!

How Do You Mix Business and Pleasure?

THERE IS ANOTHER SPECIAL situation for professional women that I want to address: company events outside of the office. Receiving an invitation to a company picnic, baseball game or even a pool party with colleagues might trigger that familiar nightmare of wearing your pajamas or, worse, only a bath towel (or less) in front of your peers.

The stakes are higher for women than for men in these situations, especially in male-dominated professions. You could decline the invitation, but this might not be the most prudent option. You could pray for rain to cancel the event. Or you could meet the dilemma of what to wear head-on.

How do you choose a look that says relaxed and fun yet still elicits a sense of proper business etiquette? You do not want to dress down to the point of looking inappropriate, and you also do not want to look like the office fuddy-duddy.

Here are a few tips to guide you:

When in doubt, ask. If you are not sure what the expectations are or what others, especially those more senior than you, will wear, simply ask. You will at least get more direction than you had and might even get some outfit descriptions. You could even discover that their definition of casual is completely different from what you had imagined. Thank goodness you asked!

Plan ahead. Shopping at the last minute in desperation is rarely productive, efficient or satisfying and will only add more angst to the situation. If you do not have what you need to feel comfortable, do a little research, take a trusted friend with you, or ask a personal shopper for help.

Compromise. Cropped pants, although please forgo the cropped cargo pants in favor of something a little more upscale, can solve the dilemma of shorts, pants or a skirt. Three-quarter-length sleeves (unless it's 100 degrees) can look comfortable and casual and will take away concern about exposing your arms, if this is something you worry about. Avoid T-shirts with advertisements on them, but do add color and embellishments or have fun with accessories. I also strongly recommend that you do not wear flip-flops unless you are at the beach. They are ultra-casual and noisy—they aren't called flip-flops for nothing—and sandals can always do the job better. And, of course, make sure you have had a pedicure; either do it yourself or go to a professional.

Keep Monday morning in mind. Refrain from wearing anything too provocative, messy or cutesy. Leave your belly shirts, tube tops, daisy duke shorts and sheer items in the closet. In fact, abstain from anything that requires you to go braless. Remember that you have to see your colleagues at work the next day.

Keep it upscale. The outfit does not have to be expensive, but it should not look like you are going to pick blueberries or clean your garage. This means nice sneakers for the company baseball game and your pretty cover-up for your bathing suit. An oversized T-shirt is not a cover-up!

It is sometimes hard to be objective about ourselves, so if you feel like you have lost perspective on the viability of your casual wardrobe, ask for feedback from a trusted friend or professional.

Remember, the idea of these company events is not torture but fun, and part of enjoying yourself is feeling good about how you look. And, remember, comfort and beauty can coexist. If you have any doubts, be sure to review "Can You Have Comfort and Beauty?" in Chapter 6.

— —

As you can see, your professional wardrobe and your personal style are not mutually exclusive. You do have to consider the parameters set by the industry in which you work and your specific employer, even if it's your own business, but dressing for work is really just one more opportunity to reflect who you are—not only as a professional, but also as a unique individual.

Chapter 8

Vegan Fashion: A New Way of Looking at Beauty

I HESITATED ONLY A fraction of a second on whether to include this chapter. Deep down inside I knew there was no question. What I have learned over the past few years is that I'm not alone in my concern over the use and treatment of animals in the clothing and beauty industries. As awareness grows, I am meeting more and more people who are also wondering how to eliminate animal suffering from their wardrobes and personal care products. Sure, there might be people who will skip this chapter, but if you continue reading, you will find support, guidance (including valuable styling information) and connection. Having a style you love does not mean you have to accept animal suffering. There are plenty of beautiful options available that do not involve animals at all, and I'm happy to share more about that with you.

I know that the concept of vegan fashion is foreign to most people, and it's easy to dismiss it as some kind of passing fad. This entire chapter explains why it is not simply a trend and why so many people are making cruelty-free choices once they understand what they are buying. There is absolutely no doubt that vegan fashion is growing by leaps and bounds as awareness grows. I have been watching and participating in it for many years now, so I know firsthand the progress that is being made.

Fashion evolves, and as it does, so does our sense of what is beautiful. That's what happened for me simply because I started researching where my food came from. Never did I think this would affect my wardrobe as well. The more I learned about the abuse, suffering and massive killing that goes on every minute of every day just so I could eat and wear clothes, the more shocked I was. I realized I could not be part of that experience. There was nothing beautiful about that part of the beauty industry.

I took a look at what this meant for my life long-term on all levels, and I realized that I had to follow my heart. I also knew in my soul that I could and would be a walking advertisement for dressing stylishly as well as cruelty-free. I chose to make it an adventure in learning rather than a dull exercise in deprivation. What I found is that the more I looked and learned, the more I realized it was far easier than I had initially expected. The beauty of this, literally, is that as more people purchase cruelty-free fashions, it sends a wakeup call to the beauty industry and the world at large, and they respond. It's already happening.

Sometimes, however, it feels a little bit like anyone over the age of twenty-five is left scratching her head trying to figure out what to wear. While those of us who are a tad older certainly don't want to look frumpy or dated, we also don't want to look like we are grasping unsuccessfully at our youth in order to align our animal-friendly values with our wardrobe.

Let me assure you that there are more than enough cruelty-free fashion options to go around, and the choices are growing daily. Sure, you might not want to wear the paper-thin fabrics or micro-minis that the younger women are wearing, but you also can look great without sacrificing your vegan ethics.

So, whether you are wondering what all the fuss is about or you are hoping to learn how to create a kinder, gentler wardrobe, this chapter will help.

Would You Wear Your Dog or Cat?

THE FIRST STEP IN making your wardrobe more animal-friendly is knowing what *not* to wear and why. Here's what you don't want to see on the label: wool, cashmere, mohair, silk, suede, leather, fur, shearling, and down.

Let's start with fur, which has the longest history as a controversial fashion choice.

I have to believe that most people buy fur because they are unaware of the pain, suffering and unfathomable abuse that go along with obtaining fur from a living being. How else could anyone wear it? To think otherwise would just make me so sad.

I must be clear that wearing fur is the same as wearing leather (see the next section). The one difference is that the issue of fur has been in the news for decades! Knowing where fur comes from and the horrors of how it is procured is not news! Although we don't often see paint-drenched fur coats on the street any more—which is good because that is really not the way to raise awareness—we all know that the wearing of fur is a divisive issue and that there is a very good reason why so many people are passionate about not wearing it.

I am keenly aware that I have absolutely no chance of changing someone's mind about fur who doesn't really care. Sadly, a number of celebrity designers and fashion spokespeople have been dismissive about the idea of not wearing fur, but for those of you who are still reading, I know you must truly want to understand.

The truth is that whether you're wearing a full-length fur coat, fur trim on your cuffs or fur-lined gloves, the problem is the same. It isn't related to volume. The fur comes from the same place—and it's not pretty!

According to Friends of Animals, an international animal advocacy organization (www.friendsofanimals.org):

"Each year more than 9 million wild animals are trapped worldwide and then clubbed, strangled and stomped for their pelts. Caught painfully in steel-jaw leghold traps, wire snares and conibear traps, many fur bearers try to free themselves by chewing off their own feet only to die later from shock and blood loss. This act of self-mutilation illustrates how incredible the pain caused by steel-jaw traps really is for wolves, beavers, coyotes, raccoons, opossums, skunks, and red and gray foxes. And for every 'target' animal caught in one of these painful devices, two to ten times as many 'non-target' animals are killed: hawks, owls, deer, and domestic cats and dogs."

And, that's just the animals that are trapped. Fur farms are equally as dreadful. Here's more from Friends of Animals: "Cages are typically kept in open sheds that provide little protection from wind, cold, or heat. In the winter, animals often have to endure sub-zero temperatures. Summers are particularly hard on minks because they lack the ability to cool their bodies without bathing in water."

And, who wants a fur coat that has unsightly marks in it? I mean really! All sarcasm aside, the animals are killed in gruesome ways just so nothing mars that beautiful fur and compromises its market value. As a result, they are subjected to anal electrocution (fox), suffocation in decompression chambers (doesn't it feel hard to breathe just thinking of that?) or have their necks broken (most mink), according to the website veganpeace.com.

I absolutely cannot, in good conscience, wear something from a living being that endured that much misery.

Here's the thing. An animal's fur is gorgeous, so it makes sense that we admire it. I look at Mickey's tail (he's my big orange kitty) and think, wow, how amazing is that plume of fur he walks around with every day? And Gracie, my little gray kitty, had fur that was bunny soft. Would it ever, in a million years, occur to me to wear it? Perish the thought! And I give the same respect to other living furry beings.

I can only hope that awareness will grow and people will look more and more for alternatives. I have to admit that I choose not to wear faux fur because it looks so real, and I don't want someone to think I am wearing the real thing. That's my choice. But, if you want the look, you can have it without the bloodshed! There are some amazing faux options.

Check out Donna Salyers' Fabulous-Furs. Salyers, the president and founder explains how she got started on the company's website:

> "Inspiration for Fabulous-Furs came nearly two decades ago when I was on my way to purchase a mink coat. On my car radio, Paul Harvey described kittens being skinned to become 'mink' teddy bears. Instead of buying a coat that day, I was inspired to create a luxurious alternative. Not in my wildest dreams did I imagine that Fabulous-Furs would evolve into fine ready-to-wear, attracting a clientele of high-profile, internationally recognized celebrities. As a real-life Cinderella, it's fabulous to see our guilt-free products in movies, on TV and Broadway. It's gratifying to know that our products, in providing a luxurious alternative to real animal fur, bring joy to people all over the world, and at the same time, make unnecessary the destruction of countless animals."

The bottom line is that it is not prestigious, elegant or in any way necessary to wear fur. We can live without it; the animals can't, so why not let them keep it?

What Do You Know About Leather?

NOT LONG AGO, I was shopping at a favorite store, and when I asked the saleswoman if the belt she was showing me was leather, she said, "Yes, but it was a by-product of the meat industry, so it's not like any animals were killed specifically to make this belt. I'm very particular about that."

I'm sure she is trying to be aware. I know she truly believes that, and her heart is obviously in the right place. But, how much truth is there to what she said?

Wouldn't it be nice if we could wholeheartedly subscribe to the beauty, glamour and delicious mystery of the fashion industry knowing that no living being suffered to provide that beauty and glamour? It certainly has a mystique and intrigue that are fun to consider. But often when you scratch the surface, the beauty industry has lots of explaining to do!

So here are three myths about leather and why they don't hold up:

Myth #1: Some leathers are better than others.

The truth is that no matter how you frame it, leather can never be cruelty-free by any stretch of the imagination. The meat industry is one of the cruelest there is, and it relies heavily on the leather industry, which is a billion dollar operation that has been around for a long time. The meat industry sells meat, but it also sells hides to remain solvent (whether they come from factory farms or grass-fed cattle ranches). The two products go hand in hand. In fact, my understanding is that as people eat less meat, the industry is depending more on hide sales for profitability.

No matter how you look at it, leather items—be they wallets, coats or couches—mean animals died brutal deaths. Whether they come from Walmart or Saks makes absolutely no difference.

This does not even take into consideration that not all leather sold is a co-product of the meat industry. Some animals, especially exotic animals, are raised just for the their skin, much as animals are raised strictly for the fur industry. There is really no distinction between leather and fur. It's just that we've heard more about the fur industry because it is seen as a luxury. Leather is often seen as a necessity, but that's changing. Keep reading.

Myth #2: Vegetable-tanned leather is better for the environment.

You might feel better about wearing vegetable-tanned leather, but the animals still suffered great pain and torment because it is still their skin you are wearing!

To be honest, vegetable-tanned leather is really not as eco-friendly as the industry would like us to believe, and it comprises only a tiny portion (somewhere around 10%, if that) of the leather available to the consumer. The hide still goes through a huge chemical bath to "leatherize" it. Remember, before leather is leather it is skin, and skin left untreated will decompose. This toxic chemical bath is necessary to transition skin into something that bears no resemblance to its original form, a product that can be worn for years and years without disintegrating. But, and this is super important, whether the leather is chrome-tanned or vegetable-tanned, it still takes a chemical soup to dehair, bleach, and finish it, among other things.

The environmental impact of leather is massive since simply raising animals as commodities is an environmental nightmare. In 2006, United Nations Food and Agriculture Organization senior official Henning Steinfeld said, "Livestock are one of the most significant contributors to today's most serious environmental problems." And as the world population grows, this situation is getting worse. When you consider the land degradation from grazing animals, water pollution from animal farms and the deforestation that is happening to keep up with the growing demand for meat, you can see that any kind of leather it is not environmentally friendly.

Saying no to leather and saying no to eating meat, eggs and dairy and going wholeheartedly vegan is the only animal- and environmentally friendly option. Stella McCartney, a well-known fashion designer who never uses leather in her shoe designs, told *The New York Times* in 2012, "Using leather to make a handbag is cruel. But it's also not modern; you're not pushing innovation." Want to push innovation and save the environment, animals and people's lives? Check out vegan shoe designs by Elizabeth Olsen (www.olsenhausshoes.com), who uses recycled television screens to make innovative polyester microfiber.

How can you use synthetic materials and call it eco-friendly? Just ask Lauren Carroll and Jodi Koskella of Charmoneshoes.com. According to the website:

> "Believe it or not, the process of creating microfiber is less polluting to the environment than the process of tanning, factory farming and processing leather. In addition, the materials are free from harmful PVCs, using instead a light polyurethane coating which is gentler on the environment. We also incorporate sustainable practices throughout the production process, from using last boards made from 70% pre-consumer waste to using recycled materials in our boxes, business cards and other printed materials."

These are not isolated companies. More and more this is becoming the norm as innovative entrepreneurs who feel a deep commitment to the environment, people and animals meet a need. This is the beauty industry at its best!

Myth #3: There are no beautiful, non-leather alternatives.

Five or ten years ago it might have been true that a lot of the non-leather accessory options were not the most stylish, and it often felt a little like choosing the lesser of two evils. But times change, and they are changing quickly! As awareness grows, the demand for cruelty-free products has grown as well, and more and more designers--especially the up-and-coming designers--are responding positively and with extraordinarily beautiful alternatives to leather.

They span all price points as well. I own the most comfy and cool pair of non-leather boots by Steve Madden as well as a stunningly beautiful handbag by Stella McCartney that I found at a high-end consignment store. Her handbag originally retailed at more than ten times the cost of the boots, so you can see there is a huge range of prices available to suit every vegan-friendly pocketbook.

I know in my heart that the more people become aware of the truly negative side effects that go along with creating some of the clothes and accessories we wear, the more they will naturally seek cruelty-free alternatives. Now is the perfect time to give your leather shoes, and all leather, the boot!

Wool: What About the Sheep?

IF YOU LIVE IN a cold climate you know how much we rely on wool when it comes to staying warm. Coats, hats, sweaters, scarves, gloves, socks, blankets: you name it, it's made of wool. It is also a less obvious example of animal suffering in the fashion industry, and as a result, it is often overlooked or misunderstood.

People regularly stare at me wide-eyed when I tell them I don't wear wool for ethical reasons. "Sheep aren't killed to make wool," they say. "They are just sheared, which is a natural process and doesn't harm the sheep." Sadly, neither of those statements is really true. Then, while still in a state of disbelief, they say, "If you don't wear wool, what do you wear?"

Here are some questions and answers:

1. **Do sheep die for us to wear wool?** Yes. Not immediately, of course, although some do as a result of the farming conditions. But once they become unproductive wool producers, they are shipped off to slaughter— and die much younger than they would if it were a natural death. Just like dairy cows, once they are past their prime, they are killed. So although we don't have to slaughter them to obtain their wool, we are ultimately responsible for their death.

   The Ugg boot trend is another thing altogether. Sheep die to make these boots because they require both sheep wool and sheep skin. Wearing a pair of Uggs is like wearing a fur coat, only the fur (in this case, wool) is worn on the inside.

2. **Does shearing harm the sheep?** We have purposely bred domesticated sheep to have extra folds in their skin thereby creating more wool per sheep. As a result, if domesticated sheep are not shorn soon enough, they can die from heat exhaustion and other issues related to too much wool being produced.

That said, they are often sheared in the early spring before it is actually warm enough for them to be comfortable without their wool, which, of course, they grow to protect them from cold temperatures. The result is that some die from exposure.

When it comes to the shearing process, some small farmers might do it delicately. But all you have to do is take a look around the stores to realize that absolutely massive amounts of wool are being produced, and small farmers are not doing the bulk of it. The wool industry is a huge agribusiness, and the sheep are their "product." Time is of the essence! But if great care is not taken when shearing, it can be extremely stressful to the sheep and result in serious injuries. You can guess how many sheep have peaceful shearing sessions.

This is just the tip of the iceberg when it comes to the journey from sheep to sweater. You can learn more online at veganpeace. com and veganmeans.com.

3. **What do you wear instead of wool?** Of course we have to keep warm in the winter. That's a given. The good news is that you do not have to rely on wool. You might have to look around a bit more and definitely read labels, but there are other options available. Here are some tips:

    - Try a thick, knit cotton, acrylic, polar fleece or manmade fiber that holds the warmth in.

    - Layer! You can find plenty of lightweight warm layer pieces that don't add bulk but keep you toasty.

    - Add a scarf. Scarves are always a plus for an outfit, and keeping your neck warm is one of the keys to staying warm all over.

    One of the trickiest concerns for any vegan in a cold climate is finding a fashionable winter coat that is not made out of wool, fur or down. Leanne Mai-ly Hilgart, the creative founder of Vaute Couture (www.vautecouture.com) is leading the way in this area both in terms of vegan options and environmental awareness. Here's what she says about the fabrics for her beautiful coats:

"Our coat fabrics are not just ethical – they are advanced new fabrics designed for weather protection, insulation, and comfort, with super pretty textures and flirty drapes. Our shell fabrics are a new advanced textured Polartec fabric, made in the USA and 100% recyclable, with a recycled option, lined in a 100% Recycled, Closed Loop, Zero Waste Satin Ripstop from the Teijin Eco Circle collection. Each coat is finished off with gorgeous buttons – either deadstock metal vintage buttons from a UK factory, or the 'vegetable ivory' Tagua Nut."

If this is news to you, do some research on how wool is produced, look for alternatives and support the companies, like Vaute Couture, that are committed to cruelty-free, eco-friendly fashion. In the long run we all benefit!

What's the Flap Over Feathers?

FEATHERS ARE NOT ON most people's compassion radar. People either don't think about where they actually come from or assume that they are harmlessly procured. To be fair, I think the former situation is more common.

For example, one day I ran into a friend whom I was delighted to see. We exchanged greetings and hugs and then she said, "What do you think of my new hair accessory?" Clearly, she was delighted with it and anticipated my exclamations about how pretty it was (because it was pretty). My heart sank as I said, "That's not a real feather, is it?" She looked at me wide-eyed and with all sincerity said, "I don't know. Why?"

Our desire to use feathers in fashion is only natural. Feathers are gorgeous, and celebrities wearing them make people only want them more.

Not surprisingly, when stars such as Miley Cyrus and Steven Tyler began wearing feathers in their hair for all the world to see, demand spiked for these "accessories," which come from roosters bred for their stunningly beautiful saddle feathers. Typically, the fly fishing industry used these roosters' feathers, but now that the beauty industry is also involved, more roosters are suffering than ever before.

But if most people knew how they get from the bird to their heads, they would—I hope—think twice about wearing them (or, for that matter, using them to catch fish). Thankfully, at least one media outlet pointed out the cruelty inherent in this new fashion trend--and the not-so-new fly fishing trend.

In 2011 a *Bloomberg Businessweek* story on the feathers said, "They come from roosters that are genetically bred and raised for their plumage. In most cases, the birds do not survive the plucking."

It's a sad irony: Because these animals are beautiful, they are subjected to life in a cage (or "apartments," as some breeders call them—oh, please!) and are killed at age one for their feathers instead of living a natural ten to fifteen years. Their lifeless bodies are then composted.

And if you think that is a terrible story, consider the plight of other birds such as ducks and geese. Not only do we farm them for their meat and their fatty livers, which get this way after the animals are force-fed until the organs become horrifically enlarged—often twelve times their natural size, but also because we want their feathers. Those soft down feathers that help to keep them warm and dry in cold weather will do the same for us. The problem is that the animals have to endure confinement, being plucked alive (depending on where they are raised) and eventually slaughter. If you consider that it takes the feathers of approximately seventy-five geese to make one down comforter, according to the 2009 *Huffington Post* article "Down With the Truth," you get the idea that procuring down is not a pretty picture. But since wearing down is less obvious than wearing fur, we don't assign the same degree of cruelty to it when, in fact, there is little difference and maybe even more suffering within the down industry, especially when the birds are plucked live.

So what do you wear when the temperatures plummet? Refer to my previous suggestions for winter coats that aren't wool and also look for:

- PrimaLoft insulation. It was originally developed for the U.S. Army as a water-resistant alternative to down and is globally recognized as the world's best synthetic insulation. The company touts it as warmer, drier and softer than any other synthetic insulation. Not only that, but the end product is less bulky than one made with down feathers.

- Patagonia and other brands that are cruelty-free and green. Patagonia says it "recycles used soda bottles, unusable second quality fabrics and worn out garments into polyester fibers to produce many of our clothes."

Is Animal Testing a Necessary Evil?

BEFORE PURCHASING YOUR CURRENT tube of mascara, you probably thought carefully about your color preference as well as whether the mascara was thickening, lengthening, waterproof or smudge proof. The beauty of the packaging might have even influenced your choice. Did you also consider whether the product had been tested on animals? Some of you are nodding your head and thinking, "Yes, I always check." Others of you might think, "Does anyone really test on animals any more? I assumed that was a thing of the past."

It might surprise you to know that there are still many beauty companies—especially some well-known larger companies—that each year test their products on millions of animals, including rabbits, guinea pigs, rats and mice. Despite growing consumer objection to animal testing and the fact that there are many accurate, cost-effective and cruelty-free alternatives to animal testing, they persist. Perhaps these companies hope that people either do not think about the fact that so many animals die excruciating deaths to create cosmetics or that people will overlook or ignore the testing because their products have become staples in consumers' lives.

According to U.S. law, skin-care products and cosmetics must only be tested if they include new ingredients. Even then, the law does not require these safety tests to be performed on animals.

It is sad that the United States is not leading the movement away from animal testing. In fact, it is a holdout. As Neal Barnard, president of the Physicians Committee for Responsible Medicine, reported on his blog at pcrm.org in January 2013, the European Union and India are set to join Israel in banning animal-tested cosmetics, so the United States "will become the last top cosmetics market to allow animal testing on cosmetics."

The more information there is available on this topic, the more we realize that blinding a bunny with mascara or rubbing abrasive ingredients onto an animal's raw skin—usually without providing pain relief—serves no useful purpose. It simply tortures the animal. As Victoria Moran notes in *Main Street Vegan*, "The government only requires that products are shown to be safe; showing this by torturing sentient beings is a *company* choice with no justification. All of us have the right, of course, to demand that the products we use on our bodies and in our homes are safe. These tests, however, are antiquated and unreliable."

Many companies committed to creating cruelty-free products draw from the thousands of ingredients that have already been determined to be safe for use in beauty and personal care products or, when introducing a new ingredient, use one of nearly fifty non-animal testing alternatives. These include the use of synthetic skin and skin tissue cultures and computer modeling. The results from these tests are often more reliable and useful because scientists do not have to account for the difference in how species respond to various chemicals that is necessary with animal testing.

It is also important to note that sometimes a brand does not test on animals, but its parent company does. Think about companies such as Tom's of Maine, now owned by Colgate-Palmolive, or Origins, which is one of the original brands of the Estée Lauder Companies. It might surprise you to know that L'Oreal owns Kiehl's. Who tests and who doesn't? It could be that the brand you use does not test on animals, but your money essentially goes to the parent company that does. Only you can decide where to draw the line. Sometimes, you have to search to find out who owns what, but it is worth the effort.

If you are wondering how to find out more, Victoria Moran's book *Main Street Vegan* contains lists of companies that do not test on animals or use animal ingredients in their products. In addition, it is very easy to stay updated on who still does animal testing by regularly visiting websites such as TheVegetarianSite.com.

To take this issue one step further, consider that even if a company does not test its products on animals, it might still use animal ingredients. The cruelty-free status of products that include lanolin (from sheep), carmine (from beetles), squalane (from shark livers or plant sources) or royal jelly (from bees), just to name a few, is disputed. You can read more on this topic in the next section, "Are There Bugs in Your Blush?".

Since 2005 when I first did my research that led me to become vegan, I have seen the cruelty-free cosmetics, skin-care and personal care industries grow by leaps and bounds. You do not have to go without a type of product because you prefer not to buy from a company that tests on animals or uses animal ingredients. There is *always* an alternative.

Purposely moving your allegiance to more compassionate brands makes a strong statement about how you want to spend your hard-earned dollars. Every time you pass up a product made of cruelly procured materials, you are making a statement—of beauty *and* compassion.

Do You Have Bugs in Your Blush?

Bugs are not cuddly or cute. Well, at least to most people they aren't. In fact, they are often scary or creepy looking. Think about it. When was the last time you cooed over a spider or hugged a beetle? So, when I tell people that, as a vegan, I do not wear silk or use lipstick with carmine in it, they shake their heads. What's the big deal?

Like most people I grew up with a fly swatter in the house, and my first apartment after college had cockroaches that we regularly exterminated. So, who would think that today I would get all riled up about what happens to bugs?!

To be honest, I never really thought about bugs as living beings in terms of their capacity for suffering. Bugs were bugs, and they didn't take up much space in my head or heart. The more I have learned, however, the more respect I have for what they do—and, most importantly—for their right to live free from our interference and abuse.

Let's look at three of the most commonly farmed insects.

Silkworms

Silk worms create their cocoons out of raw silk, which is actually one long continuous thread (1000–3000 feet). When ready, the silk worms eat their way out of the cocoons, but that action breaks the threads and renders the silk useless for our use. So, what do we do in most cases? We throw the unbroken cocoons with the silk worms still alive inside into boiling water. This kills the silkworm and leaves the thread intact.

Carmine (Cochineal) Beetles

It comes as a surprise to many to learn that the carmine or cochineal beetle is one of the primary sources of the red dyes in cosmetics. It is also used in food and by the pharmaceutical industry to color pills. Since the fact that it comes from a beetle is left off the label, most people don't give it much thought. These beetles, like the silkworm, are harvested or farmed and then boiled alive before being dried to produce the sought-after dye.

Bees

Bees are the most well-known farmed insect. This is a huge topic. The Friends of Animals Vegan Starter Guide says:

"Bees have intricate neurological systems and communicate through intricate dances, but they usually get our attention only for the consumer goods they can be made to produce: honey, beeswax, propolis, bee pollen, royal jelly, and venom. Bees make honey from the nectar of flowers, then store it to eat in winter. Honey, then, is the bees' own food. The bees might have their legs and wings clipped off to keep them from flying away—but they'll be shaken out of their hives, or removed with blasts of air, so the owner can collect the honey. Beeswax pours from the bee's underbelly glands; the bees use their mouths to shape the substance into combs, creating a foundation for the hive. Humans take the wax away for cosmetics, pharmaceuticals, polishes, and candles. Royal jelly, a blend of secretions from worker bees, nourishes the queen bee. Some people believe it has youth-preserving qualities, and take it away."

As you can imagine, given that so many people do not want to acknowledge what we do to cuddly animals in the name of fashion, it comes as no surprise that it's a lot harder to garner sympathy for creepy, crawly bugs. My purpose here is to raise awareness on a topic that most people have never even considered. I cannot help but encourage you to bring as much awareness and compassion as possible to the clothing and personal care choices you make. I promise it's easy to do and is getting easier every day.

Do You Have to be Twenty and Wafer Thin to Have a Vegan Wardrobe?

THESE DAYS IT'S TRENDY to be vegan. That is not a surprise since the term has been tossed around in relation to many well-known names, including Ellen DeGeneres, Bill Clinton, Alicia Silverstone and Dr. Benjamin Spock. Whether they are truly vegan or not, the bottom line is that not eating animals is seen as super cool.

While it's all well and good that being vegan is now fashionable, what sometimes seems to be missing from this new awareness is that going vegan involves more than just what you eat. Yes, most of us eat at least three times a day, so food is front and center in the discussion of veganism. What is often overlooked, however, is that we also get dressed at least once a day, so the clothes we wear can have a significant impact on animal suffering.

The super-cool, trendy idea is great, but when it comes to the fashion world, "trendy" usually translates to clothes for young, tall, thin women. This can make the wardrobe aspect of veganism seem daunting to anyone over the age of forty. With whisper-thin cotton tanks, adorable cotton dresses and slouchy tops leading the trend, many dismiss the idea of a vegan wardrobe as impossible if they have mature bodies and want to be age appropriate.

Let me change that perception right here and now. Vegan fashion can easily be timeless, beautiful and appropriate for any age, size, shape or coloring, and the whole concept is not as foreign as you would think. I can pretty much guarantee that you already have "vegan" clothing in your possession. In fact, you are probably wearing some now. And, guess what? You don't have to shop in special stores or go out of your way to find vegan clothes. Every store has them.

Here are five beautiful, timeless items you probably already have—or can easily add—that represent cruelty-free fashion choices.

1. **Jeans:** A great pair of dark wash jeans works well in anyone's wardrobe. Because they are made of denim (which is a form of cotton), no animals were harmed in the making of them. A few of my favorite brands are Not Your Daughter's Jeans and JAG jeans for women who carry a little more weight in their tummy. For women who have smaller waists and fuller hips Little in the Middle jeans and Levi Bold Curve jeans are great. **Fashion tip:** If you wear straight leg or bootcut jeans, make sure you wear them long enough. They should be no more than half an inch off the ground.

2. **Cardigans:** Cardigans are timeless and very trendy. Yes, a lot of them come in wool and cashmere in the winter, but there are still plenty of options available in a heavy-knit cotton, rayon and manmade fibers that mimic the look and feel of wool. Reading the label is super important here. **Fashion Tip:** Refer to "Is Your Cardigan Frumpy?" in Chapter 3 for a full description of how to buy and wear a cardigan.

3. **A Great Blazer:** Blazers seem to have gotten a bad rap lately, but they can be really pretty, stylish and versatile. They are especially handy for women with narrow shoulders and broader hips because the structure in the shoulders helps to balance your hips and bring the body into proportion. While you will find a lot of wool blazers in the winter, you'll also find them in a variety of manmade fibers (some that have a feel similar to wool), cotton, linen, rayon and a variety of other fabrics that are cruelty-free. **Fashion Tip:** Avoid double-breasted blazers unless you are absolutely sure you look great in them. They can add width and bulkiness to your body.

4. **Shoes:** This is where a lot of people become perplexed when it comes to creating a cruelty-free wardrobe. Going vegan does not relegate your shoe choices to sneakers and Crocs. Far from it. Whether your taste and comfort level runs to a fun pair of red shoes with a heel, a fashionable ballet flat or a great pair of high heel boots, there are plenty of options. The average

woman owns thirty-five pairs of shoes. If those are all leather, that's a lot of skinned animals. **Fashion Tip:** Designers Olsen Haus, Cri de Coeur, Novacas, and Neu Aura design exclusively vegan shoes, but you will also find man-made shoes among the regular designers such as Nine West, Bandolino, DKNY and Anne Klein. Most shoes indicate what they are made of. They are vegan-friendly if they are stamped *man-made*.

5. **Dresses.** Dresses are a great addition to any woman's wardrobe. You don't have to wonder how to match a dress with a top or bottom. You just put it on, add a pair of shoes and accessories, and you are all set to go. A surprising number of dresses that are comfortable, flattering are made of easy-care cotton or man-made materials such as rayon, polyester, polyamide, nylon and acetate. And many have spandex or elastane in them for stretch, which adds an extra degree of comfort. **Fashion Tip:** Make sure your undergarments support you properly. If your bra doesn't fit well, neither will the dress.

To help you get started, here is a vegan shopping guide. There are many more options out there, and they are expanding constantly. But, these are some of my favorites and can make your shopping experience fruitful and easy!

Clothes

When it comes to vegan clothing, it is less about brands and more about fabrics. Look for cotton, linen, rayon, tencel, lyocell and microfibers, which are all vegan-friendly.

You can find animal-friendly fabrics everywhere from Bloomingdale's to Kohl's. For instance, Vera Wang makes a beautiful line of clothing for Kohl's and Nicole Miller has created a line for J.C. Penney. Much of what they have designed is cruelty-free and a lower price point.

Shoes

Vegan shoes can be made from many things, but the one thing you can be sure of is that they are not made from any animal skin, fur or other animal by-product. And many, such as Olsen Haus and Melissa shoes, are eco-friendly as well.

Exclusively vegan:

- Olsen Haus – www.olsenhaus.com
- Neuaura – www.neuaurashoes.com
- Cri de Coeur -- http://cri-de-coeur.com/
- Novacas -- http://www.novacas.com/womens_s11.htm
- Melissa – www.melissaplasticdreams.com (they are made out of their signature plastic material called Melflex, which is soft, breathable and recyclable.)
- Unstitched Utilities – www.unstitchedutilities.com
- Charmone - www.charmoneshoes.com

These lines make many vegan options:

- Steve Madden
- Rampage
- Bandolino
- Franco Sarto

Handbags

- Big Buddha – www.bigbuddha.com
- Matt and Nat – www.mattandnat.com
- Susan Nichole – www.susannichole.com
- Melie Bianco – www.meliebianco.com
- R&Em by Rebecca Minkoff – www.macys.com
- OMG Handbags – www.amazon.com

- Noah -- www.noahhandbags.com
- Nahui Ollin -- www.nahuiollin.com
- Shiraleah –www.target.com, www.overstock.com and www. shoebuy.com
- Gunas –_www.gunasthebrand.com
- Jill Milan – www.jillmilan.com

Vegan fashion websites:

- www.compassioncoutureshop.com
- www.veganchic.com
- www.alternativeoutfitter.com

These are just my favorites; there are many more sites out there. You will even find that some traditional online shoe stores even have "vegetarian" sections. Whether you shop online or in the stores, be sure to read the tags before you try something on so you can make choices that flatter you *and* reduce animal suffering. It's a win-win.

— —

Although I know some of the information in this chapter is unsettling to say the least, it also is meant to inspire you. You do not have to accept the status quo. In fact, we can change it. And thankfully, it is not an either–or situation: You do not have to sacrifice your personal style to make a compassionate fashion statement. I know because I have done it, and I'm happy to help you follow this path, too.

Chapter 9

Aging with Beauty, Style and Grace

Ours is a society obsessed with being young: Our culture revolves around it, the media glorify it, and our mirrors reflect it. Or not! With each passing day, it seems we become more and more aware of whether we are meeting or falling short of these arbitrary standards.

It doesn't matter if you are fast approaching thirty or about to cross the sixty-five-year mark. The focus is the same—how to maintain a youthful appearance and a healthy, energetic attitude. It's a constant source of conversation among women as we compare notes about body parts that are changing before our eyes. On the surface, this is a good thing. Staying youthful and enjoying life is good. The problem arises when we spend an inordinate amount of time assessing how we measure up or trying to hide or ignore the fact that we are getting older.

I regularly talk about this topic with friends and clients alike. Conventional society reveres youth, and the wisdom and natural beauty that come with aging are rarely given the respect they deserve, especially for women. In most of these conversations, the discussion usually comes down to one question: How do you age gracefully? Does it mean accepting without reservation all that comes with getting older? Do you have to buy into the growing market of cosmetic surgeries and additional "beauty" treatments to be able to look in the mirror and feel youthful? If not, how do you compete (and by that I mean feel comfortable with who you are) when the standard of how youthful you are expected to look at any given age is constantly being raised?

This chapter will address these concerns, help you get some perspective and give you some guidance for making choices that will bring you happiness and peace no matter your age.

How Do You Gracefully Make Peace with Aging?

THINK BACK TO WHEN you were a child or teenager. What were the older women around you like? I remember a friend's mother putting cold cream on her face at night because that was the only "anti-aging" product available. One of my aunts, who looked exactly like the Queen of England for as long as I can remember, wore no makeup, let her hair go gray, and adjusted her dress size as her weight shifted. She had seemingly little or no angst associated with these things and offered no apologies. Few older women dyed their hair, at least in my town, and no one whitened their teeth (was that even invented then?). If someone had plastic surgery, it was very hush-hush, and you could barely tell. To be honest, I don't remember anyone in my town having it done.

I can't say all of the women I knew eagerly embraced the aging experience, but they certainly were not grasping at youth, and there was no encouragement to do so that I know of. Maybe it was easier then or maybe not. Perhaps they felt discouraged about wrinkles and sagging skin, but there was not the pressure to do something about it.

Actually, in all my wondering I decided to call my mom and ask her if my memory served me well. She didn't hesitate a second before she said, "In my thirties and forties I didn't go around with a group that worried about whether our chins sagged. We didn't talk about getting older. We were a happy group and content with ourselves."

What a gift! While I'm sure women today can be happy with themselves, they are still resisting immense pressure to address every line and age spot that appears, and the standards are certainly different today than they were thirty or forty years ago. When you see celebrities who are sixty or seventy looking forty or fifty--or at least trying to--it's hard not to consider how you, personally, measure up.

My mom addressed this a bit: "We weren't comparing ourselves to each other or to movie stars. It's not that we didn't care how we looked. We were all about fashion and loved getting dressed up. We would each buy two dresses before going to a party because we weren't sure which one we wanted to wear, and we loved having our hair done. But we didn't notice wrinkles even when they came, and we didn't feel old. There wasn't the pressure there is today to have everything fixed."

As we talked I found myself wishing that we could turn back the clock. These days it seems we have to make a conscious decision to be OK with how we look rather than have it just be a non-issue. And, it would be nice to have the playing field leveled again. Right now, there's an unattainable standard of beauty for women over age fifty—and often much younger—that bears no resemblance to how we age naturally. Even if you have taken good care of yourself all of your life, you cannot compete with women who are having multiple treatments done. So what do you do?

If you take my mom's advice, you'll "go with the flow and have fewer worries and won't wrinkle so fast." There's definitely wisdom there. But what do you do when you are already worried and wondering how to keep up? How do you embrace the aging process?

Since we can't turn back the clock or erase the awareness from our consciousness, here are six tips I use to keep me feeling good most of the time.

1. **Don't worry; be happy.** It sounds silly, but I have watched friends age before my eyes when they've been under an inordinate amount of stress. Stress causes blood flow to your skin to be restricted, it makes you frown more, and it can cause inflammation. None of this makes you look beautiful or feel relaxed. And, over time, these internal stress responses will have long-term negative impacts on your skin and your entire body.

   Regular meditation, exercise, fun distractions and positive affirmations can all contribute to happiness and positive energy. Although it's not always easy to do these things, the effects of uncontrolled stress are not fun or pretty. Yes, it takes effort and focus to move away from stressful situations, but the results are worth it in the end on many levels.

2. **Focus on your health.** When you don't feel well, you don't feel happy or beautiful. Protect your health. Eat well, avoid toxins, exercise, sleep and play.

3. **Banish your magnifying mirrors.** I understand that sometimes one is necessary for applying eye makeup, but once that is on, put it away. Do not spend time examining and critiquing your face in a five- or ten-magnitude mirror. Yikes! Everyone on the planet can find something to obsess about in one of those. And while we're on the topic of mirrors, here's another tip: Avoid mirrors that have overhead lighting. They make everyone look tired and old because they cast shadows and create or exaggerate dark under-eye circles.

4. **Always wear your best colors.** This one probably should be first! In fact, during my conversation with my mom and without any prompting from me, she told a story about a friend who is now in her mid-eighties. Every time she sees this friend, the woman is dressed nicely and wearing beautiful colors that make her glow. As you know from earlier chapters, wearing your most flattering colors is important at any age, but as you get older it is even more important. Sure, you might have to hold out a bit to find your best colors in the stores, but it's worth the wait to look radiant and beautiful all of your life. Please note that if it has been more than ten years since you've had a color analysis or if your hair color has changed over the past few years, it's time to re-evaluate the colors you wear. There is a good possibility they have changed a little or a lot.

5. **Smile.** This is my new way of coping. I don't see the lines around my lips or the softening of my jaw when I smile, so I take every opportunity to do so. See? I made you smile!

6. **Do what makes you feel good.** If seeing dark spots on your face or lines around your lips is all consuming, find out what your options are to soften those concerns. There's no right or wrong way to address your experience with aging. When it comes to making choices about feeling youthful, only you can decide for yourself.

Now go take a good look in the mirror. What do you see? Look past the lines, spots or gray hairs if they bother you, and identify what it means to be the age you are. Perhaps make a list of what makes you happy and what doesn't. Start by focusing more on what you feel good about. Then, choose one thing that is pestering you about getting older, and find out what you can do to ease that discomfort.

Maybe a good first step is to whiten your teeth, get a new haircut or buy a top in a gorgeous color instead of black. If plastic surgery or a noninvasive skin treatment is the answer, then get a referral from a trusted source, and check it out.

Here's a different kind of idea: The next time you are with friends, encourage them to talk about what they love about themselves rather than about what is making them feel old. Lighten the energy and help each other see the beauty of your current ages. We thrive on this kind of connection and need to create our own support network when the media and society ignore or harass us. Do not buy into their youth-crazed messages!

There will still be days when you wish you had firm knees, a tiny waist, or your natural hair color again. But you can look and feel great now, even if it means lengthening your dresses a bit, buying a top that skims your waist instead of accentuates it or finding out what colors make your gray or colored hair look amazing.

This is your personal journey. It is worth it to make peace with aging so you can do it gracefully and maybe even enjoy every step along the way!

Are You Dressing Too Young or Too Old?

MAKING PEACE WITH AGING is one thing, but so many women feel unsure of where to find middle ground between dressing like they did in their twenties and dressing old before their time. Kate is a perfect example. She came to me because she felt she had lost perspective. She was fast approaching forty and wasn't sure her wardrobe was doing her any favors. Many of her clothes were hand-me-downs from her mom—and it showed. When Kate put on a pair of flowy pants and a pastel shirt with a T-shirt underneath, she suddenly took on the energy of someone much, much older. The colors weren't making her sparkle, everything was way too big, and there was nothing youthful and fun about the look. She could sense that, but she wasn't sure what to do about it.

On the other hand, Angela was fifty-one and worked hard at keeping her body in shape. As a result she could fit into the super low-rise skinny jeans and mini skirts. A low-cut halter top showed off her trim arms and more. In her younger years, she had always been a few pounds heavier than she wanted to be and never felt great about herself. Recently divorced, she had started working out and had a new lease on life. She was now excited, albeit a bit nervous, about dating again. One of the things she said to me was that she was not sure how far she could or should push the envelope without appearing like she was trying too hard. She asked me to help her with guidance and a periodic reality check to help her create a classy, sexy (yet not trampy—her word!) look.

When you're eighteen, there are few stigmas attached to how you dress. You can go the route of T-shirts and jeans, or you can embrace the fashion trends with abandon and little worry about looking foolish. At most you will get a few eye rolls and people chuckling about what it was like when they were eighteen. At that age you can get away with a lot, and it's fun to experiment!

Fast forward a couple of decades or so, and the rules change dramatically. Add to that the fact that the fashion world does not change its focus from designing clothing primarily with teens and twenty-something women in mind, and it's no wonder women often feel confused.

A friend once said to me, "There has to be a look somewhere between teenage rock star and nana, but it beats me as to where to find it!" That's it in a nutshell. Being age appropriate has as much to do with not looking too old as it does with not grasping at youth.

Kate and Angela typify the contrasting ends of the wardrobe spectrum. Although most women do not go to either extreme, they sometimes have a leaning one way or the other and don't feel good in their clothes. Here's how I helped both women find the middle ground between nana and teenage rock star.

Let's go back to Kate. She felt so thankful that her mom was giving her clothes. She was quick to tell me that she was not happy with her body and didn't like shopping for clothes. With the frequent gifts from her mom, it meant she had a ready-made wardrobe and didn't have to spend a lot of time in the stores. Plus, she was touched that her mom thought of her. The problem was that her mom was nearly thirty years her senior and had a much older look going on in general. Maybe that worked for her, but it did not translate well for Kate.

The first thing we decided was that she had to let go of the hand-me-downs. It turned out that her mom was fine with not sending them to her any more. She just knew how much Kate hated to shop and was trying to spare her from having to do that. She also knew Kate was working with me, so she was happy she would have some support.

From there, I walked Kate through the steps you are reading in this book. We looked at who she was and what made her special. We identified her best colors, and I showed her the difference between something that fits and something that doesn't. She found a great tailor to help her tweak things. She began to see that she had been settling for good enough and not allowing her true self to shine through. No more mom jeans (jeans that come to the waist, are full at the hips and taper at the ankle) for her. She discovered skinny jeans with stretch, which were something she thought she could never wear, and paired them with a sweater dress and boots. Traditional cardigans were replaced with fun, casual jackets and layered tops. Now it was clear that Kate was a vibrant forty-year-old woman, and her energy exuded that youthful beauty. You could sense it the minute she walked into a room. She felt natural, comfortable and much more beautiful in her new look.

Angela, on the other hand, was full of fun, fiery energy. She wanted that to be immediately obvious in her wardrobe choices but was sensing that that message was getting lost, misinterpreted and undermined by her overtly sexy choices. After talking with me for a while, she realized that she was worried about losing the fun, flirty feeling if she dressed more conservatively, so she felt stuck.

Let me tell you that there was nothing conservative about Angela! In fact, to squash that fiery part of her would have been sad. What we wanted to do, instead, was to showcase her passionate spirit in a fresh way. To do this there's a general rule of thumb I subscribe to: Instead of wearing clothes that are low cut, tight and short, choose one of these things at a time. Also, when I say low cut, I'm talking about showing *some* cleavage—the amount depends on you—not sporting a slit down below your bustline. It also could have nothing to do with cleavage and instead mean cutouts at the shoulder or a boat neck that showcases your collarbones. Short translates into somewhere above the knee, depending on your legs and personality, but generally does not come close to mid-thigh. And it definitely doesn't include the micro minis that we see on teenagers.

In Angela's case, she was very proud of her well-toned body, so tight was naturally her first choice. We also addressed what was tight and what was *too* tight. Looking like you are busting out of something and being able to see every nook and cranny is not sexy. Wearing something that lightly skims your body and shows off your shape *is* sexy.

So, one of the first outfits she got was a beautiful dress that followed her curves in a rich crimson, which is a spectacular color for her, to speak to that fiery part of her personality. The dress was sleeveless and had a keyhole neckline that hinted at cleavage. It came to the knee, and she wore striking black high-heeled shoes with a low vamp to expose the top of her foot and elongate her legs. With this outfit, we redirected the energy from too much exposed skin to instead highlight her passion and natural beauty and add a touch of mystery.

Both Kate and Angela now had new visions of themselves as mature women. They found their own self-expression somewhere between teen rock star and nana and were delighted with what they saw.

If you are unsure if how you are dressing is age appropriate, keep Kate's and Angela's stories in mind the next time you get dressed. As always, it comes down to how you feel in what you are wearing. If you spend the entire day wondering if your skirt is too short or feeling unbearably frumpy, then something isn't right. Use this chapter and the entire book to help you figure out exactly where you fit in.

Where Are You Getting Your Fashion Advice?

I DON'T KNOW ABOUT you, but when I was a teenager I never spent time at the mall with my friends shopping for clothes. It just wasn't something we did. Maybe it was the fact that I grew up in a small town called Feeding Hills, or maybe the world was just different then. I'm not sure. Today, young women have many more fashion resources than we did at their age. In the 1970s there were no TV makeover shows or celebrity style magazines, and there was no Internet.

All of the information available to teens now means they have opinions about what looks good, and they often have a great desire to share these opinions. I hear this from my clients (their moms) all the time. Many times they tell me that their daughters love fashion and are ready, willing and able to pass along their style ideas. While their intentions are usually good, and their advice could help get you out of a rut, their insights are still limited by their age. The bottom line is that if you put something on and feel too old or too young, it's not right for you no matter what anyone else says, including a fashion–savvy teen.

Case in point: One day I went in to a fun boutique that I had wanted to explore for a long time. A young woman there showed me a fun animal print top that she was so excited for me to try on. When I put it on, it fit perfectly, and the colors were great, but I felt like I was twelve years old. She was super enthusiastic about it and said flattering things, but it had a baby doll feel with short, somewhat puffy sleeves that just didn't seem right to me. I thanked her profusely and left the top there. The store was fun, but, in general, the selection was just too young and trendy for my taste and comfort level.

As you can see, where you shop definitely affects your choices. Some of my clients share that they pick up a good portion of their wardrobes in Forever 21, H&M or Old Navy because that's where they shop for their children's clothes. It's no wonder they aren't happy! Most of those clothes have a very young styling to them. A piece here or there? Yes. A wardrobe? No.

Can I add one more thing? It is so easy, especially receiving fashion advice from much younger women, to continually compare yourself to them and come up wanting. They make getting dressed look so effortless and, in comparison, you might feel discouraged because you have gained weight or body parts have shifted. You no longer feel that ease of dressing you had when you were younger, and you miss it. Resist the temptation to judge yourself. Instead go back and reread "How Do You Gracefully Make Peace with Aging?" at the beginning of this chapter. In fact, don't just reread it. Do the exercises for the second, third or fourth time. They will remind you that while you are never going to be seventeen or twenty-six again, you can still express your natural beauty and inner vibrancy and look just as smart and engaging as someone much younger.

Are You Wearing These Fashion No-nos?

KNOWING WHAT TO BUY and what looks good can feel tricky. I regularly get questions about particular styles and whether they are suited to someone over forty or, in some cases, anyone at all—regardless of her age.

I'll be the first to admit that there is an exception to every fashion rule. And, for sure, I am a huge proponent of creating a look that expresses your own spectacular personal style.

Fashion no-nos, however, fall into a league of their own. These are looks that are almost universally unflattering. Staying away from these looks is a good rule of thumb; I know of no woman who wakes up each morning and thinks, "Why don't I put something on today that looks dreadful?"

So without further ado, here are ten fashion/makeup styles that are questionable at best and, in some cases, absolute no-no's, especially for women over forty.

1. **Leggings worn with tops that don't cover your butt:** Leggings are, by their very nature, worn very tight and, as a result, are pretty revealing. Some leggings are even relatively lightweight like tights, and those are the biggest offenders. Either way, be 100% sure your top absolutely, completely covers your butt. **Exception:** If you are eight years old!

2. **Oversized T-shirts:** There is absolutely nothing flattering about a typical T-shirt. It is shapeless and devoid of any interesting styling or detail, the neckline is universally unflattering, and the sleeves usually hit an unbalanced place on the arm and stick out to make you look bigger and wider than you are. What's to like about that? Usually women who wear these are just hiding their bodies. Throw them away immediately. They will always double or triple your size and will overwhelm the rest of your

body. **Exception:** Sleep in one if you must, although there are much prettier pajamas and nightgowns available.

3. **Pajama bottoms worn in public:** I don't know where this trend started, but it's definitely not my favorite! It takes all of five seconds to pull on a pair of jeans or pants when you want to go out. Please leave this trend at home. **Exception:** None, though I understand the attraction for college students while they are on campus. I will just have to leave it at that.

4. **UGGs and Crocs:** All I have to say is uggh! These boots and shoes are ugly on many levels. From a style standpoint, it's obvious: They are both bulky and shapeless and cause most people to shuffle awkwardly when they walk. As a vegan, it is truly upsetting at a heart level. For more information refer to "Wool: What About the Sheep?" in Chapter 8. **Exception:** None for Uggs. When it comes to the original Crocs style, I'll stay away from the safety debate over whether nurses should wear them and say that unless you are gardening, have a foot injury that requires them or really feel like they reflect who you are at your essence—which I doubt is true for most women— look for alternatives. Yes, they are out there.

5. **Pants worn too short:** I see this everywhere. Pants that end at the ankle or a little above are universally unflattering. They will always make your legs look shorter and never hit you at a place that balances your body. Mostly, they just look like you washed your pants and they shrank, but you didn't notice. Pants should generally hit the top of your shoe and be about a quarter inch to an inch from the floor in the back (depending on the width of the pant leg). **Exception:** Pants that are super slim to the leg and ankle and are worn with slim shoes, preferably in the same color or a complementary neutral color, may end at the ankle bone. This way the hem of the pants is less obvious and so does not create a wide horizontal line at the ankle bone that visually shortens your legs.

6. **Puffy short sleeves:** We are not little girls anymore, and puffy sleeves have a tendency to infantilize grown women. Yes, it can depend on the degree of "puff" and the feeling of the rest of the outfit. But if you put something on and the first thing you see when you look in the mirror is a young girl staring back at you, it's probably best to leave it to the teenagers. If these sleeves are on a babydoll-style top, don't even try it on. **Exception:** The puffiness is negligible, and it feels fun and flirty.

7. **Too tight tops:** Not too long ago, my partner and I were having lunch in our favorite restaurant and in walked a group of women—two young women and a third woman whom we presumed to be their mother. The mother was wearing a low-cut white spandex top. It left absolutely nothing to the imagination, especially from behind, and was unflattering on too many levels to count. I felt sad for her because instead of making her look younger, it made her look older.

   Yes, the style these days is to wear everything super tight, and in some cases it can have a slimming effect if the fabric has enough body to hold you in. But, more often than not, the opposite is true, especially when so many tops are made out of paper-thin fabrics that forgive absolutely nothing and reveal everything. **Exception:** The fabric has enough body that it does not show every lump and bump, and you are pairing it with something with more volume.

8. **Heavy eyeliner:** Many women get stuck in a makeup rut wearing what they've always worn because it used to work. The problem is that what was fun and trendy when you were younger can look heavy and overwhelming when you are a tad older. So many women have come to me wearing a thick pencil or liquid eyeliner that probably was chic when they were twenty but now is distracting and just too heavy on their eyes. We see the eyeliner first and never get to notice the natural beauty of their eye color.

If this sounds familiar, switch to using a dry powder liner on your upper lashline for ten days. Use a small liner brush and smudge it right between the lashes. Use a very dark brown, charcoal or even black. It can take some practice, but when done well, this look has a lot of impact without looking overwhelming.

Wearing eye makeup in a new way can be one of the hardest things for a woman to get used to. It is true that when you have seen yourself the same way for many years, you almost don't recognize your face when the makeup changes. Even seemingly subtle changes have a big impact, which is why I suggest wearing your new look for ten days before you decide. It can take you a little while to feel comfortable with a new technique and your new look. **Exception:** You are going to a costume party, or you have your makeup professionally done so it is extreme but perfectly executed.

9. **Unnatural lip line:** As we get older our lips get thinner. This is bad news for those of us who already have naturally thinner lips. Knowing how to plump them up a bit without using injectables is tricky. I've noticed women lining outside their natural lip line with a lip pencil or wearing their lipstick outside the natural line. Please don't. At worst it makes you look a bit like Goldie Hawn in *The First Wives Club,* and at best it simply looks curious. I understand this issue since I have a naturally thin upper lip. I use a very natural colored dry (not creamy) lip pencil to line just at the upper edge of my natural line. The color looks like my natural lips, and that's about as much as I can push it without it looking kind of scary! **Exception:** You are on stage playing someone other than yourself.

10. **Visible bra straps:** I have mentioned this before, but it bears repeating on the no-no list. I keep waiting for this fashion statement to go away, but I'm not sure it will. Rarely have I seen it done tastefully. Mostly, it just looks downright messy and distracting. Obviously, not everyone agrees with me, and

if this is really a look you want to wear, be sure you are doing it in a way that speaks to your personality and not just because you are in a hurry. **Exception:** None. Leave it to the teenagers, and hope they will grow out of it.

Please don't berate yourself if you fall into any of these categories. And let me assure you that I am all for self-expression and honestly believe everyone should create a look she loves without anyone else's interference, including mine, unless requested. I know, however, that most of these fashion no-nos are not being worn with intention but rather by default.

Unless you are absolutely, positively sure you can pull off the looks above, let someone else experiment with them. I promise that there are so many other beautiful styles out there that it's really not necessary to try to "make" something work. If you have to try that hard, it generally isn't worth it, and making a different choice will often suit you better.

Are You Graying Gracefully?

Do you remember that Clairol advertisement? "Does she or doesn't she? Only her hair dresser knows for sure!" If you remember that, chances are good that you are old enough to have considered the dilemma of whether to dye your hair or let it go naturally gray. And, if you are someone who is over fifty and only has a handful of gray hairs, then count yourself lucky! You are off the hook from making this decision and you just saved countless dollars and hours at the hairdresser!

Clients and friends who are starting to see gray hairs regularly ask me if it is time to start coloring their hair--they trust me to tell them. Because we live in an in-your-face, youth-obsessed culture, it is no surprise that whether to go gray is a question many of us do not take lightly. We've all heard about how gray hair "ages" a woman but makes a man look "distinguished." No wonder a woman's confidence and self-esteem often suffer as she gets older!

I'm a big proponent of keeping your natural hair color as long as possible—sometimes forever. It's just not for me. I pretty much nixed the idea of graying about forty years ago while still in my mid-teens. My sister, who is also a redhead, and I made a pact after seeing my redheaded grandmother's hair turn a blah, faded shade of yellow before it turned pure white. We agreed that we would always be redheads. That's easier said than done when it comes to red hair. Thankfully, I have a talented colorist who keeps my hair from turning unnatural shades of red or pink.

So all this is leading up to the point that gray hair can be strikingly beautiful, and it can also be extremely aging. The key is to treat it as a fashion accessory from day one.

If your goal is to let your hair gray naturally and you still want to feel fresh, youthful and stylish, then there are three things you must do:

1. **Get a stylish haircut.** This means no straggly ends and no blah, nondescript styles. I find that a lot of women who let their hair go salt and pepper have thick, coarse, wavy hair, and for sure that helps right off the bat. But, if yours is none of those things, you can still have fabulous gray hair; just be sure you keep it well shaped and well groomed.

2. **Wear only your best colors.** As you can tell by the number of times I address this topic throughout the book, when it comes to clothing color, I am a fanatic. As I have said before, color is extremely powerful, and it becomes even more important as you age. Unflattering colors can make you look pale or faded, overwhelm you or highlight lines and shadows. When you let your hair go gray, it is even more important that you wear colors that absolutely support your natural coloring, including your gray hair. And no, they are not the same colors you could wear twenty years ago! Without exception, wearing your most flattering colors makes an enormous difference.

3. **Dress your personality, not your age.** As you know, this is something I work with all my clients on no matter their age, but it becomes even more valuable the older you get. Too many women start to dress for comfort alone, and this often translates into shapeless, oversized styles. No, no, no! While it might take a tad more focus to find clothing you want to wear that feels terrific, it is out there. I have clients who are eighty-plus years old, have let their hair go gray and have beautiful wardrobes. They look great every day.

When Cynthia came to me she wasn't sure if she should dye her wavy salt-and-pepper hair. She had colored it many years ago, but one day about ten years ago she just decided to see what it looked like gray. It took a long time to grow out, and her hair looked unusual for a while as the line between the dye and her gray eased down her head. But once she made it through the growing-out process, she felt happy with her choice.

About to turn sixty, she had fallen into a rut with her personal style including her hair. When she looked in the mirror, she just felt old! She wondered if her gray hair was the major contributor to her feeling of frumpiness or if once she made some wardrobe and personal style changes she'd feel better.

Before she did anything drastic to her hair, we set to work on the three steps above as well as all the suggestions in the other chapters. She had let her hairstyle go for a long time, and she immediately felt better when she had a more up-to-date look with layers and a style that framed her face. Not realizing the importance of changing the colors she wore once her hair went gray, most of her clothes were in colors that no longer worked for her and did not compliment her beautiful salt-and-pepper hair. She was thrilled with the difference she saw with her new wardrobe colors and clothing styles that reflected her openhearted and magically free-spirited personal essence. Now when she looked in the mirror, she saw a vibrant woman staring back and felt happy with her natural gray hair. In fact, she celebrated its beauty and was excited to show off her new look.

Embrace your individuality—that wonderful spark inside you that makes you who you are. Perhaps part of what makes you *you* is your decision to go gray. If so, use the guidelines here to create a beautiful, pulled-together look. Then, rejoice, and enjoy it!

Do You Know These Makeup Secrets?

How LONG HAVE YOU been doing your makeup the same way? I bet you'll be surprised when you stop to consider this! It is easy to get stuck in a makeup rut: You learn one way of applying makeup when you're young and do it forever. Sometimes if you shake it up a little, your makeup can feel fresh and fun! No matter what your age is, these simple makeup secrets will add pizzazz to your daily routine.

I have been wearing makeup since I was thirteen. OK, in the beginning I wore only mascara. I have blonde eyelashes and really wanted dark ones like my friend Joanne, but wearing mascara changed my world. The three days I wore lipstick in junior high school don't count; they were too traumatic! My mom had given me a light-pink lipstick as a gift, and I was so excited. It was the '70s after all, and light-pink or even white lipstick was all the rage. Unfortunately, it looked shocking pink on me, and the other kids made fun of me. I threw it away after three days and didn't wear lipstick again for fifteen years. It took me that long before I learned how to choose the right colors and apply makeup properly—and not worry that others would laugh at me.

The most important thing I learned is that it's always important to know what you're doing when you apply makeup, and that is doubly true when you are a fair-skinned redhead. Even the slightest goof with color or technique can make a fair redhead look like Bozo the Clown! So believe me, these tips are tried and true!

I also know that women want their makeup routines to be simple and quick. Primping is not high on most women's to-do lists these days, myself included, so knowing what works and what doesn't lets us cut to the chase and get on with our day.

For me, part of what is so much fun about makeup and fashion is that as I learn things that make a difference for me, I am able to share these techniques with others and give them that same a-ha experience.

I use the following makeup tricks every single day and have for years, and I teach them to my makeup clients all the time. Enjoy!

1. **Apply concealer to your eyelids.** As you age, the skin on your eyelids often takes on another color—blue, purple, brown or red. This color can detract from your eyes and make you look tired, but there's an easy fix.

    Apply a light coat of concealer or foundation to your eyelids. I mean not only the part under your brow bone, which I already see a lot of women do, but also your lids. This will brighten your eye area and allow more focus to go to the color of your eyes. Use a dusting of a light color of eye shadow or translucent powder over the concealer/foundation to set it so it will last longer.

2. **Make your eye color pop.** Have you ever seen an eye makeup application in a magazine and thought, "Ooh, I'd love to do my eyes like that." So, you follow the explicit instructions and when you look in the mirror, something seems to be missing. You re-read the directions but, nope, you can't figure out what you did wrong.

    Don't worry. It's not you. For some reason, magazines often forget to tell us one very important step that their experts do that makes a huge different in how your eyeliner looks. Here it is: They are applying eyeliner to the upper inside ledge of the eye--and lower inside ledge if they are doing a smoky eye. It's a very easy technique though it takes a bit of practice if you are not used to putting something that close to your eyes. Contact lens wearers will find this super easy. I have been doing it for twenty-five years, and people always tell me how natural my makeup looks. Using a black, charcoal or dark navy pencil will look great on most people. Hint: You have to lift up the upper lid a bit to see the ledge of your eye. It's between the eyelashes and eyeball.

3. **Create your own customized lipstick color.** How many times have you gone to the cosmetics counter to find the perfect lipstick only to leave frustrated? You see other women wearing beautiful colors, but somehow you never seem to find exactly what you want.

The simple truth is that many times a beautiful, seemingly perfect lipstick color is actually more than one color, layered. And how much time does it take to create this look? About ten seconds. You apply one color and then another. Done! And reversing the way you layer them will produce a subtly different look. Or try applying a lip gloss to your lips first and then your deeper evening lipstick color over. Voila! The deeper color is slightly diffused by the gloss and now feels more like a daytime color. Layering lipstick colors is fun and easy, and it expands your lipstick options without costing you money!

While not earth shattering, these tips can have a profound impact on how your makeup looks. Play with them, and see what you think. I suspect you'll be pleasantly surprised and be sporting a new look right away!

Are You Listening, Fashion Designers?

BECAUSE I KNOW HOW hard it is for many women to find clothes they love that make sense for their age, I decided to try to aid the cause with a direct appeal to the fashion industry. So here it is, my open letter to fashion designers everywhere.

Dear Designers:

Could I talk frankly with you for just a minute? Like some of you, I have been in the fashion industry for a long time--over twenty-five years--and I love it. There is, however, one critical area where our efforts differ. While most of the fashion world is focused on very young, tall and thin women, my clients tend mostly to represent the over-forty woman. As a result, and because I fall into this category as well, I know what she likes to wear.

Perhaps I could provide some insights to help you create your collection for next season? I know that your hearts are in the right place and that you want women to look and feel beautiful, but, oh dear, have you tried your designs on women over forty who might have a few extra pounds floating around here or there and are more often closer to 5'4" than 5'9"?

Your goal, I'm certain, is to sell all your designs and not have them end up on the end-of-season sales rack or in a consignment store with the tags still on them. The problem is that there is a slight, and sometimes not so slight, disconnect between what we see in the stores and what is actually wearable by anyone with a little maturity.

I know you didn't ask me, but I also know from watching *Project Runway* that you encourage constructive criticism. So I hope you will take this all in the kind and supportive manner in which it is meant.

First of all, what I love about you:

Thank you for making your designs for plus-size and petite women. While some stores have misguidedly eliminated these departments, for those who still support them, it is wonderful to see beautiful garments for women who don't wear the traditional sizes 2–14.

Thank you for the variety of skirt lengths, shoes with heels of varying heights and widths and every imaginable boot style! There is something for everyone and that allows women to express their personality with comfort.

Thank you for the new version of the cowl neckline. It is very flattering and stays in place better so we don't have to fuss with it like we did back in the 1980s. Definitely new and improved!

Thank you for bringing scarves back. It's amazing how one piece of fabric can add so much beauty, warmth and personality!

I would also like to share a few thoughts on things that women need that seem to be missing from the choices of late. Please:

Use fabrics with substance. This is probably the most important request of all. That paper-thin stretchy fabric that so many shell/tank tops and T-shirts are made out of has got to go away. Soon! It is unflattering on most women who wear it (even young women), because it shows every little lump and bump even on women who wear a size 2. It is so frustrating to find something in the perfect style and color to complete an outfit only to discover that the fabric is dreadful. And that is not an exaggeration.

Bring brown back. We need more dark brown in basic jackets, pants and skirts. This deep brown works on so many people—especially those who cannot wear black or gray well.

Make more jackets, please. It makes getting dressed a little frustrating when you hyper-focus on one particular style to the exclusion of all else. Case in point: long cardigans. They are a great addition, but do we really need so many of them? Because there are so many of them, there is little room left for interesting jackets for women who enjoy wearing them or need to dress professionally for work. And, please, we do not need any more black or gray jackets! Take a risk and add some beautiful colors. I think you will be pleasantly surprised.

Take dresses to the next level. I cannot tell you how exciting it is to be able to buy a dress with sleeves after all these years. Believe me, when it's freezing outside, a sleeveless dress just doesn't cut it. Here are two quick things about dresses. When you do make sleeveless ones, could you please make some short cardigan sweaters in pretty colors (enough with the black already!) to wear with them? Sure, the twenty-something crowd can look trendy and cool in a long cardigan over a dress, but for the rest of us, we just look and feel frumpy!

And, lastly, not every woman wants to, or can, wear a dress that is body hugging. Many who have curvy hips and thighs look better with a slight A-line--and no gathers at the waist, please. They were here in abundance not long ago, and we loved them. Please bring them back. I think you'll be thrilled to see how many you sell!

These are just a few of our major requests for now. I want to thank you in advance for considering these ideas. If you think I am overstating this, please know that most of the women who get in touch with me say they can't find anything they like to wear. Sure, sometimes it's because they need some expert guidance, but sometimes it's because the choices are limited. I just know that together that we can remedy this, and women over forty everywhere will thank you!

Thank you again. Feel free to get in touch with me anytime!

With beauty, style & grace,

Ginger

— —

What you do with the aging process is a personal choice. But if you don't embrace the idea of getting better (remember Clairol's "You're not getting older; you're getting better" ad?), what's the alternative? Just getting older and feeling blah and frumpy? No!

Your inner essence—that sparkle that is yours alone—does not go away just because you turn forty-five or seventy. Having passion and joy for life is attractive at any age. Then, when you infuse your wardrobe with that delicious energy, you radiate beauty. Sure, it's not the same look you had when you were twenty-two, but there's nothing less appealing about it.

Don't wait for the fashion designers respond to my letter. Who knows when or if they ever will? In the meantime, you can gracefully make peace with aging just by being you inside and out.

The Next Step:
How Do You Keep the Magic Going?

IF YOU ARE READING this book, chances are good you are not a self-proclaimed fashionista. You might not go to the mall to shop for clothes when you want a relaxing afternoon. But you do want a wardrobe that works for you and expresses who you are. You just want that process to be as simple and accessible as possible. That's why this book is purposely presented in short segments and why I constantly talk about taking baby steps. Making small changes is how you get to where you want to be.

Before you read any further, take a minute to acknowledge the huge step you have just taken toward creating a personal style you love: You have read this book cover to cover and have been experimenting with the exercises. You *have* been doing the exercises, right? If so, some of what you are learning is becoming second nature. The more you practice, the more this will be true. So, now what? How do you keep the momentum going and create a look that's totally you—inside and out, from head to toe?

That's easy. Go back and re-read the book. Concentrate on the sections that still feel a bit new to you or that you completely forgot. This book is not meant to be a one-time read. It is a handbook that you can refer to over and over again for support and guidance.

As you are reading and practicing, keep these things in mind:

A complete transformation won't happen overnight. There is no magic pill or one-size-fits-all answer for creating a look you love. It takes focus, desire and perseverance, but the more you practice what you are learning here, the faster you will get results and the happier you will be. Each success—no matter how small—is exciting. If you have been stuck for a long time, you will notice that when you are making progress, you feel better and more excited about continuing to make changes. Let each success inspire you to take the next step and the next one after that and the next one after that.

There will always be more to learn. Your body changes, your lifestyle changes, you get older, and, yes, fashions change. Constantly. So, as you negotiate these changes, you are always learning what works for you at any given moment in time. If you have a setback, chalk it up to learning more about what does not work and keep going. When used regularly, the tools in this book will support you in navigating the ins and outs of creating a look you love with beauty, style and grace.

You are worth it. Life is way too short and too precious to feel bad about how you look or feel resigned to a look that's just "good enough." You deserve to feel beautiful every day, and you now know how to get there.

I know these things to be true because I have lived them and continue to do so. In fact, a recent experience showed me how far I've come and reinforced my belief in the advice I offer in this book.

There I was standing in front of the bathroom mirror with wet hair, a round brush in one hand and my hair dryer in the other. Click. I turned the dryer on, but nothing happened. No worries. I pushed the reset button and confidently flipped the switch. But there was silence in place of the usual deafening whir of the dryer. "OK," I told myself. "There has to be an explanation." I tried pushing the reset button on the outlet as well as the dryer and even plugged the dryer into another outlet. Mild panic was setting in, but I remained hopeful. I tried again and again to no avail.

All I could think was: "You're going to stop working *now*!? I have a very busy day planned starting with a quick trip to the post office to mail some client orders followed by a day of shopping with a client. Why couldn't you stop working tomorrow when I'll be in my office all day?"

I'm sure you can imagine my dismay (that's putting it mildly) when I realized I had no way of styling my hair. I didn't have time to buy a new dryer, and hot rollers weren't even an option because my hair takes a very long time to air dry, so there was no way it would be ready for rollers before I had to leave.

In case you are wondering why I was so distressed about my hair dryer breaking down, you must first know that my hair has always needed extra attention. It is thick, straight (with a slight bend) and heavy. If I don't style it, it just lays there like a mop looking flat and messy. As a result *I* feel messy, which, not surprisingly, is never how I want to feel. So my dead dryer was a catastrophic event for me, and the situation brought back memories from, dare I say it, thirty-eight years ago!

It was my first day at Mount Holyoke College, and I was meeting the other women in my dorm. I strolled into one woman's room to introduce myself, and we started talking about what we had to do the next day. I learned that we had a swimming test (do they even still do that?), *and*—here's the tricky part—we had to go right from the pool to another orientation event. There was not time to do anything other than get dressed and go.

I looked at this poor woman with horror. "Do you mean I can't dry my hair before we go?" I said incredulously. She looked at me like I was a crazy person. I'm sure she wondered if it was just me or if all the women at Mount Holyoke were worrying about their hair and, if so, she had clearly chosen the wrong school. I have to add that, unlike me, she had beautiful curly hair that could air dry and always looked great, which also meant it was no surprise she could not relate to my turmoil. (Just in case you are wondering, despite our initial conversation, we are still friends nearly forty years later!)

I spent the next twenty-four hours worrying about my hair. Everything must have worked out all right, or perhaps it was traumatic enough that I pushed the experience from my memory. I honestly do not remember what happened. I do know that I survived and that worrying did absolutely nothing to help the situation.

If took me a while learn this, though. If the hair dryer debacle had happened even ten years ago, I would have stressed myself out, worried about what others would think and said things such as, "Oh, great! Is this the way my day is going to go?"

This time, though, I was up to the challenge. I spent a few minutes reviewing my options and looking to see what other handy hair styling tools I had around the house. And, no, canceling was not an option since my client had traveled 4,500 miles to shop with me. How would I explain that? "Oh, gee, my hair looks messy, so I can't make it." I don't think so!

Instead, I decided to channel my "exquisite" energy. That's the inner beauty word I use when creating an outfit or deciding what clothes to buy. As I've said, people pick up on your energy. I knew that if my energy didn't match the look I had created, others would feel the disparity. I did not want to walk around all day feeling disgruntled or embarrassed about how I looked and pass that energy on to everyone I encountered.

Having my hair look messy was frustrating to me, but I did the best I could with a heated brush. Beyond that, I had to let my hair do what it wanted to do. I could have let the rest of my look and attitude follow suit and given up on trying to feel good about my image, but would that have made me happy and been a good representation of who I am? No. I also could have dressed in the outfit I had chosen before the hair dryer incident but apologized to everyone I saw or tried to hide or become invisible with the hope that no one would notice me because my hair looked terrible. But this would just make others feel confused, distracted or uncomfortable because my visual message, which was well put together despite my hair fiasco, did not match my energy, which would not be well composed if I felt self-conscious.

What did I do? I drew on all the information and guidance I offer in this book and promptly dismissed both of the above options. Instead, I chose to dress in the planned outfit I love and pretend I purposely styled my hair a little differently. And, I inwardly thanked my hairstylist for giving me such a good haircut. I deliberately chose not to let one frustrating experience color my day or my interactions with others. If people noticed my hair, they didn't say anything or give me any funny looks. I suspect, or at least choose to believe, it was a nonissue because I made it a nonissue.

What's the moral to the story—and this book? **I channeled my inner beauty, even when everything was not falling together perfectly on the outside.** You can do the same thing. Yes, absolutely, you can. Your personal inner beauty can directly influence the energy you express in your wardrobe choices, and this is exactly why I work closely with my clients to determine their four descriptive inner beauty words (refer to "What's Your Signature Style?" in Chapter 3).

Once you feel confident in that energy, you, too, will be able to handle challenges like my hair dryer. If something occasionally goes awry, it will be relatively easy for you to do the best you can to fix the problem in the moment and then let it go. You can also learn from the experience. In my case, I bought a new hair dryer and a travel dryer to have on hand just in case.

On the other hand, daily wardrobe malfunctions and feeling like your outfit never adequately reflects who you are different issues. That's when working with the information in this book until getting dressed feels natural and exhilarating becomes so important.

Now that you have come to the end of *That's So You*, take a minute to consider your own personal style. Is there generally a connection between how you feel inside and the look you create on the outside? If this connection is temporarily broken, can you regain your momentum easily? If not, why not? What would you need to do differently to make this happen? Which chapter(s) would it be helpful for you to revisit?

Use these questions to reflect inwardly and gain insight into the source of the disconnect—whether sporadic or constant. Then determine if there is one small inner or outer change you can make right now to inspire you to begin restoring the connection. Your solution, like mine, might be as easy as getting a backup hair dryer. Or it might require more inner reflection to determine if your wardrobe is purposefully and effectively expressing who you are.

Whatever happens, let your growing awareness guide you, inspire you and support you as you make the changes you've been longing for. You have the tools and guidance you need right here to create a lasting look that's so you and only you. Keep reading, and keep practicing. Then celebrate as your wardrobe and style come alive with your personal beauty, style and grace.

About the Author

GINGER BURR, PRESIDENT OF Total Image Consultants, has built a remarkable career as an expert personal image consultant working with women from all walks of life. A notable speaker and leader in the field of fashion and style, Ginger's adroit understanding of beauty trends and fashion has been celebrated by Fox TV News, The Boston Globe, MORE Magazine.com, cnn.com, Bloomberg Business Week, Forbes Magazine, and Worth Magazine, and she has been recognized by VegNews Magazine as one of the "25 Most Fascinating Vegetarians" in the world for her innovative and groundbreaking work as a vegan image consultant.

Ginger has directed corporate seminars for some of the world's most prestigious organizations including Harvard Law School, Harvard Business School, the U.S. Army, Fidelity Investments and Unilever. In 2009, Ginger launched her one-of-a-kind body image, self-esteem, and style coaching program "Who Taught You How to Dress?" which allows women to overcome the obstacles and learn the skills they need to create a wardrobe they love all in the comfort of their own home and with Ginger's guidance and support!

For more information about Ginger or her company, please visit her website: www.totalimageconsultants.com

What Do You Do If You Get Stuck?

THIS BOOK HAS GIVEN you everything you need to truly create a wardrobe you love. That said, I also know that sometimes it can feel lonely and a little scary to do it by yourself. This is where the power of support comes in and is exactly the reason I created the *Who Taught You How to Dress?* coaching program.

It supports you to take everything you have learned in *That's So You* and put it into action with my personal guidance--all from the comfort of your own home.

With this program you receive a 180-page workbook, 4 cd's and other support materials (as described at www.whotaughtyouhowtodress.com) as well as immediate access to a community of like-minded women through the monthly live Q&A calls and special inclusion in an online forum. Just like you, these women have struggled with their wardrobes and personal styles, too. They now use the forum to explore different looks and have their questions addressed by me and the other members of the *Who Taught You How to Dress?* community.

No more guessing if something works or giving up after trying to complete an outfit. Just jump on the forum and ask for help. With each question you ask, you have an immediate sounding board and direct support from me as you put everything you learned in *That's So You* into practice.

If you want support keeping your progress and momentum going, *Who Taught You How to Dress?* can help you do that!

For more information, go to www.whotaughtyouhowtodress.com.

CPSIA information can be obtained at www.ICGtesting.com
Printed in the USA
LVOW051949300513

336141LV00002B/638/P